Praise for

#1 NAT

Winner of the 2017 Lo ....nfiction

"Adam Shoalts is Canada's Indiana Jones—portaging in the north, dodging scary rapids, plunging into darkness, and surviving to tell the tale." —*Toronto Star*

"Adam Shoalts, twenty-first-century explorer, calmly describes the things he has endured that would drive most people to despair. . . . Rare insight into the heart and mind of an explorer." —Col. Chris Hadfield, astronaut, author, and space station commander

"Explorer Adam Shoalts's remarkable solo foray into the quietly dangerous and mysterious Hudson Bay Lowlands is the kind of incredible effort that fosters legends." —*Winnipeg Free Press*

"Anyone who thinks exploration is dead should read this book." —John Geiger, author and CEO of the Royal Canadian Geographic Society

"Move over Jacques Cartier, Christopher Columbus, and Sir Francis Drake—Adam Shoalts is this century's explorer." —*The Hamilton Spectator*

"Doing things the easy way has never been my style. There is no adventure in that! In *Alone Against the North*, Adam Shoalts does nothing the easy way. He travels to places no one has ever seen before and as a result comes back with an amazing story. As gripping to read as it must've been exciting to live!" —Les Stroud, award-winning creator, producer, and star of *Survivorman*

"While the book is a nail-biting chronicle of polar-bear encounters, brutal swarms of black flies and surprise tumbles down waterfalls, Shoalts also vividly describes an area of the country most of us will never witness." —*Metro* (Toronto)

"[Shoalts's] narrative is both humourous and honest, and at times intensely gripping." —*St. Catharines Standard*

"[*Alone Against the North*] is a story of brutal perseverance and stamina which few adventurers could equal." —*Life in Quebec Magazine*

"Shoalts's love of nature, cool professionalism, and almost archaically romantic spirit draw us into his adventure. . . . [He] is a knowledgeable and observant guide." —*Quill & Quire*

ADAM SHOALTS

A HISTORY OF CANADA IN TEN MAPS

EPIC STORIES OF CHARTING A MYSTERIOUS LAND

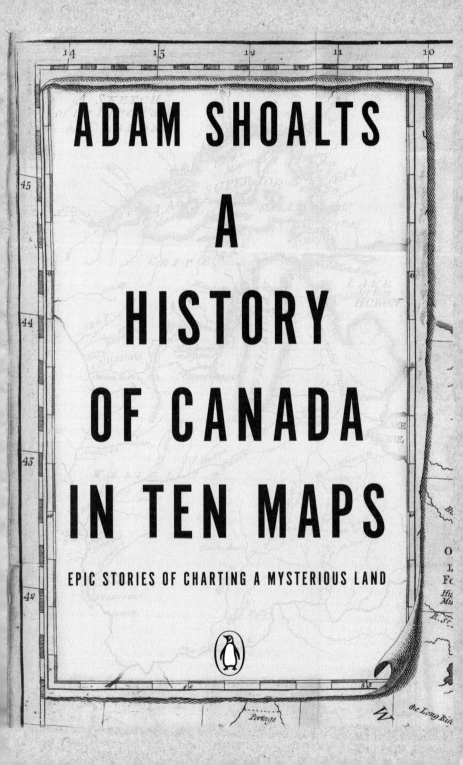

PENGUIN

an imprint of Penguin Canada,
a division of Penguin Random House Canada Limited

Penguin Canada, 320 Front Street West, Suite 1400, Toronto, Ontario M5V 3B6, Canada

First published in Allen Lane hardcover by Penguin Canada, 2017.

Published in this edition, 2018

7 8 9 10

Book design: Leah Springate
Cover images: (photo) Duncan Andison/Arcangel; (map) Samuel de Champlain's
map of New France (1632): Library and Archives Canada/Alexander E. MacDonald
Canadiana Collection/e010694118; Interior image: (title page) A General Map of the
Middle British Colonies, in America. Robert Sayer and John Bennett (Firm), 1776:
David Rumsey Map Collection.

Printed and bound in Canada.

Library and Archives Canada Cataloguing in Publication available upon request.
ISBN 978-0-14-319398-2
eBook ISBN 978-0-14-319400-2

www.penguinrandomhouse.ca

Penguin
Random House
Canada

To my father

CONTENTS

INTRODUCTION

Geographers . . . crowd into the edges of their maps parts of the world
which they do not know about, adding notes in the margin to the effect
that beyond this lies nothing but sandy deserts full of wild beasts, and
unapproachable bogs.

—PLUTARCH, *Plutarch's Lives*, FIRST CENTURY AD

The best adventures, it seems, often start with a map—typically a tattered old map that has yellowed with age and happens to be missing a crucial piece, like the precise location of buried treasure. Who as a child did not at least daydream of such a map and such an adventure? Consider the treasure map the sailor Edmond Dantès followed to find the fabulous fortune of Monte Cristo, or the ones that were always leading Indiana Jones (or more recently, Lara Croft) on some harrowing quest. These maps and stories are, of course, fiction. But hidden away in archives or carefully preserved in temperature-controlled museum cases sit real, historic maps that are *even more* fascinating.

The ten maps at the heart of this book span nearly a thousand years. They tell stories—stories of adventure, discovery, and exploration, but also of conquest, empire, power, and violence. After all, few maps are wholly innocent—the interesting ones usually aren't.

But what exactly is a map?

In the most basic sense, it is a graphic representation of the geography of a particular place—including natural features like mountains, islands, rivers, lakes, and oceans or political features like boundaries, cities, towns, empires, and nations. Often maps combine both the natural and the political. But a map is more than just a representation of a particular bit of land or sea.

A map is also a cultural artifact—a window into the past and a clue to understanding the worldview of the person or persons who made it. It is a glimpse at what they may have valued and what they didn't, what they desired and what they didn't. What they might have known and certainly what they didn't.

The first maps were probably simple sketches drawn in the sand or mud by our ancient hunter-gatherer ancestors tens of thousands of years ago. They might have delineated a hunting territory, or perhaps a lone hunter might have gone ahead of the main group to scout out fresh hunting grounds, or an area for a camp, then reported back on what he or she found by drawing it with a stick. The earliest maps traced in the sand in Africa would have disappeared with the first strong rain or wind. Those maps, if we could see them, would tell us about what our ancestors valued: good hunting territory with large game animals, sources of fresh water, shelter in caves or elsewhere—and maybe even an area where flint could be found for tool making and fire-starting.

Not until people started making their maps in more durable materials was it possible for them to survive. The oldest cave paintings in the world date back an astonishing 40,000 years—and the oldest maps, while not quite that old, are also found drawn on cave walls. These earliest surviving maps don't depict what we might expect—simple hunting territories—but instead chart the stars. One of the oldest is a map dated to around 16,500 years ago found painted on the wall of the famous Lascaux cave in France. This mysterious cave painting appears to show the Pleiades star cluster, as well as the three bright stars known as the Summer Triangle. A similar star map showing constellations has been discovered by archaeologists in a cave in Spain; it's thought to have been painted around 14,000 years ago.[1] Humankind, it seems, has always dreamed of the stars—of distant horizons and the unknown.

Today, 15,000 years later, we're still working on mapping the unknown mysteries of our solar system.

Other prehistoric maps may be even older than these maps of the night sky. A curious carved stone unearthed in a cave in Spain has been dated to nearly 14,000 years ago; archaeologists believe it's a map of the surrounding landscape, including rivers, ponds, and mountains. Another cave, near Pavlov in the Czech Republic, contains a landscape map that may be older still, which through radiocarbon dating has been tentatively dated to nearly 23,000 years old.[2] Maps, in other words, are older than the earliest writing, cities, or the invention of agriculture. Indeed, maps are one of the oldest examples of abstract human reasoning.

Leaving aside cave drawings and rock carvings, the oldest clearly recognizable maps that have survived the ravages of time are found on clay tablets in ancient Mesopotamia. Mesopotamia, roughly the modern Middle East, is the "cradle of civilization": the place where humans first practised agriculture, founded cities, invented the wheel, and developed writing. In the 1930s, archaeologists digging in the desert outside the city of Kirkuk in northern Iraq uncovered an ancient clay tablet with a map etched into it. Dated to 2500 BC, the map shows an area of land between two hills with a river or stream running through it. Cuneiform writing on the tablet explains that the map depicts an estate of 354 iku (roughly twelve hectares) owned by a man named Azala. Three circles on the tablet seem to indicate the cardinal points north, east, and west, though an alternative theory holds that these circles are meant to represent cities.[3] Regardless, the meaning of the clay tablet is clear: it is a property deed or estate map—a reminder that from the very dawn of civilization maps have been instruments of power, of saying that this patch of ground belongs to one person and not another.

The oldest world map is also one found on a clay tablet unearthed in the ancient Near East—though few would likely guess that this is what the map shows. Dated to around 600 BC, the tablet shows at the centre of the world the city of Babylon, with the Euphrates River draining into the Persian Gulf, and these lands surrounded by ocean. The idea that the world was flat and surrounded by water was a common belief among early civilizations—as was (and is) the notion that one's own civilization is the centre of the world.

When the ancient Egyptians invented papyrus—a type of paper made from the pith of the marshy papyrus plant—it became possible to create maps that could easily be folded or rolled up and taken anywhere. Dry conditions in Egypt's sandy deserts have sometimes allowed pieces of these ancient maps to survive to the present. One of the most famous examples is the Turin Papyrus Map, which depicts the route to an Egyptian stone quarry as well as a separate gold mine. It's considered by some geographers to be the oldest example of a geological map. Dated to an astonishing 1150 BC—the late Bronze Age, or roughly the time of the mythical Trojan War—it may also be the world's oldest surviving paper map. Other ancient Egyptian papyrus maps illustrate the elaborate layouts of pharaohs' tombs.[4]

While the surviving maps of ancient Babylon and the other early centres of civilization in Mesopotamia and Egypt are the oldest, every civilization made maps. Some of these ancient maps have survived the centuries and are now carefully preserved in museums around the world. Others—most—have been lost forever. Besides the Mesopotamians and Egyptians, the ancient Greeks made maps displaying their view of the world and the layout of their cities. The Romans created maps of their extensive road network. Ancient Chinese maps, drawn on pine wood and silk, show topographic features and cities; maps from ancient India depict sacred rivers and plans of monasteries; elaborate maps of trade routes and different lands were made by early Arab geographers. And in the western hemisphere, there are ancient Mayan maps painted on palace walls and in their famous codexes; Aztec maps of their great cities and the territory they ruled; Olmec maps of the cosmos that have been etched in stone; Incan maps of the road system throughout their empire. They testify that maps are a nearly universal feature of human culture.

Of all these ancient cultures, it was the Greeks who made the greatest strides in cartography. The Greeks were the first to deduce that the world was spherical instead of flat—knowledge that was to revolutionize human understanding of maps and geography. They were also the first to create globes and to devise a grid system of longitude and latitude that allowed for scientific mapping. The Greek geographer Eratosthenes, a mathematical genius, was the first to attempt to calculate the circumference of the Earth and the tilt of its axis—at a time when almost everyone else still believed the Earth was flat. Eratosthenes's calculations, which he worked out by carefully observing shadows in different places and the distance between them, proved amazingly accurate.[5] Seventeen hundred years later, when the Italian navigator Christopher Columbus proposed crossing the Atlantic, he dismissed Eratosthenes's calculations, believing instead that the world was much smaller, which would make it possible for him to sail from Europe to Asia in a matter of weeks by heading west across the Atlantic. Columbus was mistaken—he ended up in the Caribbean instead of India.

The oldest map in this book dates back surprisingly far—indirectly to the Viking Age, over a millennium ago. The actual map, at least the copy that has survived to the present, isn't nearly that old—it's a later copy of a 1590 original made by a scholar in Iceland. But his map is the oldest genuine map incorporating knowledge gained from the Norse voyages to North America—and it may have been partly copied from a much older map from the Viking Age. The Vikings have long fascinated people; many have hoped to uncover one of their faded maps in some forgotten archive. Alas, none have ever come to light. But the single most controversial map in history—the so-called Vinland Map—was unveiled to the world in 1965 by Yale University as an authentic map from the 1400s showing North America based on knowledge passed down by

Vikings. This map, if genuine, would have been the oldest European map showing the New World—except, much to Yale's embarrassment, chemical analysis of its ink later exposed it as a twentieth-century forgery.[6]

Many of the maps featured in this book, although drawn by Europeans, incorporated the knowledge and expertise of aboriginal persons—who very often assisted in their creation. In the yellowed pages of explorers' journals stashed away in archives, like those of Simon Fraser, Peter Fidler, or Alexander Mackenzie, it's common to find mention of aboriginal guides sketching out maps for an uncertain explorer. European explorers were often astonished by the accuracy of these aboriginal maps drawn purely from memory. The fur trader Daniel Harmon, for instance, marvelled:

> The Indians possess a quick perception, and strong curiosity, and a very retentive memory . . . [A]t the expiration of twenty years after they have passed only once through a country, to the distance of several hundred miles, they will return by the same way in which they came. Mountains, hills, prairies, lakes, valleys, remarkable rocks . . . are the objects they especially notice, and by these they are enabled to follow a former track. Almost any Indian, who has passed once through a country, is able to draw so correct a chart of it, with a piece of charcoal, on bark, that an entire stranger, by its assistance, would be able to direct his course to a particular place, several hundred miles distant, without varying a league from his object.[7]

The maps made by aboriginal guides, hunters, or other wayfinders proved invaluable to European explorers—and Harmon's comments were echoed by many of his colleagues. The Inuit in particular were highly regarded for their abilities as mapmakers. The whaling captain and explorer Charles Francis Hall, in his 1864 account of his Arctic voyages, discussed the skills of the Inuit mapmaker Koojesse:

Koojesse finished drawing his chart of the coasts, bays, and islands
from Northumberland Inlet to Resolution Island, and both sides of
the so-called Frobisher Strait to its head. The original of this chart is
now in my possession, and it has always astonished me for its remarkable skill and general accuracy of detail . . . The knowledge that the
Esquimaux possess of the geography of their country is truly wonder-
ful. There is not a part of the coast but what they can well delineate,
when once it has been visited by them, or information concerning it
obtained by others. Their memory is remarkably good.[8]

Sadly, few aboriginal maps have survived. Aboriginal people, like
other hunter-gatherers, tended to make their maps quickly from memory in sand, snow, or dirt, or with charcoal on a piece of birchbark or
tanned animal skin. Most of these maps have been lost, though a few
precious examples have been preserved and can still be seen today. One
of the oldest is incised on birchbark and appears to be a map of the
Mattawa River in northern Ontario. It was discovered in 1841 by a surveying party; the officer in charge of the survey, Captain Bainbrigge,
found the map attached to a tree and believed it had been left there to
show the route that a group of natives had taken in their canoes.
Although it was only an ordinary map quickly incised on birchbark of
the sort that were probably once common, Bainbrigge preserved the
map as a memento, and for that reason, it survived.[9]

But most surviving aboriginal maps are copies, drawn by explorers
or fur traders who based them on the originals that their native guides
made on the spot. This is the case with a map drawn by the famed
Chipewyan travellers Matonabbee and Idotlyazee—men who ranged
over a greater extent of Canada than almost any other person of their
time. In 1767, Moses Norton, the governor of Prince of Wales's Fort on
Hudson Bay, dispatched these two wayfinders to chart the lands and
rivers north along Hudson Bay. They created a map showing in rough

outline the west coast of Hudson Bay across to Great Slave Lake; Norton copied it; and fortunately, that copy still survives. It was to be the inspiration for the incredible journey made a few years later by Matonabbee and his friend Samuel Hearne on foot across thousands of kilometres of Arctic tundra and subarctic forest.

In rare cases, we have surviving maps that were made directly by aboriginal people—drawn in their own hand rather than copied by a fur trader or surveyor. The Hudson's Bay Company's archives has at least thirty such native maps dating from the eighteenth and nineteenth centuries that were drawn to assist various explorers and fur traders— especially the eighteenth-century surveyor Peter Fidler, who was keenly interested in indigenous mapping.[10] Later cartographers working for Canada's Geological Survey in the late nineteenth and early twentieth centuries frequently had their aboriginal guides draw sketch maps in their journals for them—of these, over a hundred survive.[11] Of the ten maps featured in this book, at least seven incorporate contributions from aboriginal guides and pathfinders. So how were aboriginal people able to make such impressive maps purely from memory?

It's a matter of conditioning the mind to "read" the landscape and commit it to memory to the point where it becomes second nature. In the past, many people had these skills, but today, as we've become ever more technology-dependent, such skills are increasingly rare. In an age of smartphones, GPS, and expanding digitization, most people have poor spatial memories and would likely struggle to accurately plot on a map from memory even a small area where they live and work.

There is, however, at least one notable exception to this decline in our mental mapping abilities—the taxi drivers of London, England. To navigate the notoriously complicated streets of London, taxi drivers are required to pass a rigorous test that involves memorizing the city's 25,000 streets as well as many common destinations. Would-be taxi drivers on average require three to four years of meticulous study before they're able to pass the examination. Such a real-life test of mental mapping has given neurobiologists the perfect opportunity to study how our brains handle making new spatial memories. In a ground-breaking study that examined the brains of both taxi drivers and ordinary people, neurobiologists found that London's taxi drivers tend to have significantly more grey matter in their posterior hippocampi—the part of the brain that handles long-term memory and navigation. Even more important, however, was the study's finding that before they began studying London's streets, taxi drivers' brains were no different from an average person's: the change in brain structure came through the process of learning extensive mental maps of the city. The most enlarged hippocampi were found in the most experienced drivers; as for those who failed the test, the grey matter in their posterior hippocampi remained unchanged.[12] The good news is the study reveals that, with rigorous training, it's possible to increase brain functioning and memory even as adults—so you can still become an expert mapmaker if that's your dream.

As an experiment to see whether this is a feasible career option, get some paper and, along with your family or friends, each draw maps from memory of your neighbourhood or hometown. Then, extend the map outward to incorporate as much of the surrounding area as you can confidently draw from memory. With practice, you can gradually increase the amount of territory you can map—something I make a habit of practising for any given location before heading into the wilderness. Wherever possible, on my canoe journeys I prefer to follow the example of aboriginal travellers of Canada's past and rely on mental maps rather than printed ones or GPS—this allows for faster travel, saves time in the field, is more enjoyable, and encourages a deeper connection to the land.

✳

I've long been fascinated with maps. As a child, I had several breakfast placemats that were maps of Canada, which I studied each morning before school as I ate my Frosted Flakes. One of my hobbies became drawing maps of Canada from memory—trying to remember the maze of Arctic islands proved the trickiest part. Oftentimes, bored at school, I'd start doodling Canada maps in the margins of my notebooks. To the annoyance of my teachers, I made hundreds of these maps—a few of the better ones I still have tucked away in a folder with other faded mementoes of my grade-school education.

But my real understanding of maps came from growing up in Ontario's countryside, where with my twin brother, Ben, and our dog Max I would explore the local woods that surrounded our family's home. We'd wander the deciduous forests in all directions—trying to walk silently, barefoot or in moccasins, like the aboriginal hunters in the stories we had read to us. Our rambles often involved searching for fox dens, deer trails, animal skulls, or bird nests. In the summer we'd build "forts" out of sticks and sleep in them—keeping our Swiss Army knives in hand for fear of prowling coyotes, axe murderers, or other bogeymen of our imaginations. Most of all I wanted to be like the native people we learned about in school or in our children's books; I wished, like them, to be able to wander the forest and tell my way by certain signs known only to the ablest woodsmen and native peoples— to find my way by reading the trees, moss, streams, and the sun and stars. We spent an inordinate amount of time in the woods, building rafts to paddle the swamps, among other adventures, and learning by trial and error what plants and berries to eat and especially not to eat— chewing on the jack-in-the-pulpit root is not something I intend to do again. (In the words of the naturalist Bradford Angier, it "burns the mouth like liquid fire."[13]) Our concerned mother, when she hadn't heard from us for a good while and shouting our names proved to no avail since we were usually a long way off, took to pushing on the car horn until we heard the faraway echo through the forest and wearily returned.

Sometimes in our little rambles we'd pause to clear away the leaf litter of the forest floor and with a stick draw out a map: a rock might represent the family home, a piece of bark the barn, some lines the various creeks we'd follow or cross, another stick our "fort," and an "X" the particular spot we were seeking—often some deer hunter's old tree stand, which we'd climb up in order to survey the woods in our quest for our own game, typically squirrels or sasquatch. By far the greatest discovery we ever made was an abandoned trailer deep in the forest. We promptly concluded that it must be the home of an old hermit— who would, naturally we assumed, kill us if he ever caught us trespassing. This mysterious trailer in the woods became the centrepiece of all our maps—the fascinating yet terrifying endpoint of many an adventure, where we believed that our lives would be in great peril should the hermit catch us. We'd sneak about silent as the grave through the ferns that surrounded the rusty old trailer, dashing from oak tree to birch to keep out of sight, crawling forward on our chests through the sarsaparillas and maple saplings to get as close as we dared. (Only later did we learn that it was actually an abandoned hunting trailer.) Eventually, we came to know every nook and cranny of the local woods; nearly every hollow and old tree was recognizable to us for a particular memory it held; and in due time we could, as in the stories about the native hunters we idolized, map from memory the whole of our forest.

While my brother and I may never have found any buried treasure, murderous hermits, gingerbread houses occupied by witches, or other fantastical imaginings of our childhood minds, we did acquire certain basic skills—the mental ability to create a map in one's head based on ground travelled—which helped prepare us for the wilderness canoe trips our father took us on. On these journeys through the lakes of the

Canadian Shield, we'd paddle a cedar-strip canoe lovingly crafted by my father's own hands. We never had a GPS or even topographic maps issued by Canada's Ministry of Natural Resources. Instead, our maps were pencil or ink sketches our father had drawn on lined paper, with a North arrow marked in the corner and a crude scale copied from a canoe book. We would follow these maps to the backcountry lakes accessible only by portages in northern Ontario, where we'd hope to catch our meals of bass and pike. In other words, maps, I learned, could be a lot of fun.

Although I never quit making sketch maps from memory, in school I began to learn more about the science of cartography. First I learned about reading topographic maps and orienteering. Then in archaeology field courses I gained a deeper understanding of the actual process of topographic mapping with a traditional surveyor's transit: the meticulous attention to detail required and the mathematical knowledge needed to triangulate points and reproduce on paper an accurate representation of every hill, valley, depression, and feature of the landscape. My subsequent education included more cutting-edge cartography tools and methods—laser-guided transits, satellite-powered GPS, lidar (air laser), air photos, and GIS computer software programs. But I always remained curious about the older way of doing things, and on my own time I continued to explore earlier methods. From an antique store I purchased a sextant—a type of navigational device invented in the eighteenth century for measuring the angle between the horizon and the sun, stars, or moon. Eventually I learned enough about how to use it to appreciate with sheer awe the superlative skill, patience, and solid mathematical knowledge of the old-time mariners, explorers, and cartographers who charted the world with these and similar instruments. But you don't have to squint at the sun through a strange-looking instrument to appreciate maps.

At some point or another nearly everyone makes use of maps. Maybe it's a car GPS when you're stuck in traffic and trying to find a shortcut.

It could be using Google Maps on a smartphone to find the nearest Tim Hortons or some other important place. Perhaps it's that map you sketched out on a napkin to show the route to a friend's cottage, or the one you hurriedly jotted down on a scrap of paper on campus to indicate how someone can find their lecture hall. Maps of a seating plan at a wedding; maps of the shortest route to a destination; park maps of campsites, hiking trails, or canoe routes; maps of a shopping mall's layout with the location of the store you're looking for; maps of rides and pavilions at amusement parks. Maps on a plane's seatback monitors that display the aircraft's progress; trail maps of ski hills with their black diamonds and other symbols revealing information about different runs; maps of property lines, building blueprints, office fire escapes, airport terminal layouts, public transport systems, city walks, or mountain bike routes. Clearly, the modern world still has many uses for maps.

If I've learned anything about maps, it's that each one tells a story. The maps reproduced in this book were made by First Nations, Scandinavian, French, English, Scottish, Canadian, and American cartographers. Together they tell the story of the land that came to be called Canada. They remind us that there was nothing at all inevitable about the country's borders or geography. The familiar image of Canada's geographic outline—which today occupies such a conspicuous chunk of the world, nearly the whole northern half of an entire continent—might have looked very different. Indeed, it might not have existed at all. That such a vast and diverse land—or really, many lands—ever came to be united in a single state called Canada, with the shape that now seems so familiar, is only one of a whole range of possibilities.

In the beginning, on the earliest maps, "Canada" was not the immense extent of land and sea it comprises today. Originally, "Canada" referred merely to the land on either bank of the St. Lawrence River—territory that was to become the heart of the French Empire in the New World. As the French colonists spread, so too did the name Canada—and by the end of the seventeenth century, "Canada" was being used on maps to indicate everything from the upper Great Lakes to northern Acadia.

By the time of Confederation in 1867, Canada had come to signify the land between Lake Superior in the west and Nova Scotia in the east. Within a few more years the map of Canada had been redrawn to stretch all the way west—across the grasslands of the interior and the snowy peaks of the Rockies to the rainforests of the Pacific coast. By the dawn of the twentieth century the map of Canada had continued to expand northward to the desolate reaches of the High Arctic, beyond even where the Inuit lived. And by the mid-twentieth century Canada had expanded farther still to encompass Newfoundland as well as the mountainous wilderness of Labrador—giving the country its modern shape. Some 9,984,670 square kilometres in all, an immense area nearly larger than the whole of Europe combined, with borders on three of the world's five oceans and more coastline than any other country. Accurately mapping such a vast part of the globe took centuries, persistent effort, and ingenuity—the final 1:50,000 scale topographic map of the last bit of Canada's Arctic was completed only in 2012. As for the undersea bed of Canada's maritime waters, there are parts that still remain uncharted.

Most of that mapping was accomplished peacefully, but national borders are more often than not forged in war—and Canada's are no exception. Though few would probably guess it from how peaceful life now seems in Canada, there is hardly a place anywhere in the southern part of the country that hasn't seen some battle or other—battles that sometimes resulted in the redrawing of maps. Canada was for centuries the battleground of empires. The Iroquois Wars, King William's War, the War of Spanish Succession, the War of Austrian Succession, the Seven Years' War, the American War of Independence, and the War of 1812 were all major conflicts that saw blood spilled in part over who was to rule Canada. During this turbulent era many hundreds of pitched battles were fought on Canadian soil and much of the country-side was laid waste.

Nearly every Canadian settlement, farm, and town from the Detroit River east to Lake Ontario was plundered or torched by marauding American armies and their turncoat Canadian collaborators between 1812 and 1814. Upper Canada's colonial capital, York, was pillaged and burned in April 1813 by American troops under the command of the explorer Zebulon Pike, who was killed in the attack when he was crushed by falling debris from an explosion. The Americans torched the provincial legislative assembly, which included the colonial library. Niagara-on-the-Lake shared the same fate in 1813, in the midst of a December blizzard that left survivors destitute and later prompted bitter reprisals from Canadian colonial forces—who bayoneted much of the American garrison they took by surprise at Fort Niagara, and then, in revenge for their lost homes, burned towns on the American side of the Niagara River. The following year American troops retaliated, again invading Upper Canada and burning the town of St. Davids as the start of a final bloody campaign that saw thousands of casualties in hard-fought battles at Lundy's Lane, Chippawa, Fort Erie, and Cook's Mills. Two and a half years of war had transformed much of Upper Canada into a charred, smouldering wasteland. Hundreds of Canadians were killed or wounded in the fighting at a time when the colony's population numbered only 75,000—a casualty rate comparable to what the country suffered in the World Wars. The memories left were bitter and deep.

This is not the PG-13 version of Canada's past taught in schools. Canada's history was nothing if not bloody. For the better part of a hundred years the French and their aboriginal allies, especially the Wendat, warred with the powerful Iroquois Confederacy of Five Nations—and that war had roots in conflicts that dated back even before the French settlements. Quebec City has been attacked and laid siege to numerous times—the bloodiest of which left much of the city in ruins. Montreal was nearly wiped out by an Iroquois attack in 1660; the city was later fought over by British and French armies, and endured occupation by an American force in the Revolutionary War. Nearly every town in southern Quebec—the heart of Old Canada—was the scene of some violent raid or skirmish between English colonists and Canadien settlers or Iroquois warriors. Newfoundland's English settlements were laid waste in a brutal campaign between 1696 and 1697 by the Canadien pirate and adventurer Pierre Le Moyne d'Iberville and his Canadien troops, and Nova Scotia and New Brunswick saw interminable wars involving colonial New Englanders, Acadians, British and French regulars, and Mi'kmaq and other First Nation warriors— to say nothing of piracy in the offshore waters. Rival fur empires clashed in the Northwest with wholesale slaughter at places like Seven Oaks; the French and British battled on the seas of Hudson and James Bays; the Inuit fought repeatedly with their Dene and Cree rivals, who were also at war with each other; and the Great Plains warfare between the Sioux, Blackfoot, Plains Cree and other First Nations raged for centuries. In a single day in 1870, a Blackfoot war party killed three to four hundred Cree on the banks of the Belly River near Lethbridge, Alberta—the final battle in a conflict that had lasted off and on for centuries. The Métis were locked in a long-running feud with the Assiniboine, and on the Pacific coast, large-scale raiding and warfare was the norm among the Haida, Tlingit, Kwakwaka'wakw, Nuxalk, Nuu-chah-nulth, Coast Salish, and other First Nations, which persisted right up until the late nineteenth century. In southern Ontario, the largest aboriginal nation, the Neutral or "Chonnonton," as they called themselves, were annihilated in warfare with the Iroquois Confederacy, as were other First Nations. Rebellion erupted in Upper and Lower Canada in 1837, with fighting on the streets of Montreal and Toronto and forgotten skirmishes in little out-of-the-way places like Saint-Denis and the Short Hills. In Lower Canada, the fighting was more bitter and protracted—culminating in the bloody battle at Saint-Eustache and the burning of a Catholic church with rebels trapped inside it. The following year, 1838, saw violent border clashes with American marauders on the St. Lawrence, Niagara, and Detroit rivers as well as on Pelee Island; many feared these violent episodes would spark renewed war with the United States. Further war scares occurred when tensions flared between loggers in the forests of New Brunswick and Maine—the so-called Aroostook War—and on the Pacific coast in 1859 in a dispute over the St. Juan Islands. On the very eve of Confederation were the Fenian raids at Ridgeway and elsewhere; shortly afterward came violent clashes between Métis and Canadian settlers as the new Dominion sought to expand westward, as happened again on a larger scale in 1885. Many of these border wars and conflicts were fought for land, and for much of the time it seemed probable that the map of Canada would be completely redrawn—if not altogether erased. It is the faded, sometimes torn or water-stained maps featured in this book that reveal much of the cut-and-thrust of this violent history.

Out of this chaos and disorder emerged in 1867 a new polity, the Dominion of Canada, which was much smaller than the country we know today. It included just four provinces: Nova Scotia, New Brunswick, and two new creations, Ontario and Quebec, which were carved out of the original colony that had been called Canada since the days of the French Empire. Gradually, the map of Canada grew larger—through diplomacy, political union, land acquisition, and military force, and by dispatching explorers on official expeditions to seek unknown lands in the uninhabited wastes of the High Arctic. It was for a long while a rather uncertain thing—Canada could easily have shared the fate of Mexico, losing much of its territory to American territorial expansion.

That Canada escaped American conquest was not through lack of interest on the United States' part—the Americans launched full-scale military invasions in 1775–76 and again in 1812–14. For nearly the whole of the nineteenth century the Canadian–American border remained militarized; dozens of border fortifications like Fort Lennox, Fort Ingall, Fort Henry, and Fort Mississauga testify to this era of occasional violent clashes and other tense incidents that threatened war. Even as late as 1901, American president Theodore Roosevelt was prepared to use force to redraw the border to his liking. Roosevelt planned to dispatch troops to Alaska to settle a simmering border dispute over the Alaskan panhandle if an international committee didn't rule in the United States' favour—which it did, though Canada refused to accept the decision. In the 1920s the Canadian military, led by veterans of the grim battlefields of the Western Front, still had secret plans and classified tactical maps to fight the United States in the event of another invasion. Canada's borders, in other words, were for over a century contested spaces—forged in war and conflict, subject to change, and with an unfriendly and much larger nation on the opposite side.

Empires have come and gone in Canada. Cultures have flourished and vanished. Communities have bustled then turned into ghost towns. Maps have been drawn and redrawn. It is the nature of human creations that nothing lasts forever; culture and politics are always in a state of flux. But in political terms, 150 years is a surprisingly long time—few political settlements endure that long. Indeed, though we are accustomed to think of Canada as a "young country," the reality is that as a constitutional nation-state, which is what Confederation at its core was about, Canada easily ranks as one of the world's oldest.[14] Few people in 1867 predicted that Canada would last as long as it has—many believed the union would fall apart amid infighting and that annexation by the United States was inevitable. But this book is not about celebrating the past 150 years. It is about taking a look at what led up to 1867 through the maps that have come down to us and the stories they tell.

Pierre Trudeau, who of all of Canada's prime ministers probably saw more of the country and surely spent the most time in a canoe, once reflected, "I know a man whose school could never teach him patriotism but who acquired that virtue when he felt in his bones the vastness of his land and the greatness of those who founded it."[15] Whether one agrees with Trudeau or not—whether one feels a sense of patriotism when reflecting on Canadian history or not—the story of the creation of "Canada," the exploring and settlement of it, the mapping, and the wars fought to define it, is an epic one.

THE VIKINGS: THE SKÁLHOLT MAP

Fearlessness is better than a faint-heart for any man who puts his nose
out of doors. The length of my life and the day of my death were fated
long ago.

—"SKIRNIR'S JOURNEY," VIKING AGE POEM,

CIRCA TENTH CENTURY AD

The ship under sail pitched and swayed as a bearded warrior gazed across heaving seas at fog-bound cliffs. Hidden beyond those grey mists might be a land of frost giants, fire-breathing dragons, deadly serpents, or other strange beings. It was a land no man on board the ship had ever seen before—it was Canada, long before that name had any meaning.

If you were to visit Denmark's Royal Library, you might find stashed away in a temperature-controlled room a curious map. Known as the Skálholt Map, it was drawn by an Icelandic scholar named Sigurd Stefánsson in 1590 based on knowledge passed down from the much earlier Viking voyages to the New World. Stefánsson's original map has been lost, but a 1669 copy of it is what now sits in Denmark's archive. [1] This ancient Icelandic map reveals two incredible exploration stories separated by nearly a millennium: the Viking voyages to North America five hundred years before Columbus, and the modern discovery of "Vinland" by the remarkable husband-wife duo of Helge and Anne Stine Ingstad. As far as ancient maps leading to astonishing discoveries go, it's the stuff of legend.

The Vikings were among the greatest seafarers, warriors, and adventurers the world has ever known. From their homelands in the modern countries of Norway, Sweden, and Denmark—which in their time were divided into hundreds of small chiefdoms and kingdoms that frequently warred with each other—they began an extraordinary expansion in the year 793 AD, launching lightning raids on the Christian lands to the south in their dragon-headed longboats. The bearded, sword- and axe-wielding warriors of the North terrified southern kingdoms that viewed them as barbarians. The Vikings eagerly raided these lands for gold, silver, and slaves, or "thralls," as they called the unfortunate souls carried off as prisoners to work on their farms or in their households. Their attacks and seafaring exploits took them across the North Sea to England, Scotland, and Ireland, which they raided, plundered, and eventually conquered and colonized. Other Vikings sailed along the coasts of France and Spain, plundering as they went—even sacking Paris—and eventually rounding the Cape of Gibraltar into the warm waters of the Mediterranean Sea. Here, they raided the islands of Corsica, Sicily, Sardinia, the southern coasts of France and Spain, North Africa, and Italy. They travelled to Greece and Byzantium, where they traded their wares with Greek, Jewish, and Roman merchants. They were respected, and they were feared. The Eastern Roman emperor at Constantinople even created an elite, all-Viking bodyguard composed of these exotic northerners. The famed "Varangian Guard," as it was known, served Byzantine emperors for centuries.

Other Vikings departing from their homelands in Sweden, Denmark, and the island of Gotland sailed their ships across the Baltic Sea and up the wild rivers of Russia, rowing where necessary against the current. When the rivers became too shallow or swift to make headway, rather than retreat, the Vikings amazingly pressed onward by portaging their ships overland through the Russian wilderness—eventually making it all the way to the great inland bodies of water known as the Black Sea and the Caspian Sea. Large boulders elaborately incised with runes—the writing of the Vikings—testify to their exploits in these distant lands. One such example found on a Swedish runestone reads: "Tóla had this stone raised in memory of her son Haraldr, Ingvarr's brother. They travelled valiantly far for gold, and in the east gave food to the eagle. They died in the south in Serkland."[2] To give "food to the eagle" meant to slay one's enemies—a major Viking preoccupation.

The Vikings pushed on in their ceaseless, restless quests southward to the deserts of the Middle East—and their trade routes eventually extended all the way to distant India. In an era when most people lived and died within a short distance of where they were born, the Vikings were exceptional in the extreme: almost no other people in the world had ever travelled and ranged over such a large portion of the globe, encountering so many different lands, kingdoms, cultures, and environments. What motivated these northern farmers to risk all on such dangerous voyages to unknown lands from which many never returned?

Some historians have theorized that it was overpopulation in Scandinavia that drove the Vikings to seek new farmlands and opportunities abroad. Others argue that it was a desire to maintain their restless sense of freedom as their homelands gradually became subjected to the centralized control of powerful kings. The Vikings, after all, had a rough sense of justice and personal honour that often led to violent duels to redress perceived wrongs. Like his father before him, Eirik the Red, the founder of Greenland, had been involved in several such fatal affairs. But ultimately the most plausible reason behind the Viking expansion is the one offered by the Norse themselves. A medieval Norwegian manuscript from 1250, known as "The King's Mirror," offers this explanation for why Norse seafarers would risk journeys to distant shores, in this case Greenland:

You ask what men are looking for when they go to Greenland, and why they travel there at such great risk to their lives. The answer lies in the threefold nature of man. One element is competitiveness and the desire for fame, for it is in a man's nature to travel to places where dangers are to be encountered, in order to win renown. Another element is curiosity, for it is in a man's nature to enquire into things that he has heard about and to find out for himself whether what he has been told is true or not. The third element is acquisitiveness, for men will look for wealth wherever they hear they can get hold of it, even though acquiring it involves great danger. [3]

In the stormy North Atlantic, the Vikings, using their ingenious ships—the most technologically advanced vessels of their time—managed to sail to remote and isolated islands like the Shetlands, Faroes, Hebrides, and Orkneys, all of which fell under their sway. By the year 870 they had pushed into the open ocean and discovered Iceland—a wild land of fire and ice that must have struck the first Viking settlers as something straight out of their myths.[4] The lava-filled volcanoes, boiling hot springs, shooting geysers, glacier-fed waterfalls, and snowy mountains of this remote island in the northern ocean was a setting worthy of the stories told about Thor, Odin, Loki, and the other Norse gods. Aside from a few Irish monks who may have inadvertently drifted ashore in their diminutive skin boats, the Vikings were the first humans to set foot on Iceland.

What is perhaps most impressive is that the Vikings did all this before the invention of the compass, quadrant, sextant, or other navigational devices. To navigate the formidable seas in their open boats with a single square sail, which, it must be remembered, few people ever dared attempt—even among the Norse the seafaring raiders known as Vikings were exceptional—they relied on the sun and stars. With these celestial bodies, skilled Norse mariners could reckon their latitude fairly accurately so that they would know roughly how far north or south they had gone, but they had no means to estimate longitude. Dead reckoning, birds, sea currents and seaweeds, and a degree of luck—or faith in their gods—were often their only means of estimating their distance from land in unfamiliar waters. On days when thick clouds hid the sun, the Vikings may have used "sunstones"—a type of mineral known as Icelandic spar, a transparent variety of calcite found in Iceland—to locate the sun through its polarizing qualities. With only these relatively primitive navigational methods at their disposal, the Norse were able to plot on a map a wider portion of the earth than almost any other people of their time. Alas, no Viking maps have survived down through the ages for us to examine today—but we do have later copies, notably the Skálholt Map.[5]

From Iceland, in either 982 or 983—the exact year is uncertain—the ever-restless Vikings pushed on, crossing frigid and dangerous seas to a land of towering glaciers, fjords, and snow-capped mountains. This was, as Eirik the Red named it, the huge island of Greenland. It had been, at the point the Norse discovered it, a wilderness populated only by polar bears, walrus, seals, reindeer, and a few other hardy Arctic animals. Greenland must have at first seemed like the end of the known world. The Viking settlers, however, managed to carve out a life in this harsh land—hunting reindeer, polar bears, walrus, seals, whales, and birds; catching fish; and raising livestock at the grassy heads of the deep ocean fjords. From shore or in small boats they hunted narwhals; back in Europe, they would sell the long ivory tusks as "unicorn horns" discovered in enchanted lands in the far North. On Greenland there were no trees aside from small stands of dwarf birches; but, resourceful as ever, the Norse made their houses out of sod blocks cut from the ground and stones. The Norse settlements on Greenland would flourish for centuries—which later led some to wonder: had the Vikings managed to push on farther still across the seas to North America?

There were, after all, the ancient sagas: oral stories told and retold for generations about voyages to distant lands, heroes and kings, old feuds, and the history of the Norse. Icelandic scholars eventually wrote these down in the 1200s and 1300s—centuries after the events they purported to describe. Of the hundreds of sagas that have been preserved in archives and museums, there are two in particular, the *Saga of the Greenlanders* and *Eirik the Red's Saga*, that describe in detail voyages to unknown lands west of Greenland, which the Norse had explored and even settled—as well as scattered references in other surviving medieval documents. In addition to these sources, there are a few mysterious old Icelandic maps—the earliest of which is the Skálholt Map—that show lands across the Atlantic from Europe. In the nineteenth century, long after the Vikings had vanished and their descendants assimilated into the European mainstream, some historians began to speculate about whether the sagas might be more than just myth. Could it be possible that, five hundred years before Columbus, the Vikings had made journeys across the stormy, iceberg-filled North Atlantic to America? In Iceland, where the Viking legacy was strongest, historians had almost always accepted the voyages to "Vinland" as real history that had become embellished with legend, rather than just pure myths.

Not everyone was convinced. Skeptics pointed out that if the Vikings *had* made voyages to the New World, what happened to them? Why hadn't anyone found any Viking ruins or artifacts anywhere in North America? Why hadn't later European explorers like Cabot, Cartier, and Champlain met with any of their descendants? The sagas, cynics said, were just old legends, little more than campfire stories, unreliable oral traditions that could not be taken as real history. They mingled the names of real people, like Thorvald and Leif Eriksson, with stories of monsters, strange creatures, and talking ghosts.

Still, starting in the late nineteenth century, settlers in Canada and the United States claimed to find strange stone carvings incised with runes—the writing of the Vikings—as well as iron swords and other mysterious artifacts. In northern Ontario, in the little logging town of Beardmore, north of Lake Superior, a medieval sword, axe, and part of a shield turned up in the 1930s—proof, it was claimed, of Vikings having once been there. Farther south, in Rhode Island, an old stone tower was claimed by some to have been built by Vikings, and later a Norse coin was supposedly unearthed in Maine. Yet none of these artifacts and runes withstood close scrutiny—they were all proven to be fakes, or real artifacts that had been planted as hoaxes, or simply things unrelated to Vikings, as was the case with the stone tower, which turned out to be the ruins of a seventeenth-century windmill. There remained no definitive evidence that the Vikings had ever set foot on North American soil other than in Greenland. But this fact didn't discourage people from continuing to speculate on the matter.

The sagas describe multiple voyages to, and one substantial settlement in, "Vinland," a country with grapes somewhere southwest of Greenland. One of the major clues to the unravelling of the centuries-old mystery of where the Vikings settled in North America—if they settled at all—was the half-forgotten map made in 1590 by the Icelander Sigurd Stefánsson. He created it based either on what he knew of the Viking voyages as told in the sagas or quite possibly on an even older map that had survived from the time of the Vikings—which, if it ever did exist, now no longer does. The sagas were already centuries old by the time Stefánsson made his map, but knowledge of them had been much better preserved and kept alive in Iceland than elsewhere. Stefánsson's original map has since been lost, but fortunately for posterity, it was copied in a 1669 book about Greenland, which has survived. By carefully examining Stefánsson's map—known as the Skálholt Map after the town in Iceland where he lived—in connection with what the sagas relate about the Viking voyages to Vinland, we can glimpse a part of Canada as it existed a thousand years ago. But to decipher Stefánsson's map we first need to consider the Vinland sagas.

The sagas do not agree on all points—they have certain contradictions—but overall there is enough agreement between them to stitch together a coherent narrative of the Viking discovery of North America. It begins in Norway with an ambitious young man named Eirik the Red, so called because of his red hair, and perhaps also his fiery temper. While Eirik was still a youth, he and his father left Norway "because of some killings," as the saga puts it. [6] They sailed to Iceland and settled in the northwest of the island at Drangar. Here Eirik initially prospered—he married into a prominent family, established a farmstead, and had a son named Leif. But, as is common among Vikings, he soon fell into quarrels with his neighbours, and killed two men. Eirik was then forced to relocate to a different part of Iceland. Here things followed a similar pattern—Eirik, though charismatic and popular, became embroiled in a dispute with some neighbours who had borrowed his property and failed to return it. This dispute sparked fighting between Eirik and his friends against their rivals, and several more people were killed. This time, the local assembly voted to banish Eirik from Iceland for his crimes. Eirik had to pack up his belongings and with his family and followers seek a new future elsewhere. He must have been truly brave or truly desperate—or likely both—to have embarked on the course that he did. In his ship, Eirik headed west across icy seas to seek an unknown land that other Norsemen had reported earlier but that no one had ever successfully settled. It turned out to be a wasteland of desolate glaciers, windswept rocks, ice and snow. Naturally, Eirik called it "Greenland." An appealing name, he figured, would be more likely to attract other settlers. After exploring the barren land for three years and eking out an existence there off reindeer, fish, and a few farm animals, Eirik returned in his ship to Iceland to recruit more settlers to join him in the new country.

Of the twenty-five ships that departed that summer from Iceland with Eirik to seek Greenland, only fourteen reached their destination. The others were blown off course and had to turn back or were lost at sea—a stark indication of how dangerous sea voyages were in the Viking Age. The icy waters of the North Atlantic were incredibly deadly: sailors could be swept overboard, storms could capsize or swamp even the best-built ships, and there were no lighthouses or nautical charts to warn of the many thousands of reefs, shoals, and rocky islands that could spell doom for any vessel. Thick fogs often further hid these dangers, and shipwrecks were commonplace. The fact that Eirik was able to convince so many to follow him—twenty-five ships in all, holding three or four hundred people—is a testament to his powers of persuasion as well as the restless, adventurous spirit of the Norse Icelanders.

Shortly after the colony was established, in 986 the Icelandic trader Bjarni Herjólfsson attempted to visit his father in Greenland, who was one of the new settlers there, but was blown off course by dangerous storms. When the sea calmed and the fog lifted, Bjarni and his crew found themselves off the coast of a mysterious land none of them recognized. It was, in the words of the saga, "well wooded and with low hills."[7] Bjarni and his men did not set foot on shore but kept sailing, passing more unfamiliar lands, including ones with mountains and glaciers. The crew wanted to go ashore to investigate, but Bjarni refused. After several weeks of sailing they eventually crossed the sea again and made it safely to Greenland, unsure of where they had been.

In Greenland, Bjarni met Eirik's son Leif and told him about the mysterious lands he and his crew had sighted to the southwest. Intrigued by what he heard, Leif resolved to seek out these unknown lands and explore them. He purchased Bjarni's ships and recruited a crew of thirty-five brave men willing to accompany him. The crew was a mix of Greenlanders, Icelanders, and at least one German. Leif asked his father, Eirik, to lead the expedition. Eirik was reluctant; as the saga puts it, "he said he was getting old, and could endure hardships less easily than he used to."[8] But Leif dismissed his father's concerns and managed to persuade him. The Vikings, however, were superstitious— and on the day they were to depart Greenland to seek the unknown, an ill omen occurred. As Eirik was riding on horseback down to the sea to board the waiting ship, his horse stumbled and he was thrown off, injuring his leg. According to the saga, Eirik concluded, "I am not meant to discover more countries than this one we now live in. This is as far as we go together."[9] Thus it fell to Leif to lead the expedition.

Leif was well suited for the undertaking. The *Saga of the Greenlanders* describes him as "big and strong, of striking appearance, shrewd, and in every respect a temperate, fair-dealing man, wise, and an outstanding leader."[10] Leif was already a seasoned sailor by the time of his fateful voyage, which was around the year 1000; he had sailed across much of the North Atlantic, including voyages to Iceland, Norway, Greenland, and perhaps also the British Isles. Tradition held that while in Norway Leif had served as an attendant to the great King Olaf Tryggvason, who was later killed in battle. In the Hebrides he had apparently had a passionate romance with a local woman of noble birth named Thorgunna. And while sailing to Greenland, at some point—the exact chronology is uncertain—he had rescued a party of shipwrecked sailors who were clinging to some floating wreckage in the sea. This fortunate event gave rise to Leif's nickname: "Leif the Lucky."

On the voyage in search of the lands sighted earlier by Bjarni, Leif lived up to his nickname. His ship survived the crossing of the rough seas immediately west of Greenland and came upon a shoreline that matched what Bjarni had described. The saga records this event of world historical significance in a straightforward, almost nonchalant, manner:

The first landfall they made was the country Bjarni had sighted last. They sailed right up to the shore and cast anchor, then lowered a boat and landed. There was no grass to be seen, and the hinterland was covered with great glaciers, and between glaciers and shore the land was like one great slab of rock. It seemed to them a worthless country.

Then Leif said, "Now we have done better than Bjarni where this country is concerned—we have at least set foot on it. I shall give this country a name and call it Helluland."[11]

The old Norse word "Helluland," translated into English, literally means "Slab-Stone Land," or more loosely "land of flat stones." This descriptive name is a close match for much of Canada's northeastern Arctic, which has endless miles of desolate flat grey rocks. Such an environment would not have offered the Norse anything they couldn't already find in Greenland, so Leif and his crew continued sailing south from Helluland deeper into the unknown. The saga explains that they reached a second land, and as before, boldly rowed ashore in their ship's small boat. This time the land was thickly forested, with sandy white beaches all along its shores. Leif again decided to name it— calling it "Markland," which in English means "land of forests."

Markland was probably southern Labrador, which is cloaked in subarctic boreal forest and has white sandy beaches along its wind-swept shores. A wooded country would be highly valuable to the Greenlanders—coming as they did from a land that lacked forests. The Vikings needed wood not only to build their all-important sailing ships and smaller fishing vessels, but also for fuel, carvings, tool handles, and wooden nails.

Next Leif led his crew south from Markland. They sailed for another two days before sighting land again, where they once more ventured ashore. The saga records:

They went ashore and looked about them. The weather was fine. There was dew on the grass, and the first thing they did was to get some of it on their hands and put it to their lips, and to them it seemed the sweetest thing they had ever tasted. Then they went back to their ship and sailed into the sound that lay between the island and the headland jutting out to the north.[12]

At this third land, the most promising of them all, Leif and his crew decided to build houses and overwinter. Compared with Greenland, to the Norse this new country seemed remarkably mild and blessed with resources. Near where they made their camp were a lake and a river, with "bigger salmon than they had ever seen."[13] There was also plenty of grass for their livestock to graze upon. Moreover, since they were considerably farther south than their homes in Iceland and Greenland, the variation in daylight was less extreme throughout the year—something that would strike any Arctic dweller visiting a more southerly latitude. The saga mentions that "in the depth of winter the sun was aloft by mid-morning and still visible at mid-afternoon."[14]

From their base camp, Leif divided the company into two parties: one was sent to explore more of the surrounding country, while the other was to remain behind and maintain the settlement. On one of these exploring journeys, Tyrkir, the German, made a discovery that was to greatly influence subsequent events. The *Saga of the Greenlanders* describes Tyrkir as rather homely, small in stature, and frail-looking—but very skilled with his hands. One evening it was reported that Tyrkir had gone missing, news that alarmed Leif, as Tyrkir had been part of his family's household and had helped raise Leif, who still affectionately called him his "foster-father." Leif organized a party to search for the missing German. They found Tyrkir in such an excited state that at first he spoke rapidly only in his native German, which no one else could understand. After Tyrkir calmed down and finally spoke in Norse, he explained that he'd come across something that would have seemed almost mythical to Arctic Vikings—wild grapes. When Leif, astonished, asked if it was true, Tyrkir explained that he'd often seen grapes and vines where he was born, so he at once recognized them.

Grapes are not found in Greenland or Iceland, which are too cold for them, nor in the Viking homelands in Scandinavia, which are also too far north. Instead the alcoholic beverage of choice for the Vikings was mead, made from fermented honey. But the Norse would have known wine and grapes through their travels and trade, and Leif instantly understood the great value of Tyrkir's discovery. He resolved that the party would on alternate days cut vines and gather grapes, and continue to fell trees, until their ship had a full cargo. The *Saga of the Greenlanders* records: "In the spring they made ready to leave and sailed away. Leif named the country after its natural qualities and called it Vinland."[15] Or, translated into English, "Wine Land."

The Norse returned in their ship to the settlement in Greenland that spring—carrying with them their precious cargo. It was on this return journey that Leif apparently rescued the shipwrecked mariners, gaining his nickname "the Lucky." News of Leif's explorations and cargo would have spread rapidly throughout the isolated Greenlandic settlements and to Iceland, and indeed to the wider Viking world. Mention of "Vinland" can be found in various medieval documents—proof that the story reached Europe. The earliest of these is the German chronicler Adam of Bremen's *Descriptio Insularum Aquilonis*, written circa 1075.

Back in Greenland, there was much talk of Leif's discovery. Leif's younger brother Thorvald was eager to follow up his brother's explorations. Leif agreed, and allowed Thorvald to use his ships as well as the sod houses he'd already constructed in Vinland. Under Leif's guidance, Thorvald prepared the ship for the journey and engaged a crew of thirty men. They apparently reached the houses in Vinland without much trouble. The Norse overwintered at the settlement, living off fish. In the spring, Thorvald divided the party, keeping one group in the main ship with him and sending the other in a small boat to explore westward along the coast. The *Saga of the Greenlanders* explains:

> They found the country there very attractive, with woods stretch-
> ing almost down to the shore and white sandy beaches. There were
> numerous islands there, and extensive shallows. They found no traces
> of human habitation or animals except on one westerly island, where
> they found a wooden stack-cover. That was the only man-made thing
> they found; and in the autumn they returned to Leif's Houses.[16]

The Vikings again overwintered at the settlement—a mild experience compared with what they were used to in Greenland. The following summer Thorvald set off in his ship along the coast, seeking to
explore more of these mysterious lands. A fierce storm, however, drove
their ship ashore, damaging the vessel and forcing the Norse to stay put
for several weeks as they worked to repair it. Soon after refitting their
ship, the Vikings came upon a large, heavily wooded fjord with towering cliffs plunging down into the sea. The spot's beauty appealed to
Thorvald, who, after exploring the area on foot with his companions,
remarked, "Here I should like to make my home."[17]

Alas for Thorvald, this was not to be. When the Norse were on their
way back to the moored ship, they spotted three overturned skin boats
lying on a sandy beach. Under each boat they could see three sleeping
men—not Norse. This chance meeting was the first recorded encounter between Europeans and Native Americans, some thousand years
ago. It did not go well. The Vikings and natives, no doubt surprised by
and suspicious of each other, fought. The sagas are vague about the
details, but the Vikings would have been armed with swords, axes,
spears, bows and arrows, and shields. The natives most likely relied on
their bows and arrows, but perhaps also had spears. Thorvald and his

men—who apparently had the element of surprise and likely terrified their opponents, who'd never seen anything like them before—killed eight natives; only one escaped alive by fleeing in a skin boat.

The man who fled sounded the alarm to the rest of his companions some distance away. With what must have been remarkable courage considering the circumstances, they returned to face these strange men and avenge their fallen comrades. According to the saga, Thorvald and his companions were sleeping when they were startled by a swarm of skin boats paddling down the fjord. Now it was the Vikings who were outnumbered and on the defensive. Thorvald and his men took cover in their ship as the natives fired arrows at them before retreating. An arrow slipped past Thorvald's shield and struck him under the armpit, mortally wounding him. Realizing that he was dying, Thorvald asked his men to bury his body at the headland that he had wanted to make his home. The Norse carried out this sad task, and now leaderless, spent the winter at the base camp that Leif and his crew had established earlier. They loaded their ship with grapes and wood, and in the spring sailed back to Greenland.

Meanwhile, back in Greenland, Eirik the Red had died. Leadership of the settlements had passed to Leif, which meant that he'd be unable to make any further journeys of exploration. Still, he and his family were eager to retrieve Thorvald's body and return it to Greenland for proper burial. The task of leading a new expedition to Vinland to recover Thorvald's body—and, presumably, to gather more wine and wood—fell to Leif's youngest brother, Thorstein. The saga records that for this journey, Thorstein "selected the biggest and strongest men available. He took a crew of twenty-five and his wife Gudrid as well."[18] However, their ship never reached Vinland. All summer long they were blown off course, finding themselves at the mercy of storms and unfavourable winds—a reminder that those who would seek unknown lands did so at the risk of their lives.

Eventually, just before the winter set in, Thorstein's ship returned to Greenland, having failed to reach Vinland. The winter proved a harsh one—disease broke out in the Norse settlements, and Thorstein was among those who died. His widow, Gudrid, went the next summer to live with her in-laws on Leif's farm. There, she caught the eye of the captain of a merchant ship that had arrived from Norway—a wealthy Icelander named Thorfinn Karlsefni, who was on friendly terms with Leif. Karlsefni fell in love with Gudrid, who was still young, and the two were soon married.

Together the Viking newlyweds Karlsefni and Gudrid decided to make a new voyage to Vinland on a much larger and more ambitious scale than anything yet attempted. The expedition involved sixty men and five women according to the *Saga of the Greenlanders*, but according to *Eirik the Red's Saga* it was even larger, with 140 people divided between three ships. Unlike the previous voyages, this was no mere exploring journey or resource-gathering trip, but rather an attempt at full-blown settlement. Sheep, pigs, cattle, and even a bull were loaded onto the ships and taken on the voyage to Vinland.

Karlsefni's expedition was given permission by Leif to use the houses he and his crew had previously erected. The expedition sailed first to Helluland, then along the shores of Markland—where reefs and rocks would have presented great danger, and where they saw an island with polar bears on it. Several more days of sailing brought them along a peninsula with exceptionally long sandy beaches, which they named Furdustrandir ("Wonder Beaches"). They may have wintered somewhere near here or a little way south; *Eirik the Red's Saga* mentions that the party endured a harsh first winter, surviving off a whale that washed ashore. There were tensions between those who worshipped the old gods—and saw the beached whale as a gift from Thor—and the converted Christians. Thorvald the Hunter, an old pagan who'd been a close friend of Eirik the Red's and was said to have a wide knowledge of "uninhabited regions," led a splinter group that went off on their own in one of the party's ships.[19]

The majority, however, remained with Karlsefni and Gudrid, and seem to have reached Leif's base camp. During the Norse's second summer at the settlement, or perhaps on one of their exploratory journeys southward, they encountered natives—whom they called "Skraelings," a word meaning something like "wretched." Possibly the name referred to the size difference between the Norse and the natives, since the sagas describe the Skraelings as small in stature. Maybe this was just idle boasting on the Vikings' part, but from the skeletal record we do know that the Norse were exceptionally tall for their era—when the average human height was considerably shorter than it is today.[20] The Skraelings were most likely the ancestors of either the Innu, Mi'kmaq, or Beothuk peoples.

The natives were eager to trade with these strange visitors from beyond the waves—especially for their weapons and tools, which were made of smelted iron, a material entirely unknown to them. Karlsefni, however, forbade his men from trading weapons. Instead, he had the Norse women offer the natives goat milk, which proved so popular that they traded all the tanned animal skins and furs they had for more of it. But the Norse remained suspicious of the natives—who must have outnumbered them— and Karlsefni, more cautious than Thorvald had been, ordered that a palisade be erected around the settlement. Gudrid, meanwhile, gave birth to a son named Snorri—the first child of European descent to be born in North America outside of Greenland, and the first in what would become Canada.

The following year, the Norse and natives again traded on the same terms as before: milk for hides. The Norse also offered red cloth in exchange for skins.[21] But suspicions remained high—and one of the Vikings killed a Skraeling after he was caught trying to steal weapons. This caused the others to flee, abandoning their furs and what they had to trade. Karlsefni realized that the killing would spark retaliation, and so he and the Norse prepared themselves for battle. In the ensuing fight, several Norsemen and natives were killed. Sporadic clashes between the two groups continued thereafter.

Despite the dangers, Karlsefni and the Norse made additional exploratory voyages from Leif's settlement farther south—much farther south. They sailed to a place where there were extensive tidal lagoons, grapes, forests, and many more Skraelings. They called this place "Hop," a word meaning tidal lagoon. It was said to have many wild grapes and "self-sown" wheat as well as a great many salmon in the rivers. Karlsefni and his ship's crew spent one winter at Hop before leaving because of hostilities with the natives—who were far more numerous here than farther north. Several more Norsemen were apparently killed in the fighting near Hop. After more than three years in Vinland, Karlsefni, Gudrid, their son, Snorri, and the rest of the Vikings returned to Greenland and Iceland. They brought with them more grapes, pelts, and wood.

Other voyages to Vinland followed. One was led by Leif's strong-willed half-sister, Freydis. Eirik the Red had fathered her out of wedlock after his wife converted to Christianity and, so the saga says, refused to sleep with him any longer because he wouldn't abandon the worship of the old gods. Freydis took after her fiery father. She resolved to lead her own voyage to Vinland and settle there.

However, Freydis's venture ended in disaster. The natives returned and attacked the settlements; during the fight, Freydis herself, disgusted with the cowardice of her male companions, grabbed a sword from a slain Norseman and brandished it at a group of natives in the woods—who fled in terror at the sight of this wild woman. Despite this triumph, divisions later arose in the Norse settlements, centred on the rivalry between Freydis and two Icelandic brothers who had outfitted their own ship and crew and were supposed to be co-leaders of the settlement. If the sagas are to be believed, Freydis led a cold-blooded massacre of the brothers and their followers, catching them off-guard while they slept in their sod houses. After the men were killed, the saga records that

> soon only the women were left; but no one was willing to kill them.
> Freydis said, "Give me an axe."[22]

Such, at any rate, were the stories preserved in the Icelandic sagas. But how much truth there was to them could ultimately be settled only by the discovery of the Norse settlements described in the sagas. It was the Skálholt Map that proved the crucial clue in deciphering the saga's geography.

On the lower right of the map, or southeastern portion, are the familiar outlines of Ireland and Great Britain—both raided and colonized by Vikings for centuries. Just north of them in the Atlantic are the various islands of the Orkneys, Shetlands, and Faroes, all of them important waypoints for Norse seafarers as sources of fresh water and safe harbour. At the top right of the map is Norway, land of deep-ocean fjords and mountains, homeland of the Vikings who dared to cross the open ocean. West of there we see drawn on the map a slightly larger island—this is Iceland, and beyond that is the immense expanse of Greenland, extending northward to the Arctic ice pack, which is drawn on the map as if it were land. In these mysterious nether regions of polar ice is labelled at the top right Jötunheimr—the mythical home of giants in Norse mythology.

But where the map gets really interesting is on the left-hand side, or western portion. Here we see, about halfway down, Helleland: the "Stone-Slab Land" named by Leif Eriksson in the sagas. The latitude, noted in the map's margins for Helluland, is around 62 degrees north, which happens to correspond to the actual location of southern Baffin

Island. The sagas' description of Helleland—a bleak place of mountains, glaciers, and large, flat stones—also closely matches southern Baffin Island's landscape. Immediately south of Helleland is a body of water—this appears to be Hudson Strait, which separates Baffin Island from Arctic Quebec and Labrador. Next on the map appears Markland—"land of forests." The sagas' description of Markland as a heavily wooded country suggests a match with the dense forest cover of southern Labrador. The sagas' fabulous "Wonder Beaches" are probably Labrador's actual Porcupine Strand, a section of long, sandy white beaches that extends for nearly forty kilometres. After Markland the map indicates another body of water extending inland—this might be Hamilton Inlet, which penetrates deep into Labrador's interior. Immediately south of this on the map is "Skraeling Land," which appears to be southern Labrador and Quebec. This territory would have been inhabited by the ancestors of the Montagnais, an Algonquin-speaking group known to have made canoes from moose skins—again as described in the sagas.

Directly across a narrow bay from Skraeling Land is labelled Promontorium Winlandiae, or in English, "Wineland Promontory." The shape of this long, relatively narrow peninsula matches the outline of Newfoundland's Great Northern Peninsula, which is famous today for its fjords and spectacular scenery. The Great Northern Peninsula is separated from mainland Labrador and Quebec by the narrow Strait of Belle Isle, which might be mistaken for a large bay or fjord—as it seems to have been on Stefánsson's map. The latitude given in the margins doesn't match that of the Great Northern Peninsula—something to be expected, given the hazy nature of Stefánsson's sources—but rather intriguingly, if we trace a line across the map from the tip of the Vinland promontory east across the ocean, we see that it matches up with southern Ireland—and indeed, the actual latitude of L'Anse aux Meadows, on the very tip of the Great

Northern Peninsula, corresponds to that of southern Ireland. Such, then, are the clues offered by the Skálholt Map.

Most researchers searching for evidence of Vikings in the New World, however, didn't pay much attention to the Skálholt Map. Given that the sagas describe wild grapes, it was assumed that if the Norse had made it to North America, the New England coast was the most likely location—because it, unlike Newfoundland and Labrador, has wild grapes.

But one researcher who did pay close attention to the Skálholt Map was William Munn, a marine insurance broker in St. John's, Newfoundland. Munn had no formal background as either a historian or an archaeologist, but he did have an active mind and a good sense of geography, and he tried to unravel the Vinland mystery. He was convinced that the promontory marked as Vinland on the Skálholt Map depicted Newfoundland's Great Northern Peninsula. With this assumption as his starting point, Munn closely scrutinized the sagas' descriptions of islands, fjords, bays, and rivers, and tried to plot them on a modern map of eastern North America.

He concluded that the location where Leif and his crew first landed was the little fishing village of L'Anse aux Meadows, on the very tip of Newfoundland's Great Northern Peninsula. In 1914, Munn self-published a pamphlet outlining his novel theory. He figured that Leif probably built his houses on Pistolet Bay, about fifteen kilometres west of L'Anse aux Meadows. Munn's pamphlet, at the time, attracted little notice—since he wasn't an archaeologist or historian, few paid much attention to his claims. They were, after all, just speculations, with no hard evidence to back them up, and many others had already published articles and books speculating about the Vikings' "Vinland" voyages. Some thought that Cape Breton, with its forested mountains and salmon streams, was the most likely location for where the Vikings had landed. Others argued that it might be New Brunswick, the Gaspé

Peninsula, the Bay of Fundy, Maine, Cape Cod, or even as far south as New York. Indeed, most scholars still favoured somewhere in New England because of the emphasis placed on wild grapes.

But with nothing convincing turning up anywhere, other researchers began to give Munn's ideas a second look. In 1948 an American, Arlington Mallery, inspired by Munn's pamphlet and similar theories published by a Finnish geographer, set off for Newfoundland's Great Northern Peninsula to search for ruins around Pistolet Bay. Mallery found nothing but rocks, which he believed were somehow connected to Vikings—though this proved wishful thinking when archaeologists declared the rocks natural formations. A Danish archaeologist, Jørgen Meldgaard, also searched around Pistolet Bay—but again came up with nothing. Maybe, it began to seem, the cynics were right that the sagas were nothing but myths.

Undiscouraged by these failures, in the 1950s a colourful Norwegian explorer, woodsman, and sailor by the name of Helge Ingstad took up the search for evidence of the Vikings. Ingstad had travelled and hunted in Canada's northern wilderness. Moreover, he was married to Anne Stine, a professional archaeologist with experience excavating Norse ruins in Scandinavia and Iceland. Both of them had already explored much of Greenland and the ruins of the Norse settlements there—so they knew exactly what they'd be looking for in Canada. Together, their unique talents made them an ideal team to search for the ruins of their ancient ancestors, and like Munn, they paid close attention to the Skálholt Map. After carefully studying the map and the sagas, Helge concluded that it was based on an older Viking map, and that the promontory marked as Vinland was indeed Newfoundland's Great Northern Peninsula.

Armed with the Skálholt Map, the Ingstads set sail for Newfoundland. They had decided to conduct their search primarily from sea in their own sailboat, so that they'd see the land just as the Vikings would have a thousand years earlier. Scattered along northern Newfoundland's windswept, rocky coastline are isolated little fishing villages, and it was to these fishermen the Ingstads turned for further clues. They asked if anyone had ever come across strange, rectangular-looking turf ridges in the grassy meadowlands that grow on Newfoundland's Great Northern Peninsula. The initial response they received was not encouraging. Few believed that there could be a Viking site anywhere around there.

After first not finding anything, the Ingstads arrived on the tip of the Great Northern Peninsula at L'Anse aux Meadows, where they met an old fisherman by the name of George Decker. Decker informed them that while he knew nothing about Viking ruins, just beyond the little village were some "old Indian mounds." He offered to lead the Ingstads there to see for themselves. When Helge and Anne followed Decker to see the unusual, rectangular grassy mounds, they must have felt chills down their spines. They realized almost at once what they were looking at—these were no "Indian mounds": they were the remains of Viking longhouses and other buildings.

But after so many false claims of evidence of Vikings, few at first believed the Ingstads' supposition that the inconspicuous grassy mounds were Norse ruins. Only a painstaking archaeological investigation conducted with the most scientific methods available could settle the question—a task that fell to Anne Stine Ingstad. Beginning the following summer, in 1961, she led a team of international archaeologists in carefully excavating the mounds, a process that continued for the next seven summers. Radiocarbon dating fixed the age of the site at around 1000 AD—almost exactly matching the year given in the sagas for Leif the Lucky's Vinland voyage. Gradually it became clear that the site was, beyond question, a Viking settlement: iron slag, the waste product from blacksmithing, was unearthed, as well as a forge or smithy—proof that the site was European, not native, as no aboriginal culture in the western hemisphere smelted metals. Distinctive Norse artifacts like a spindle whorl, a bronze clothespin, a glass bead, iron nails, and jasper fire-starters that could be traced to mineral sources in Iceland and Greenland were found. Evidence of boat repair at the site was unearthed, and social divisions between the Norse leaders and their followers were clear from the different dwellings—some eight or nine different buildings constructed of sod in all. Some of these houses were exceptionally large, including a great hall or longhouse, with partitions into various rooms. This longhouse, which was even larger than Eirik the Red's in Greenland, would have served as the leader's household. The settlement might have accommodated upward of about ninety people, as well as domestic animals, and appears to have been occupied for about a decade before the Norse abandoned it—taking almost everything of value with them when they sailed away and burning the buildings so that no one else could use them.

So was this the long-sought Vinland? The question is misleading—Vinland was a "land," not a single place, and to the Norse it evidently meant the whole of the Gulf of St. Lawrence, or what today are Canada's Maritime provinces. The settlement at L'Anse aux Meadows functioned as a base camp for the Vikings: a strategically situated gateway into the riches of Vinland. In a straight line it was around 2500 kilometres from Eirik the Red's farm in Greenland to Leif's settlement at L'Anse aux Meadows—though this distance in practice was longer if a ship closely followed the coast of Labrador. But the Ingstads' discovery still left some questions unanswered. Where did the Norse find the grapes so vividly described in the sagas? Wild grapes have never grown in Newfoundland—not even during the "Medieval Warm Period" when the climate was several degrees warmer than it is today. Or was the whole idea of grapes just a later embellishment added to the sagas?

Archaeological excavations were continued at L'Anse aux Meadows in the 1970s under the Swedish archaeologist Birgitta Wallace. Wallace and her team found some extremely interesting new clues—butternuts and a wood burl from a butternut tree that had been carved with an iron tool. Butternut, a member of the walnut family, is a type of deciduous tree that has also never grown in Newfoundland. Nor do butternuts grow in Europe—they're native only to eastern North America. The nuts were too large to have been carried by birds, and the prevailing sea currents wouldn't have taken them to L'Anse aux Meadows. The discovery of butternuts, then, could only mean that the Vikings had travelled somewhere south of Newfoundland—to a place not only where butternuts grew, but also wild grapes. Where could this have been?

The sagas provide tantalizing clues. It says of Karlsefni's journey south from Leif's settlement at L'Anse aux Meadows:

> They sailed a long time, until they came to a river which flowed into a lake and from there into the sea. There were wide sandbars beyond the mouth of the river, and they could only sail into the river at high tide. Karlsefni and his company sailed into the lagoon and called the land Hop. There they found fields of self-sown wheat in the low-lying areas and vines growing on the hills. Every stream was teeming with fish. They dug trenches along the high-water mark and when the tide ebbed there were flounder in them. There were a great number of deer of all kinds in the forest. [23]

A ship sailing south from L'Anse aux Meadows on an exploratory voyage would have sailed down the Strait of Belle Isle, with Labrador on its starboard side and to port the western coast of Newfoundland. The Strait of Belle Isle acts as funnel leading into the Gulf of St. Lawrence, and from here the Vikings would likely have reached Anticosti Island, the Gaspé Peninsula, New Brunswick, Prince Edward Island, and the Gulf shores of Nova Scotia and Cape Breton. But wild grapes and butternuts do not naturally occur on Anticosti, Prince Edward Island, Cape

Breton, or Nova Scotia's Gulf shores—so that rules them out as a location for "Hop."

"Hop" in Old Norse means a tidal lagoon. Extensive tidal lagoons that are accessible to ships only at high tide, like those described in the sagas, are found along New Brunswick's Gulf of St. Lawrence coastline. That fact, combined with the butternuts uncovered in the 1970s at L'Anse aux Meadows, points strongly to northern New Brunswick's Gulf coastline as the place where Karlsefni and his crew landed. New Brunswick is the northernmost limit for both wild grapes and butternuts. The "self-sown" wheat described in the sagas was almost certainly wild rye or dune grass, both of which closely resemble wheat and grow naturally along New Brunswick's coast. The waterways would have teemed with salmon, and flounder can be caught in the offshore waters, just as the sagas record. Indeed, Jacques Cartier, in his explorations of the Gulf of St. Lawrence in the 1500s, noted both wild grapes and wild wheat growing along these same shores, as well as spawning salmon. Coastal New Brunswick alone has the sandbars, salmon, grapes, and butternuts that match the sagas. It would not be surprising if one day Viking artifacts are discovered somewhere in New Brunswick, perhaps around Miramichi Bay, which seems to most closely match the description of Hop.

Other Viking artifacts have continued to be found across a wide area of Canada's eastern Arctic, extending from Labrador to the northernmost Arctic islands. These finds include whetstones, wood carvings, bronze bowls, and a piece of chainmail and bronze folding scales from what appears to have been a Viking shipwreck off Ellesmere Island—the northernmost part of Canada's Arctic. The archaeologist Patricia Sutherland has even identified a second Norse settlement, or at least several encampments, on a small island off the coast of Baffin Island in Nunavut. According to Sutherland's research, it looks like the Norse used the site as a place to trade with the indigenous Dorset, the people who inhabited Canada's Arctic before the arrival of the Inuit. It is now becoming increasingly clear that the Norse presence in Canada was far more extensive and prolonged than what was previously thought. Although the settlements in Newfoundland were abandoned after no more than a decade, the Greenlandic Norse would have continued making voyages to Markland (Labrador) for perhaps four hundred years to gather wood needed in Greenland. An entry made in 1347 AD in the *Icelandic Annals*, a contemporary record of events, notes that a ship arrived in Iceland that year after being blown off course while returning from Markland—the impression given by the brief passage is that voyages to Markland were still common practice.[24] Since the Norse in Greenland needed wood, there is every reason to think they would have remained regular visitors to Labrador until the mysterious disappearance of the Greenlandic Norse sometime in the late 1400s.

There is no doubt that other Viking sites still await discovery, but the area of northeastern Canada with potential Norse sites is so vast that it's like looking for a needle in a haystack. Anyone who has excavated an archaeological site can probably appreciate just how enormous a challenge it would be to locate any of the Norse campsites or places they overwintered in such an immense area. In Sweden, I once spent five weeks excavating several square metres of ground in a sheep field as part of a team of archaeologists investigating a Viking Age settlement and harbour site. Weeks of careful digging and meticulous recording are needed to properly uncover just one small area and reconstruct the history of what happened there—which can be challenging enough in a sheep field, but in the Canadian wilderness is an entirely different order of magnitude.

Although we've exhausted what clues can be gleaned from the Skálholt Map, a new generation of satellite and aerial mapping might hold out hope for the discovery of unknown Viking sites. Indeed, in 2016, on the southwestern tip of Newfoundland, archaeologists led by

Sarah Parcak discovered through the use of satellite imagery what they believe may be another Viking site. Early excavations at the site have so far proven inconclusive, and it remains too early to tell whether it's a genuine Norse site or just something from a later time period. But the search will go on . . . The spirit of the Vikings, their restless wanderlust, their desire to seek the unknown and probe the world's mysteries, lives on in the spirit of Canadians who continue to search for traces of these ancient wayfarers.

2

THE BIRTH OF "CANADA"

I am rather inclined to believe that this is the land God gave to Cain.

—JACQUES CARTIER, 1535

When did Canada first come into existence? If we think purely in geological terms, then the land we're standing on in Canada has been around for several billion years—but it wasn't in any real sense "Canada," nor would anyone alive today have recognized it. The modern physical geography of Canada we know— the rivers and lakes and different ecosystems—was mostly formed only at the end of the last Ice Age as immense glaciers retreated northward, gouging out thousands of lakes and forming other features. It was also around this time, about 11,000 years ago, that the first humans arrived in Canada by crossing over from Siberia into what is now Alaska. They spread slowly and gradually across Canada as more of the country became ice-free and habitable, reaching the eastern Arctic last, only about four thousand years ago. But to these people "Canada" wasn't Canada—it was many different lands and territories, with different names, and not necessarily any more related to each other than traditional territories in Europe or Asia could be thought of as forming a single place. To the Haudenosaunee, as well as other Iroquoian peoples, it was "Turtle Island," or A'nó:wara tsi kawè:note in Mohawk; the Haida knew their homeland as Xhaaidlagha Gwaayaa, meaning "Islands at the Edge of the World"; and the Inuit used the term "Nunavut," meaning simply "our land."

So when did the name "Canada" first come to signify a particular land? That'd be 1535, when the French explorer Jacques Cartier misapplied an Iroquoian word he had recently learned—"Kanata," meaning village—and used it to denote the country along the St. Lawrence River. From that moment on, "Canada" became the name Europeans called the country around the St. Lawrence and started to mark it as such on their maps.

But to make sense of those maps and how a land named "Canada" first appeared on them, we need to cast our gaze a bit further back. When the Italian sailor John Cabot made his fateful voyage across the Atlantic in 1497, Europe was no longer the same place it had been in the Viking Age. The catastrophic outbreak of bubonic plague—the "Black Death," one of the most lethal pandemics in human history—had devastated the continent and killed half of Europe's population.[1] The disease had originated far away in central Asia or China, where it first spread to humans from fleas carried on rodents. The plague was then carried west along trade routes, reaching southern Europe by the mid-1300s and spreading north across the continent. According to some sources, it may have first reached Europe in 1347 during the Mongol siege of the Black Sea port city of Kaffa, where the Mongol warriors invented a type of biological warfare by supposedly catapulting infected corpses over the city walls.[2] The Italian traders inside the walls fled in terror at their earliest opportunity, inadvertently carrying the disease with them to Italy and from there to the rest of Europe.

The horrifying plague manifested itself in tumours the size of apples that first appeared in the groin or armpits; then came decaying skin that turned black, followed by acute fever and vomiting of blood. Most victims died within just two to seven days after the first symptoms. Whole villages and towns became depopulated as the plague spread. The Italian writer Giovanni Boccaccio, a resident of Florence, provided an eyewitness account of the horror the Black Death unleashed:

The plight of the lower and most of the middle classes was even more pitiful to behold. Most of them remained in their houses, either through poverty or in hopes of safety, and fell sick by thousands. Since they received no care and attention, almost all of them died. Many ended their lives in the streets . . . and many others who died in their houses were only known to be dead because the neighbours smelled their decaying bodies. Dead bodies filled every corner. Most of them were treated in the same manner by the survivors, who were more concerned to get rid of their rotting bodies than moved by charity towards the dead . . . they carried the bodies out of the houses and laid them at the door; where every morning quantities of the dead might be seen . . . Such was the multitude of corpses brought to the churches every day and almost every hour that there was not enough consecrated ground to give them burial . . . Although the cemeteries were full they were forced to dig huge trenches, where they buried the bodies by hundreds. Here they stowed them away like bales in the hold of a ship and covered them with a little earth, until the whole trench was full.[3]

The densely populated cities of Italy and southern Europe were the hardest hit, with death rates of 80 percent in some places.[4] Such widespread death and scenes of unimaginable horror—decaying corpses were piled everywhere—caused a breakdown in the social order; many, believing the end of the world was at hand, gave themselves over to all kinds of depravity. Others, fearful of contracting the plague, shunned society, even their own family, and fled to the countryside. Northern Europe, particularly Scotland and Scandinavia, because they were more sparsely inhabited, were the least severely affected—though even here vast numbers died. The height of the outbreak lasted from 1346 to 1353, during which half or more of Europe's population perished.[5] But even then the horror did not end. Seemingly without mercy, the plague recurred again and again in the fourteenth century through to the mid-sixteenth century—never in this whole period was Europe entirely free of plague. These were harsh times in which life could be extinguished without warning and all were vulnerable. Overall, the death toll had been so severe that it would take nearly three hundred years for the world's population to recover to its pre-plague levels.

The Black Death wasn't the only major upheaval that had transformed Europe since the time of the Vikings. The Vikings themselves had been assimilated and converted to Christianity—ending the worship of the old gods. Much of southeastern Europe—including Greece, the cradle of Western civilization—had fallen under Turkish imperial rule. But by the late 1400s the Moorish invaders in Spain and Portugal had finally been defeated and driven out, allowing for Spanish unification and overseas expansion. Despite the devastation brought by the Black Death, Europe managed to recapture the dynamism it had enjoyed in antiquity when the civilizations of Greece and Rome flourished. There was a rediscovery or rebirth—a "renaissance"—of classical learning, as well as new advances in ship technology, navigational instruments, and cartography. Larger kingdoms like Spain, France, and England began to emerge through the unification of smaller realms that had long been ruled by petty kings and feudal lords.

Major changes had also taken place in Canada since the time of the Vinland voyages. Archaeology, ethnohistory, and DNA studies are shedding new light on North America's distant past, allowing for a much richer understanding than was possible until very recently. A new people had emerged in Newfoundland since the Vikings had been there—the Beothuk. In the Arctic, the Dorset people had nearly disappeared and were displaced by the Inuit, migrants from Alaska who reached Baffin Island around 1200 AD—several centuries after the Norse.[6] Meanwhile, south of the Great Lakes, protracted internal warfare among the Haudenosaunee (Iroquois) had finally led to a resolution in the form of a confederacy of five nations; this peace pact brought an end to the internal strife and allowed the Confederacy to redirect their actions against surrounding peoples, especially their northern neighbours the Wendat (Huron). Both the Haudenosaunee and the Wendat had given up hunter-gathering in favour of farming around the southern Great Lakes—enabling the creation of the first permanent villages in what became Canada. In 1497, with the voyages of John Cabot and others who followed in his wake, these two very different worlds were once more about to collide.

The question of what drove the European expansion across the oceans beginning in the late 1400s has long been debated by historians. It seems clear that there was no single factor that led to the European "Age of Discovery." The Turkish conquest in 1453 of one of Christian Europe's oldest and most important cities, Constantinople, spurred incentives to find a shorter and more direct trade route to Asia. It also led many Greek intellectuals to flee their native Constantinople and seek refuge in Italy—which helped stimulate a revival in classical knowledge and thereby the spirit of the Renaissance. But there were other factors as well. The Canadian historian W.J. Eccles provided one of the best summaries of the underlying reasons for European exploration:

> This great wave of European expansion is frequently attributed to
> the new spirit of individualism released by the forces that accompa-
> nied . . . the Renaissance. It may well be that the movement was an
> outgrowth of this spirit, but to be more specific one has to examine
> the motives of the Europeans who were willing to venture across
> uncharted oceans to conquer unknown lands against incalculable odds.
> Their motives were fourfold. The European had, first, an avid desire
> for recognition and fame, to distinguish himself among his fellows
> and achieve a higher social status, to acquire those intangible qualities
> that the French refer to as *la glorie*; second, an insatiable curiosity, a

thirst for knowledge, to know what is on the other side of a mountain, around the next bend in a river, on the other planets; third, highly developed acquisitive and competitive instincts, a desire to acquire more of this world's goods than his neighbor, an inability to accept what he had, no matter how much, as enough; fourth, a marked intolerance in religious beliefs, the conviction that his particular branch of the Christian Church possessed the only true faith and that all peoples everywhere should be converted to it, that those who resisted thereby merited extermination, or, at best, a lifetime of servitude.[7]

In these motives we can recognize many of the same considerations that spurred the Vikings to brave the unknown seas—except the added factor of Christianity, which, of course, had not been a concern for pagan Vikings.

None of this, however, would have much mattered without technological innovations in navigation and ship design. Whereas the earlier wave of European overseas exploration had arisen from northern Europe, with the Norse sailing out of the fjords and bays of Scandinavia, this time it was southern Europe that had the edge, with the seaports of Italy, Spain, and Portugal leading the way. In Portugal, Henry the Navigator, a prince with an insatiable thirst for geographic knowledge, became a patron of exploration and mapmaking. Despite his name, Henry was more of an armchair explorer—from the safety of his court he dispatched Portugal's most skilled mariners and chart makers to probe the coasts of Africa, the Mediterranean Sea, and the open Atlantic. Whereas the Vikings had "island-hopped" across the North Atlantic—generally never straying more than three hundred kilometres from land—this new generation of Portuguese mariners mastered sailing far from shore. They had figured out the mysteries of the trade winds—the so-called *volta do mar*, or "turn of the sea"—the means by which it was possible, by sailing counterintuitively farther from land, to catch the prevailing winds that would allow a vessel to return to Europe. Without mastering this knowledge, the later transatlantic voyages would have been impossible, as mariners would have been stranded on the far side of the ocean. In other words, to cross an ocean is one thing, but to return is quite another.

By 1418 Portuguese mariners had reached the uninhabited Madeira Islands. A short time later, in 1427, the Portuguese, having continued to gamble with their lives on the high seas, discovered an archipelago of otherworldly volcanic islands nearly 1400 kilometres off mainland Portugal in the Atlantic: the Azores. Other Portuguese explorers sailed along the coast of Africa—steadily expanding their sea charts as they mapped the unknown coastline. They as yet had no idea how large Africa truly was—all sorts of strange tales and legends were told about what might lie in these unknown latitudes; like mermaids, cannibals, and dragons. The Portuguese hoped to find a route around Africa to the Indian Ocean, where they could trade for spices, silk, and other commodities. Gradually the Portuguese sailed farther and farther along the dangerous African coast—each generation adding fresh details to their sea charts—until finally, in 1488, the explorer Bartolomeu Dias managed to round Africa's southern tip and reach the Indian Ocean.

Although the Portuguese were the leaders in these voyages, they weren't the only ones active in exploration. Italian sea captains, in the service of merchants in city-states like Venice and Genoa, were also dreaming of finding a faster and easier way to trade with Asia. As it was, they had to rely on the long and dangerous overland caravan routes through the heart of Asia—across vast deserts and mountains—which could be ambushed by bandits and led to high prices. One eccentric in particular, the Genoese sailor Christopher Columbus, believed that he could sail directly to India by boldly crossing the Atlantic. Few, however, took Columbus's scheme seriously. To many it seemed little short of lunacy.

Columbus spent years languishing at the Spanish court of Queen Isabella and her husband, King Ferdinand, trying to persuade them to back his scheme. Finally, in 1492, the queen agreed and gave Columbus three ships for his voyage. Columbus, of course, never reached India— he made landfall somewhere in the Caribbean Sea, probably in the Bahamas, though he insisted that it was India, and that the inhabitants were therefore Indians. Despite this blunder, for better or worse, Columbus's voyages were to have world-altering significance: they brought the Old World into contact with the western hemisphere on a scale vastly larger than what the Vikings had done—and this time, the contact would transform both.

Other Italian mariners were eager to imitate Columbus's example and offer their services to foreign princes. One such sailor was Giovanni Caboto, or John Cabot as he's known in English. Cabot had been a trader in Venice and had read about the fabulous travels of his country-man Marco Polo, which may have been what inspired him to first dream of distant horizons. He toiled over globes and maps, had sailed the Mediterranean, and had made trade journeys to the Middle East, sup-posedly even visiting Mecca. His contemporaries described him as an "a most expert mariner," and the evidence of history would seem to indicate as much.[8] In any event, Cabot must have been daring to have resolved to take the ultimate of gambles: attempt in his ship to cross the North Atlantic.

Cabot, eager to find a patron to sponsor his proposed voyage, left Venice for Lisbon—the Portuguese, after all, were still the leaders in maritime exploration and might be happy to find an intrepid Italian will-ing to replicate what Columbus had done. But the Portuguese weren't interested in Cabot. They shot his offer down. Discouraged, Cabot cast about for other options. If the Portuguese didn't want him, maybe the Spanish would. Cabot set off for the Spanish court to make his case that he could be as valuable as Columbus. But the Spanish already had their

Italian explorer in Columbus, and they too rejected Cabot's offer. Twice jilted, Cabot must have been pretty despondent. But he was still eager to risk his life on a trans-oceanic voyage, and so, increasingly desperate, he swallowed his pride and turned to a small, semi-barbaric backwater on the edge of Europe: England.

England's population at the time was less than a third of Spain's and only one-seventh of France's. The Renaissance had as yet made few inroads in the damp island, which had frequently been plagued with internal quarrels. The kingdom had endured years of strife in the War of the Roses—a war that pitted noble house against noble house to determine who would sit on the throne of England. Finally, in 1485, with many of the country's nobles already dead, Henry Tudor emerged victorious when he vanquished his rival at the Battle of Bosworth Field—and thus claimed the crown for himself and his bloodline. It was to this self-made king, who ruled as Henry VII, that Cabot made his proposal.

This time Cabot met with more receptive ears. Despite the kingdom's turmoil, for some years before Cabot's arrival English fishermen sailing out of Bristol had been seeking lands rumoured to exist in the western Atlantic. There is even evidence that they may have already reached the coasts of Newfoundland. But the objective of these daring fishermen was to find new sources of cod and other fish, not to discover a trade route to Asia, and for obvious reasons they tended to keep their fishing grounds a closely guarded secret. What Cabot had in mind when he approached King Henry was something altogether different: he proposed making a voyage across the ocean to China—and as a trained cartographer, he'd be able to map the route there for others to follow. The benefits that such a discovery would bring to a relatively poor kingdom like England were obvious—riches from the trade would funnel directly into London and the royal treasury. The king liked what he heard. He agreed to provide Cabot with financial support and granted him the authority to discover any unknown lands and seek trade partnerships on behalf of the realm.

Cabot put to sea in 1496, only to be hampered by bad weather and troubles with his crew. These difficulties forced him to prematurely turn back to England. Not in the least discouraged, Cabot tried again the following spring with a small crew of twenty men—most of them English fishermen. This time he succeeded in crossing the open Atlantic in five weeks, making landfall in what was probably Newfoundland. Armed with crossbows and swords, Cabot and his crew came ashore on a wooded coast. But they found no cities or people, which cast doubt on whether they were in China at all. They coasted along these wild shores for three hundred leagues, and not meeting anyone to trade with, headed back to England—eventually arriving safely back in Bristol, to much adoration. Despite not finding any cities, it was said that Cabot had reached "the country of the Grand Khan" (China).[9] Cabot's feat made him a celebrity, to the point where, in the words of another Italian who happened to be in England at the time, "he is called the Great Admiral, and vast honour is paid to him, and he goes dressed in silk, and these English run after him like mad."[10] The king was pleased and paid Cabot a modest sum—in the belief that this first journey would lead to more profitable discoveries.

Cabot made a world map and a globe showing where he'd been—or rather where he thought he'd been, as he still imagined that the land he'd reached was somewhere in East Asia. He was sure he was close to finding the fabulous cities of great wealth described by Marco Polo, and resolved to cross the ocean again—this time on a much larger voyage, with five ships under his command. Cabot had every intention of reaching the ports of China, where he could trade for silk, jewels, and other luxuries.

He sailed out of Bristol's harbour for a third time with his fleet of five ships in 1498, but what happened next is uncertain. Cabot's fate and that of his ships remains one of history's unsolved mysteries. For a long time most historians assumed Cabot had been lost at sea or that some other disaster had befallen his ships—since no further mention of him or his expedition could be found in any surviving records. But recent research in previously overlooked archives has turned up fresh clues that suggest Cabot may have lived to return to Europe after all.[11] Much uncertainty remains, and the mystery may perhaps never be solved. Whatever his fate, Cabot had mapped the route to Newfoundland and inspired others to risk their lives in sailing into the unknown. Other explorers, including his son Sebastian, would carry on his exploratory voyages. In 1508 Sebastian Cabot led his own voyage across the ocean to the "New Founde Lande," as other English seafarers seem to have done from 1499 onward.[12]

Cabot's discoveries, and those of his contemporaries, expanded the map of the known world for Europeans and other Old World cultures. Whereas before there had been only myths, legends, and the barely known stories of the Vikings, Europeans now had definite knowledge that lands existed far across the Atlantic Ocean. But whether these lands were part of Asia or perhaps something altogether different remained a mystery. There was as yet only a very hazy sense of what lay across the Atlantic—no European suspected the true size of the landmass. Nor was there any hint yet of a place called Canada. The name "Canada" did not appear on maps until Jacques Cartier entered the picture.

Cartier is not a particularly likeable explorer—he was something of a rogue, perhaps even an occasional pirate; he kidnapped aboriginal people on his journeys to serve his needs; and he became the butt of jokes after he loaded his ships with what he thought were diamonds and gold, only to find out back in France that they were worthless quartz crystals and iron pyrite—fool's gold. But for all his faults, Cartier had salt water in his veins—he was a highly skilled navigator and mariner who made at least three successful voyages to North America at a time when such undertakings were fraught with great danger. To have done so, he must have been a person of exceptional courage, sound mind, and amazing sang-froid in braving so many unknown inlets where even a single unseen reef or shoal could have spelled disaster. And for better or worse, it was he who gave us the name "Canada"—again it was something of a blunder; he misapplied an Iroquoian word for village to the land itself—but the name stuck, and at any rate, there are probably worse names for a country.

Cartier was born on France's northern coast in the port of St. Malo, and like other youths in the ports of Europe, he must have gone to sea at a young age to have become the navigator that he did. Surviving records are scant, but it seems likely that Cartier had been part of a ship's crew that had sailed to Newfoundland and even Brazil prior to his appointment by the French king, Francis I, in 1534 to seek unknown lands. His instructions were "to discover certain islands and lands where it is said that a great quantity of gold, and other precious things, are to be found."[13] He was also supposed to search for a route to Asia— which, in European eyes, still remained the real prize.

In April 1534, Cartier set sail from France's northern coast to seek the "New Founde Land." The conditions on board ships crossing the ocean in the 1500s were almost unimaginably dreadful. Cramped, filthy quarters and the lack of fresh food and clean water made sickness and disease almost inescapable. One contemporary account of an Atlantic crossing noted about the food rations on board that:

> With the heat and the damp sea, the biscuits had become so full of mag-
> gots that, God help me, I saw many men wait until nightfall to eat their
> porridge so as not to see the maggots in it; others were so used to it that
> they did not even take the trouble to throw the maggots away when
> they saw them since in so doing they might have lost their supper.[14]

After thirty-three hellish days at sea, Cartier arrived off Newfoundland's Great Northern Peninsula. These were the same waters the Vikings had plied more than five centuries earlier. But Cartier's outlook could not have been more different. Whereas the Norse—accustomed to the harsh life of Greenland—had looked upon these lands as wonderfully mild and bountiful, to Cartier, reared in France's countryside, the place looked like a nightmare. "I am rather inclined to believe that this is the land God gave to Cain," he wrote as he sailed down the Strait of Belle Island and gazed upon the bleak, rocky shores of Labrador from his ship's quarterdeck.[15]

The Vikings had felt at home in these lands—recognizing many of the edible berries, lichens, moss, trees, birds, and animals as the same ones found in Greenland. But to Cartier and his crew, the fog-draped shores of Labrador and Newfoundland were mysterious and forbidding. Cartier pressed on southward in his ship, leaving the strait and reaching a large expanse of water—what we know as the Gulf of St. Lawrence—where he came upon the windswept, uninhabited Magdalen Islands. Then he arrived at a place far more promising than anything he had yet seen: "the finest land one can see, and full of beautiful trees and meadows."[16] This was Prince Edward Island—though Cartier mistook it for part of the mainland and headed northwest in his ship without realizing his error. Yet none of these lands, however miserable or pleasant they seemed, bore any resemblance to the rich cities of Asia that Cartier was expecting to find.

Cartier's ship cruised along the coasts of what later became New Brunswick and the Gaspé Peninsula, searching for an outlet that would lead him to "Cathay." Along these coasts, Cartier and his crew rowed to shore in their smaller longboats to explore the land. Somewhere, they figured, there must be a passage that would lead to China.

As the French explored the coasts they encountered, paddling in birchbark canoes, both Iroquoian- and Algonquian-speaking peoples who were extremely eager to trade for their iron tools and other commodities—a fact that probably indicates they'd had previous dealings with Europeans, as they did not seem startled by the sight of strange bearded men in unusual clothes with a giant wooden vessel with sails. Most likely, any number of the Basque, French, and English fishermen who were sailing the waters around Newfoundland had previously traded with them.

But Cartier, his head filled with dreams of silk, spices, and jewels, wasn't impressed with what the natives had to trade—tanned animal skins. As he wrote in his journal, "They offered us everything they owned, which was, all told, of little value."[17] Of a second encounter with more natives eager to trade Cartier recorded, "This people may well be called savage; for they are the sorriest folk there can be in the world, and the whole lot of them had not anything above the value of five sous, their canoes and fishing nets excepted."[18] Nonetheless, Cartier offered the natives iron knives, axes, and European clothing—in the hopes that good relations might lead them to help him find the route to the East he was seeking.

Cartier's indifference to trading for animal skins might seem surprising given that the fur trade is customarily regarded as a key foundation of Canadian history. But that didn't happen until later. In the 1500s, Europe's population was still recovering from the ravages of the Black Death, and the continent was still a fairly wild place with vast forests. Animals many associate with Canada—wolverines, lynx, brown bears, mink, sable (martens), and even beavers—were in fact still common in much of Europe. Scandinavian and eastern European trappers could meet the demand for fur, so Cartier saw little value in the skins or furs the natives could offer. Cartier, after all, had not risked his life on a voyage across the ocean just to trade for things he could already find in Europe. He was after the rare spices, silks, rubies, and other gems that came only from India and China.

Before leaving the Gaspé shore, Cartier had his men erect a thirty-foot cross in a conspicuous spot overlooking the sea. They attached to the cross one of their shields with the fleur-de-lys of the French monarchy. On the shield were the words LONG LIVE THE KING OF FRANCE.[19] The local Iroquoian chief with whom Cartier had been trading, a man named Donnacona, took exception to this—he was offended that the French would erect something of evident importance without first consulting him. Cartier, however, managed to placate him with gifts and in sign language claim that it was only a marker to allow them to find their way back on a future voyage. Pacified, Donnacona permitted two of his sons, Domagaya and Taignoagny, to accompany Cartier on his return journey. This would allow them to learn each other's languages and facilitate future relations. In setting off across the ocean with the French, Domagaya and Taignoagny had also become explorers heading into the unknown—they would be the first aboriginal people from Canada to explore Europe. And like the French, they'd be able to expand their geographic knowledge and report back to their nation about what they had discovered across the ocean. Exploration, in other words, had become a two-way street.

The French and their new friends survived the treacherous crossing back to Europe—enduring several days of rough seas in the mid-Atlantic along the way. Cartier, meanwhile, began to learn the Iroquoian language from Domagaya and Taignoagny, who in turn started to learn French. Back in France, King Francis was pleased with Cartier's explorations, and agreed to outfit a larger expedition involving three ships and a crew of 110 that was to depart the following spring.

On this new crossing back to North America, rough seas and storms caused Cartier's three ships to become separated. When the skies finally cleared, Cartier's other vessels were nowhere in sight—the storms had blown them far off course. Each of the ship's captains had agreed that in such an eventuality they would rendezvous in Newfoundland on the

Strait of Belle Isle. Cartier arrived there first, and anxiously waited to see whether the other two French ships had survived. Luck was still on Cartier's side—in a few weeks his other two ships appeared. Before continuing, they refitted the ships, bringing on board supplies of wood, fresh water, and birds they'd shot (most likely the now extinct great auk) to augment their maggot-infested rations.

Cartier's knowledge of the geography of these lands remained hazy—apparently he still didn't realize that Newfoundland was an island, and believed that the only outlet into the body of water we know as the Gulf of St. Lawrence was through the Strait of Belle Isle. He was as yet unaware of the open sea that separates Newfoundland from Cape Breton. Nor could Domagaya and Taignoagny be of any help in these matters. But they did tell Cartier that near where they lived was a great river leading far inland—and that if he sailed up this, he would come to the village of their father, Donnacona. From there, Cartier could explore inland and possibly find a route to Asia. On his maps and in his journal, Cartier referred to this country—roughly the north shore of the St. Lawrence River from about modern Trois-Rivières east to the Gulf—as "Canada." This name he derived from an Iroquoian word Domagaya and Taignoagny had taught him: "Kanata," meaning village.

Seeking "Canada," Cartier piloted his ships past Anticosti Island and headed for the wide opening of the river described by his Iroquoian guides—a river they said was "so long that no man has seen its end."[20] It was plainly a very large river, bounded on both sides by small mountains and vast forests. Cartier's ships sailed up it to the point where it narrowed: the modern site of Quebec City. Here, beneath imposing cliffs, stood the small palisaded village of Stadacona. Donnacona welcomed them with feasting and celebrations.

But the festive mood cooled when Donnacona learned that Cartier planned to head farther upriver—his sons had told him about a larger village called Hochelaga on an island (the present site of Montreal).

Beyond that settlement, Cartier was told, there were freshwater seas and a possible route to the rich cities he sought. Donnacona was displeased by the idea of Cartier heading inland. He'd hoped that Cartier would venture no farther than Stadacona, allowing Donnacona to create a lucrative monopoly on the trade in European goods with all the other nations that lived upriver. Ignoring Donnacona's wishes, Cartier headed upriver in one of his smaller vessels to find China. The other two ships, along with most of the crews, remained behind near Stadacona.

Cartier arrived at Hochelaga about a week later—but not without first having to leave his ship behind when the river became too swift to navigate; the French were reduced to rowing in their longboat. At the island of Hochelaga, Cartier found a much larger, fortified village numbering some two thousand people. The people here were friendly, and welcomed these unexpected and strange visitors with feasting, dancing, and celebrating. Cartier, however, was eager to carry on upriver—believing that gold and other riches were soon to be found. But just beyond the island lay furious, impassable rapids, forcing the French to turn back. Convinced that these rapids were the final obstacle in the long-sought route to China, the French called it "La Chine" (in English, "China"), a name that has endured for the nearby town of Lachine, Quebec.

Cartier and his men returned downriver to Stadacona and over-wintered there in a crude fort they hastily constructed. This was their first Canadian winter, and it proved a brutal one. The river froze over; ice coated the inside of the French huts and ships; the snows were nearly four feet deep. Lacking fresh fruit or vegetables, Cartier's crews began to develop the horrifying symptoms of scurvy: their arms and legs swelled, their gums turned black, and their teeth started to fall out. The French, shivering in the freezing cold inside their huts, grew weaker by the day. As the winter wore on, almost one-quarter of them died. All hope seemed lost until Cartier learned from Domagaya, one of his two interpreters, that a cure for scurvy could be made from the inner bark and leaves of the eastern white cedar, which is rich in vitamin C. Tea made from the bark and needles of this wondrous tree quickly restored the French to health.

Despite this, relations had soured between the French and Donnacona—who did not fully trust the mysterious visitors from across the sea. In the spring, when the river became ice-free, Cartier prepared to return to France. With his crews decimated by scurvy, one of the ships had to be abandoned as there were enough able hands to man only one vessel. He promised the natives at Stadacona that he would return the next year—but just before departing Cartier committed a foolish act of treachery. He ordered his men to seize Donnacona and nine other natives as captives to take back to France to present to the king.

Cartier had expected to return to Canada the following year, but developments in France had made the king less interested in sponsoring costly ocean voyages. King Francis had his hands full fighting a war with the Spanish crown, and no ships or expense could be spared for exploration. Cartier would have to wait another five years before the king agreed to support another venture to the land the French were now labelling on their maps as "Canada." It seemed that Cartier's long wait for a chance to return was rewarded when, in October 1540, King Francis named him "Captain General" of a new and much larger expedition. This venture would be aimed at colonization and the continued search for a route to China.

But in January 1541 Cartier was demoted when the king named Jean-François de La Roque de Roberval, an influential courtier, as the new commander of the expedition, with Cartier as his second-in-command. The demotion was likely spurred by the huge size of the undertaking, which was to involve numerous ships and a staggering 1500 people. Cartier had certainly proven his worth as a navigator and a sailor, but his leadership abilities on dry land were open to question.

Meanwhile, of the nine aboriginal people Cartier had kidnapped and taken back to France with him, eight had died, including Donnacona. The only survivor, a young girl, was left in France when the expedition sailed for Canada in the spring of 1542.

Cartier left France in advance of Roberval, who was to rendezvous with him in Canada at a later date with more colonists and supplies. When Cartier and his ships eventually arrived back at Stadacona, he found that—with good reason—the natives no longer trusted him. Cartier admitted that Donnacona had died in France, but he lied about the fate of the others, claiming that they "had remained in France where they were living as great lords; they had married and had no desire to return to their country."[21]

Cartier and his colonists weren't welcome at Stadacona, but they settled nearby anyway on the banks of the river in a fort they erected. With the leaves on the trees turning and the first chilling frosts settling over the land, there was still no sign of Roberval with his reinforcements and provisions. Cartier and his followers would have to make do through the long winter without them.

The harsh, bitterly cold winter, however, again decimated the colonists, and by spring Cartier had given up any hope of finding China or surviving long-term in Canada. He ordered the ships refitted and planned to sail back to France. But not before filling the holds with what he believed were gold and diamonds—in reality, fool's gold and ordinary quartz crystals. Off Newfoundland on his return journey, Cartier's ships encountered Roberval and his fleet—who ordered them all to sail back to Canada. Cartier, his ships loaded with what he thought was a fortune in diamonds and gold, and not willing to endure another brutal winter, ignored the order and sailed straight for France.

Roberval pressed on without Cartier to try again at colonization. On board one of his ships was his young niece, Marguerite de Roberval. Unknown to Roberval, she had fallen in love with a member of the ship's crew. When the ships had anchored off Newfoundland for three weeks to take on fresh water and other supplies, Marguerite and her secret lover had spent the time on shore picking berries, wandering the coast, and making love. A loyal servant had stood guard over them and helped keep their romance secret. But few secrets endure for long on crowded, confined ships—and when Roberval learned of the affair, he was furious. Naturally, he did what any concerned uncle would do and marooned Maguerite on an uninhabited island. He chose the appropriately named Île des Démons.

Roberval, to teach the servant a lesson as well, also abandoned her on the island with his strong-willed niece. As for the young man, his punishment was being forced to stay on board Roberval's ship as they left Marguerite and sailed away. But completely out of his mind with love and passion, the young man jumped overboard and swam to the island—choosing to share Marguerite's fate.

For a time, the three of them managed to survive by gathering bird eggs, wild berries, and shellfish, and hunting and fishing. But to complicate matters, Marguerite soon became pregnant. Her lover—whose name has been lost—after about eight months on the island took sick and died. Devastated, Marguerite soon after gave birth. She, her baby, and her devoted servant had to carry on as best they could. But things only got worse. After about a year the baby died. Then the servant died, too—leaving Marguerite alone. Exiled on an uninhabited island at the edge of the known world, Marguerite must have felt like the last person left on earth. But she was strong and determined; faced with appalling circumstances, she by necessity became an adept hunter and refused to give up. After surviving some two and a half years on the island, she was finally rescued by some passing Basque fishermen, who returned her to France.

As for Roberval, his venture was no more successful than Cartier's—scurvy, internal quarrels, the brutal winter, and poor relations with the natives, who attacked and killed many of the settlers, all doomed the colony. In 1543 the survivors limped home to France, abandoning any further thought of colonizing Canada for the immediate future. From today's perspective, successful European settlement in Canada might seem inevitable. But it sure didn't seem that way in 1543. As Cartier's and Roberval's disastrous ventures indicate, a ticket to Canada on board a 1500s-era ship was a near death sentence.

Things weren't exactly idyllic in France, either. The kingdom had become consumed by a bitter civil war that pitted Catholics against Protestants. As a result, no further colonizing attempts would be made until 1598. That year, a new king granted an aristocrat, the Marquis de La Roche, the authority to trade and colonize in Canada— giving him the grand title "lieutenant-general of the territories of Canada, Newfoundland, Labrador, and Norumbega."[22] That last land, Norumbega, didn't technically exist. But when planning grand colonizing ventures, one must not let minor details about whether such and such a place actually exists stand in the way of history.

La Roche had earlier attempted to organize an expedition to Canada, but his main ship was lost at sea and the voyage came to nothing. He was then captured by rebels in the civil war and spent seven years imprisoned in a castle. Finally freed in 1596, and with apparently nothing more promising to do, he petitioned the king to let him try establishing a colony in Canada. For his venture, the king authorized La Roche to recruit prospective settlers from among France's prisons as well as among the kingdom's "vagabonds and beggars."[23]

With these promising colonists, La Roche set sail for the New World. He chose for the site of his colony the uninhabited, windswept, and treeless Sable Island far out to sea in the Atlantic. Surprisingly enough, it turned out that settling hardened criminals, vagabonds, and beggars on a spit of sand was not, in retrospect, the best plan. La Roche settled the colonists on the island's north coast, where they erected huts and were to survive by hunting seals and seabirds, fishing, and planting what gardens they could amid the sand dunes. La Roche left two deputies in charge, and then in his two ships sailed to Newfoundland to engage in the fishery there—with the understanding that he would return each year to reprovision the colony. But storms and treacherous shoals made it difficult for ships to land at the island—later Sable became known as "the graveyard of the Atlantic" for the hundreds of wrecks around it—and in 1602 no supply ship arrived at all. Isolated and cut off from the world on a stormy, windswept island, the colonists, in a desperate state, butchered La Roche's two deputies. More murders followed as the island fell into anarchy. Within a few years the colony had disintegrated.

※

Cartier's significance lies not in his failed colony but in the new geographic knowledge his voyages generated. For the first time they allowed world maps to be made that showed not only the Old World continents of Europe, Africa, and Asia, but much of northeastern North America as well. Cartier had, literally, put "Canada" on the map. He had increased not only European geographic knowledge, but in transporting Iroquoian people to France, aboriginal geographic knowledge. The world, in other words, was shrinking—the mysteries of what lay beyond the oceans were gradually being solved.

This is illustrated perhaps most forcefully in a new map of the world made in 1550 by the French cartographer Pierre Desceliers. Desceliers's huge creation—it measures 7 x 4.5 feet, or 2.15 metres x 1.35 metres—was a special project made for the French king, Henri II. Desceliers incorporated Cartier's discoveries into his map—thus exhibiting Canada in a global context for the first time. (Cartier's original maps, like Cabot's, have not survived.) Desceliers's map combined the latest in cartographic discoveries with fantastic illustrations of animals and sea creatures. The portion of the map showing the New World has "CANADA" prominently labelled.

The geography at first appears hopelessly confused, but the key to deciphering it is to turn the map upside down—unlike on modern maps, here south is oriented at the top and north at the bottom. Once flipped over, we can recognize the hazy outlines of eastern North America from the Florida peninsula all the way up to Labrador. Newfoundland appears as a large, ill-shaped island, although the outlines of the Great Northern and Avalon peninsulas are clearly apparent. Nova Scotia juts out into the Atlantic, and the St. Lawrence River, all things considered, is quite accurately charted. Near its mouth, slightly off its correct location, is Anticosti Island. The villages of Stadacona and Hochelaga are both labelled, as is the Saguenay River. Nearby on the map stands a bearded figure in a long cloak gesturing to some natives—this is Jacques Cartier. Other aspects of the map appear more imaginative: there are unicorns roaming the wilderness, explorers hunting ostrich-like birds, palm trees, and strange beehive-like dwellings. In the sea is a fierce toothed whale with two blowholes spouting water. Labrador has more realistic bears, with two adrift on an ice floe and one on the shore.

For a long while yet, to European mapmakers Canada would continue to be a land of mingled fantasy and reality—a mysterious nether region on the edge of the known world.

3

CHAMPLAIN'S MAP OF NEW FRANCE

A captain must give proof of manly courage, and even in the face of death make light of this.

—SAMUEL DE CHAMPLAIN

Inside the palisade walls of the little wilderness fortress, a severed head impaled on a pike stood as a grim warning. It had been put there by Samuel de Champlain—perhaps the finest mapmaker in Canada's history. The head had belonged to a man who'd plotted to overthrow Champlain, and now served as grisly proof of the founder of Quebec's unflinching determination to succeed where all others before him had failed. Champlain may well have been one of the greatest dreamers and doers Canada has ever seen. He moved through a world of courtly intrigue, the slippery decks of storm-tossed ships, the brooding spruce forests and roaring rivers of a continent he could scarcely imagine, and the longhouses of his Wendat friends and allies. He survived the arrows of his Iroquois enemies and the treachery of more than one of his own countrymen. The beautiful maps of astonishing accuracy that he left behind are the enduring traces of his many journeys and adventures.

Champlain was born sometime around 1570 in France's southwest, probably in the Atlantic seaport of Brouage, not far from the shadow of the Pyrenees. It was a good place for an explorer to be born. Champlain came from a fishing family and grew up dreaming of the mysteries and adventures offered by the sea. He later wrote that he had an interest "from a very young age in the art of navigation, along with a love of the high seas."[1]

From childhood, Champlain was making fishing voyages far offshore with his father. He learned to read the waves and currents, to sense storms, to know when to trim and hoist sails, to navigate by the sun and stars, and to chart unfamiliar waters. To survive on an unforgiving ocean in the 1500s for anyone—let alone a young boy—took courage and strength. Not only that, to endure weeks at sea one had to have a strong stomach and the dexterity to scramble up a ship's rigging in fierce storms. The slightest slip and a sailor could fall to his death. Many did. It was a hard, dangerous life.

But Champlain was more than just a tough seafarer; he was also an aspiring artist. The dreamy side of Champlain's personality manifested itself in his paintings. He would later adorn his Canadian maps with sketches of the people he met and the places he saw. Though he had little formal schooling, Champlain was a quick study—he learned, perhaps from his father and uncles, the science of cartography, and he had a natural talent for picking up languages. The port of Brouage was a place where seafarers from across Europe mixed—in addition to his native French, Champlain learned to speak Spanish, English, and a smattering of Basque and other tongues.

Besides the score of fishermen he must have known who were lost at sea, the France of Champlain's time was torn by the horrors of religious war. Protestants, seeking to break away from the Catholic Church, were pitted against Catholics in a fanatical conflict that saw mass executions, sadistic torture, royal assassinations, and wholesale slaughter that lasted for decades. Heretics had their tongues cut out; people were burned alive or hurled headlong off city walls.

Champlain's own family were likely part of France's Huguenot Protestant minority—the southwestern region of France where they lived was the heartland of Protestant France. In a country where upward of 90 percent of the population was Catholic and Protestants were routinely executed, Champlain at some point in his young life made the prudent decision to convert to Catholicism.

By the 1590s Champlain was serving in the army of the French King Henri IV—a man who, like Champlain, had once been a Protestant but converted to Catholicism. "Paris is worth a mass," as Henri famously put it. But not everyone believed the king's conversion was sincere— some regions remained bitterly hostile to him. To further complicate matters, Spain declared war on Henri while savage fighting between the king's Protestant and Catholic subjects persisted. Champlain rose rapidly through the ranks of the army. That he showed merit in the fighting is clear from the fact that he won the confidence of the new king, who entrusted the young adventurer with covert missions, though nothing is known of the details of these missions. That Henri would show such favour to a commoner led to later rumours that Champlain was secretly his bastard son. More likely, in a time of war and chaos, Henri simply needed good men to rely upon—wherever he could find them. In an era when kings were often assassinated and the air was thick with plots and intrigues, one could never have too many loyal retainers, especially rising stars like this talented sailor from Brouage. The blood-shed finally ended in 1598 when the Edict of Nantes granted—at least on paper—some degree of freedom and autonomy to Protestants while uniting the volatile kingdom under Henri.

With the war over, Champlain sheathed his sword and returned to his real love: the sea. In 1598 he joined the crew of his uncle's ship. Their immediate destination was Spain's Atlantic seaports. Spain's bloody conquests in the New World—its conquistadors had subdued the mighty Aztec and Incan empires—transformed the kingdom into the most powerful nation in the world. Spain now ruled a vast empire consisting not only of its New World possessions but also much of Italy, the Netherlands, the Mediterranean Sea, and through dynastic inheritance, a large swath of central Europe. To keep such a vast, trans-oceanic empire running required great numbers of skilled sailors and navigators, regardless of their nationality. Champlain's uncle, a veteran sea captain, received a contract to transport Spanish troops across the ocean to their possessions in the Caribbean. The young Champlain, who despite the hellish nature of ocean voyages probably couldn't resist the opportunity, managed to secure for himself a place on board the vessel.

This gave Champlain the chance to see the New World for the first time. He was gone for two years and visited much of Spain's empire in the Caribbean as well as Mexico. He saw on his journey strange and wondrous things—monkeys, colourful birds and fish, unusual people, beautiful sandy white beaches, and lush tropical rainforests. All kinds of rumours and legends circulated about what might live in the mysterious jungles. Champlain recorded one story he heard about reports of a griffin, "said to haunt certain districts of Mexico," with the head of an eagle, bat wings, and an alligator's tail.[2] But here, too, he also saw a darker side. The Spanish Empire, like the Aztecs, Mayas, and Incas before them, entailed warfare, slavery, and barbaric cruelties. It was not a vision Champlain found to his liking. He kept careful notes on everything he saw and heard—and reported back to the French king.

The horrors Champlain witnessed as a young man in France and in the Caribbean profoundly affected him. Sickened by the religious fanaticism and bloodshed, he dreamed of a different way of doing things. Champlain's background in the multicultural port of Brouage, along with his experience as a religious minority in a time when violent oppression was the norm, helped nurture in him a rare tolerance and broad-minded attitude toward other people and cultures. His talents as a sailor, navigator, cartographer, and soldier; his facility with languages; and his sensitivity to injustice and commitment to tolerance made

Champlain uniquely suited for what destiny had in store for him in the wilds of Canada.[3]

Although earlier attempts at colonization in Canada and on Sable Island had ended in disaster, the French, like the English, Spanish, and Basque, had continued crossing the ocean to fish off Newfoundland and, increasingly, to trade for furs with the Montagnais and Mi'kmaq people. By the end of the sixteenth century, the French had established a trading post on the St. Lawrence River's mountainous north shore at Tadoussac—a place best known today for its whale watching. In 1600 the French had even experimented with a short-lived colony on the site, but it too, like previous efforts, had ended in misery and death.

In 1603, Champlain, filled with irrepressible curiosity about the New World across the sea, was able to secure a place on board a ship sailing to Tadoussac. Although a skilled navigator, he had no official role and was merely a private passenger. That he would risk the hardships, bad food, and chance of shipwreck on a voyage across the stormy Atlantic for a venture in which he had no official role is testament to Champlain's overwhelming urge to explore.

The voyage introduced Champlain for the first time to Canada. Unlike Cartier, he liked what he saw. He enjoyed the challenge of trying to communicate with the local Montagnais, a nomadic Algonquin tribe of the Laurentian Mountains. Champlain was keen to befriend them and learn as much as he could—inquiring about the plants, animals, trees, and local geography. He also noted that the soil along the St. Lawrence, if cultivated, would be, in his words, as fine as that in France.

After a summer of trading and fishing, Champlain returned to France in the fall with the other mariners. That winter the French court—at last free from any immediate wars—finally resolved to again attempt more serious exploration and colonization in the New World. The king named the soldier and aristocrat Pierre du Gua de Monts as lieutenant-general of "the coasts, lands and confines of Acadia, Canada and other places in New France," and instructed him to establish a colony at a suitable site while carrying on a trade in furs. For the venture, De Monts would need to recruit strong, talented subordinates who had experience at sea and could aid in the settlement.

Among De Monts's lieutenants was the dreamer Champlain, who was to serve as the expedition's cartographer. In the spring of 1604 they sailed to what the French called Acadia—the modern Maritime provinces—and up the waters of the Bay of Fundy, a place where the tides were so extreme that boats at low tide were stranded on the ocean floor. Champlain set to work making maps of the coastlines and potential anchorage places for ships. It was exciting work for a person of Champlain's temperament; wildlife abounded everywhere. The sea teemed with whales and fish. While rowing around in a smaller boat to scout out shoals, reefs, islands, and bays, Champlain took careful measurements with his astrolabe—a navigation tool used to work out latitude by measuring the position of the sun or stars above the horizon. Champlain's talents and energy were such that he was soon much more than just the expedition's mapmaker—important as that role was—and rapidly became an indispensable man in the enterprise. He took a lead role in exploring the land, making contacts with Mi'kmaq bands that hunted and fished in the area, and examining the soil with an eye to farming. Champlain, unlike most Europeans of the era, had a unique talent for winning friends and making alliances with people from different cultures—a trait that made him invaluable.

De Monts appointed Champlain to go off exploring in one of the expedition's vessels and to search for a suitable place for them to over-winter. Champlain selected an island in the mouth of the St. Croix River in what is today New Brunswick. The French built cabins here and lived off the land, hunting birds, snaring rabbits, collecting mussels, clams, and oysters at low tide, and catching fish.

But the winter proved an exceptionally harsh one, and scurvy took a heavy toll. Thirty-five of the seventy-nine settlers died and many of the others were near death. Champlain's iron constitution seems to have spared him any illness—indeed he seems never to have suffered much from scurvy. In the spring, the surviving colonists decided to relocate across the Bay of Fundy to a more sheltered site the French named Port Royal. Here they felled trees, erected cabins and a fort, and tilled the soil. Champlain, meanwhile, used it as his base while he continued to probe more of the Atlantic coastline. In his ship he ranged south along the coastline as far as present-day Cape Cod, gathering more coordinates and details for his amazingly precise maps.

Back at Port Royal, Champlain was ever busy hunting for food, catching fish—which he began to stock in a pond—and exploring the land. To make the brutal winters more bearable, he founded an "Order of Good Cheer" to keep spirits high by staging parties and banquets featuring wild game, fish, berries, and whatever else they could muster. But life remained difficult, and danger was everywhere—to the south, the French had been involved in violent clashes with the Basque and the English as well as some natives. Then, in 1607, after three years surviving in the wilderness of North America, De Monts's fur monopoly was revoked, and on his orders Champlain and the other colonists abandoned their settlement and returned to France. Although many of them were discouraged by the experience, seemingly nothing could dampen Champlain's optimism. He had fallen in love with the wilds of the New World, and was now more determined than ever to make a French settlement across the ocean a reality.

De Monts shared Champlain's dream, and together they hatched a new plan for trade and colonization. They decided to shift their focus from Acadia to the more northern land they'd visited in 1603—the place Cartier had called "Canada." The climate was harsher there, but this prospect apparently didn't discourage them. Moreover, there was the mystery of the great river to consider, the "River of Canada"—the St. Lawrence. Cartier had been told by his native scouts that it led far inland to cities of great wealth, but he hadn't managed to make it beyond the first major rapids. Seventy years later, Champlain and De Monts still wondered if the river might ultimately be the key to reaching Asia.

With De Monts's backing, in the spring of 1608 Champlain sailed from France in command of a fleet of three ships to seek Canada. Their aim was to lay the groundwork for a self-sufficient colony in the wilderness. Despite Champlain's irrepressible optimism, for the rest of the colonists it could not have been a promising prospect—every previous attempt at colonization had ended in misery and death. The Vikings had been unable to make any lasting settlement; Cartier and Roberval had both failed; the Sable Island colony had resulted in murder and starvation; the French attempts at Tadoussac had ended badly; and the colonies in the Bay of Fundy had had to be abandoned. What made Champlain think he could succeed where all others before him had failed?

Champlain had a crazy idea: unlike previous colonizers, he'd actually seek to make friends with aboriginal nations rather than antagonize them. He'd already made a good impression on the Montagnais bands in his 1603 journey and then later on the Mi'kmaq on the Bay of Fundy's coastline. In contrast to Cartier's condescension and treachery, Champlain admired aboriginal people and treated them with respect.

As he piloted his flagship up the "River of Canada," with two other vessels close behind, Champlain's first critical task was to select a strategic and viable location for his planned settlement. But before the French could do that they found themselves already facing violent opposition—not, however, from any native people, but from other Europeans. Off Tadoussac, Champlain's compatriot, François Pont-Gravé, who commanded the second French vessel, met with Basque whalers and fur traders. Pont-Gravé, brave but impetuous, demanded they vacate the harbour as it was claimed by the king of France. The Basque, not much caring for diplomatic negotiations, responded by opening fire from their ship with cannons and heavy, unwieldy firearms known as arquebuses.

When Champlain arrived, he found his friend Pont-Gravé severely wounded and the Basque in command of Tadoussac. Rather than being angry with the Basque for attacking his countrymen, Champlain was, as he put it in his journal, "much annoyed at the brewing of a quarrel we could well have dispensed with."[4] Champlain's dismay at Pont-Gravé's rashness reveals his conciliatory attitude and his desire to avoid conflict wherever possible—resorting to violence only as a last resort. With characteristic self-assurance, Champlain went aboard the Basque ship to face Pont-Gravé's attackers. He managed to smooth things over and broker a truce that would allow both sides to carry on their business in peace.

Champlain's business was exploration. He wanted to find out where the mighty river of Canada led—a river so long that the natives had told Cartier "no man had ever seen its end." For Champlain, the wide, dark blue waters of the St. Lawrence leading into the heart of the mountainous wilderness were an irresistible mystery. But he couldn't just sail one of his large ships up the river, against the current. In order to make decent headway, Champlain would need a smaller, more manoeuvrable vessel. He ordered his carpenters to outfit a pinnace—a smaller type of boat that could be equipped with oars and a single sail.

While his carpenters prepared the pinnace for the journey upriver, Champlain could not resist wandering off into the mountains and forests around Tadoussac. He climbed up some of the mountains overlooking the sea and found it a cold, harsh country—windswept and rather sparsely treed, with few signs of animals. He did, however, shoot some birds (likely spruce grouse) for food. Champlain also encountered some Montagnais who had come to Tadoussac to trade with the Basque. He befriended them, and learned about a saltwater sea said to lie some fifty or sixty hard days' journey to the north. Champlain concluded that this must be the great northern sea that the English under Henry Hudson had been exploring in their quest to find a passage to Asia.

These Montagnais, however, were recent arrivals in the area. The Iroquoian farmers who had inhabited the St. Lawrence Valley in the time of Cartier and Roberval had disappeared—their settlements were now nowhere to be found. No trace was left of the little village of Stadacona, which had rotted away and been swallowed up by dense forest. What had happened to the Iroquoian-speaking people? Historians are divided. Some think they might have been pushed out in warfare with their Algonquin rivals, relocating to the area south of the St. Lawrence around the Adirondack Mountains. Another theory is that the climate, which was cooling in the "Little Ice Age" of the era, had driven them southward. But probably the most likely explanation is that they'd been fatally weakened by their exposure to Old World diseases unknowingly transported by the French. In any event, they were nowhere to be found in the St. Lawrence Valley when Champlain and his colonists arrived.

What confronted Champlain was a vast wilderness of ancient old-growth forests that towered above the land. There were black bears, timber wolves, elk, moose, deer, lynx, beavers, and strange creatures the French had never seen before—bizarre, ungainly animals covered in sharp spines that we know as porcupines; strange bandit-masked creatures familiar today as raccoons; flying squirrels; and elusive mountain lions. In the mouths of tributary streams flowing into the St. Lawrence, the French caught salmon—a welcome addition to their diet.

As they retraced Cartier's route upriver, Champlain navigated his vessel past dangerous shoals and rocks and numerous islands. In his journal, he noted the different types of trees on shore—pine, spruce, birch, and oak, species he recognized from his native France, as well as other, less familiar trees like butternut and tamarack. As the river changed from salt to fresh water, on the north shore the French passed by an immense, thundering waterfall some eighty metres high—the spectacular Montmorency Falls.

A league beyond this wondrous cataract, on July 3, 1608, from the deck of his ship Champlain gazed across the waters of the wide blue river at a massive dark stone cliff. This was what the Montagnais called "Kebec," meaning the place where the river narrowed—the point of land where Cartier had been seventy years earlier and where the village of Stadacona once stood. Now it was a dense forest consisting of a great number of butternut trees. It was here at this strategic place—ideal for defence—that Champlain resolved to plant the seed of an empire.

The French rowed ashore beneath the towering cliff in their small ship. The soil looked promising, and the butternuts would make an excellent addition to their diet. Under Champlain's direction, the colonists felled trees, planted gardens, dug cellars, and began work on a palisaded fortress. They erected three two-storey buildings complete with chimneys, interconnecting balconies, a watchtower, and cannons. Outside the palisade, Champlain had a moat dug for additional protection. All told, it was an impressive structure in an imposing location—and it made a strong impression on the Montagnais and other Algonquin, who'd never seen anything like it. Locked in brutal warfare with the more powerful agricultural nations to the south, they were naturally keen to make an alliance with the people who could build such things.

Champlain was just as eager to encourage good relations. He conversed with the Montagnais as best as he could—asking them about their lands, customs, and spiritual beliefs. He learned that they came to Quebec in the fall to fish for eels, which they dried as part of their winter food supply. Evidently the Montagnais saw in Champlain something they didn't see in other Europeans; they trusted him enough to ask if he would store their dried eels until they returned in midwinter from their hunting and trapping. Champlain happily agreed.

Unlike the other French leaders, Champlain didn't treat natives with suspicion or make a habit of remaining armed in their presence. Instead, his style was a light-hearted one; he liked to smile and laugh, talk and ask questions about everything around him. But in an era when violence was the norm, his tolerant style did not win over everyone. Among Champlain's colonists was a locksmith, Jean Duval, who mistook Champlain's friendly ways toward natives for weakness, and despised him accordingly. Duval made his views known to others among Champlain's party; the worst malcontents, numbering four or five, began to plot against him. Soon, their whispers against Champlain as a weak and ineffectual leader came to disaffect much of the rest of the group. Duval's plan was to murder Champlain and hand the colony over to the Basque or Spanish downriver at Tadoussac.

The conspirators waited until Champlain's closest companions had left the colony in the pinnace on a mission to retrieve more supplies at Tadoussac. Their intention was to either catch Champlain off-guard and strangle him or sound a false alarm at night and shoot him as he stepped out of his quarters. With Champlain out of the way, they would then invite the Basque or Spanish to take over the fort.

But one of their number—who'd been threatened with death if he refused to go along with the mutiny—secretly informed Champlain of what was brewing. With characteristic coolness, in the forest outside the fort Champlain calmly interrogated the informer—determining who the key instigators of the plot were. Then he told the informer to go back to his chores and carry on as if nothing had happened. Champlain, meanwhile, laid a trap for the conspirators. He arranged for Duval and his three main confederates to be invited that night on board the pinnace, which had just returned, for some wine. When the conspirators climbed aboard the ship, they were taken by surprise and immediately seized by Champlain and his loyalists, who'd been waiting with arms.

It wasn't Champlain's style to arbitrarily put anyone to death—not even when as guilty as Duval and his companions appeared to be. Instead, Champlain convened a court of four officers, including himself, to cross-examine the accused and get to the bottom of the matter. The men confessed to plotting to murder Champlain. Duval himself said he deserved death for his treason—but begged for mercy. There was to be none. The council unanimously voted to execute him. Duval was hanged and then decapitated so that his head could be exhibited on a pike—a stark message to the colonists that Champlain's mercy had limits. The other, lesser ringleaders, however, were clapped in irons and sent on one of the returning ships back to France to be dealt with there. Never again would Champlain have to face a mutiny.

The first winter at Quebec proved a cruel one, and not only for the French. One by one Champlain's little band succumbed to dysentery and scurvy, while several parties of starving Montagnais arrived at the fort. One such band appeared on the far side of the river, desperate for help. Their condition was so dreadful that, faced with starvation, they attempted to paddle across the half-frozen St. Lawrence in their birchbark canoes. Champlain watched in horror from his settlement. The canoes were smashed and broken into pieces by the shifting ice, trapping the Montagnais on ice floes. It appeared as if they were doomed. But then, to the relief of all, the floes broke onto the north shore, delivering them to safety. Champlain rushed to their aid, and later noted: "They came to our settlement so thin and emaciated that they looked like skeletons, most of them being unable to stand. I was astonished at their appearance."[5] Champlain provided them with all the food he could spare, but there were so many starving Montagnais that he couldn't provide for them all. Their plight was so desperate that they ate the decomposing remains of dogs that had been left out as trap bait for foxes and martens.

Enduring their first Canadian winter, it must have been a horrifying

CHAMPLAIN'S MAP OF NEW FRANCE   85

prospect for the French to see even the native Montagnais—whom Champlain judged to be the most skilful hunters he'd ever encountered—facing starvation as a fact of life. The grim reality was that starvation could be inescapable in an environment like the boreal forest: cyclical fluctuations in animal populations caused starvations among all predators, including humans. Modern archaeological findings have confirmed this: periodic famines, especially in late winter and early spring, were for millennia part of life in Canada's North—one reason why population density and life expectancy remained extremely low. Champlain noted that because of the precarious nature of their food supply, the Montagnais were often reduced to eating the tanned skins they wore for clothing or their domesticated dogs. But starvation wasn't their only concern. War was also widespread.

The Montagnais lived in constant dread of their enemies, a fact that surprised Champlain, who hadn't expected to find such a degree of warfare in Canada.[6] The Montagnais so feared the warlike tribes to the south, whom they called "Iroquois," that they begged Champlain to let their women and children stay inside the fort to keep them safe—as the pitiless war they were caught up in spared no one, not even children. Champlain tried as best he could to help his Montagnais friends, who camped nearby under the protection of the fort's cannons.

When the long winter finally ended, only eight of the original twenty-eight French settlers were left alive. Thirteen had died of dysentery and another seven of scurvy. Champlain speculated that the scurvy might be caused by the salted meat they depended on, although he wasn't able to figure out that all around him lay the cure: evergreen boughs steeped in boiling water to make a vitamin-rich tea.

A relief ship from France arrived in the spring. It's worth taking a moment to reflect on the nature of the choice that confronted Champlain. The majority of his companions had just died horrible deaths, their fresh graves a reminder of what a Canadian winter entailed. The country was so harsh that even its own native people—skilled hunters and trappers as they were—frequently faced starvation. Many of Champlain's own followers had plotted to murder him. Downriver were hostile Basque and Spanish vessels that would also, given the chance, attack his isolated and weakened post. They were cut off from their homelands, on the far side of the ocean in an unforgiving wilderness. Cartier, when confronted with the same circumstances, took the first opportunity to escape back to France. But Champlain was made of sterner stuff. He had every intention of pressing on upriver into the unknown interior. He ordered a shallop—a type of light, easily manoeuvrable sailboat—to be fitted out, and with twenty men and his Montagnais friends in their canoes, set off upriver.

The journey took the French through territory that Champlain felt was "delightfully beautiful" to behold, with green forests and rolling hills.[7] What a contrast it all made to the bleakness of the long winter. The river, however, given its many rocks, shoals, and strong currents, was very dangerous to navigate. In order to proceed safely, Champlain used a "sounding-lead" at the bow of his little vessel to keep watch for any obstacles. On an island in the river the French came upon two to three hundred Wendat and Algonquin warriors, who had been on their way to Quebec to meet the French. In exchange for helping Champlain in his explorations and settlement, the Wendat and Algonquin wanted the French to join them on the warpath against their mortal enemies, a powerful confederacy of five related nations located in what is now upstate New York. These were the people the Montagnais called the "Iroquois"—but their own name for themselves was Haudenosaunee, meaning "People of the Long House." The Wendat and Algonquin warriors told Champlain that there could never be any true alliance between them if he wouldn't help them in their wars. Champlain, knowing the importance of establishing an alliance with the natives, agreed.

First, though, the Wendat and Algonquin wanted to see Quebec—and Champlain, eager to please, agreed to return there with them. This done, he left the settlement under the charge of Pont-Gravé, who had arrived from France, and with twelve French companions headed back upriver with his new allies. All through their shared journey Champlain was busy studying the land—examining the trees, plants, soil, rivers, and lakes, and making inquiries about what lay beyond in each direction.

At the Iroquois River (now the Richelieu River), the party divided. The river was the gateway into the homeland of the most powerful and feared of the five nations that comprised the Iroquois Confederacy—the Mohawks. Now that the party was leaving the St. Lawrence, some of the Wendat and Algonquin became nervous and quit the expedition, returning to their villages or hunting territories. The warriors who wished to continue and the French pushed on up the Iroquois River's swift current.

When the French reached rapids that couldn't be navigated in the shallop, they faced a critical choice: if they were to press on, it would have to be in birchbark canoes. Many of the French were understandably anxious about leaving the protection of their ship. Champlain, however, knew he had to fulfill his promise to help the Wendat and Algonquin against the Iroquois. So he did something no other European in Canada had ever done—he climbed into a canoe, and told his native allies they'd carry on that way. As for the others, Champlain allowed each man to make up his own mind. Only two of the French were willing to risk it; Champlain permitted the others to return in the ship to Quebec. They must have thought they'd never see their captain again.

As Champlain and the natives portaged around the rapids in their canoes, they took stock of their force: sixty warriors in twenty-four canoes, plus Champlain and his two French companions. It was an alarmingly small party to be entering Mohawk territory.

The river's source was a large, beautiful lake studded with forested islands and surrounded by green mountains. The whole country was full of wildlife—in part because it was a no man's land in between hostile nations. Among the wonders the lake contained was a species of monstrous fish that the natives called the Chaousarou. Champlain noted:

> The largest of them, as these tribes have told me, are from eight to
> ten feet long. I have seen some five feet long, which were as big as my
> thigh, and had a head as large as my two fists, with a snout two feet
> and a half long, and a double row of very sharp, dangerous teeth. Its
> body has a good deal the shape of the pike; but it is protected by scales
> of a silvery gray colour and so strong that a dagger could not pierce
> them. The end of its snout is like a pig's. This fish makes war on
> all the other fish . . . And, according to what these tribes have told
> me, it shows marvellous ingenuity in that, when it wishes to catch
> birds, it goes in amongst the rushes or reeds which lie along the shores
> of the lake . . . and puts its snout out of the water without moving.
> The result is that when the birds come and light on its snout, mistaking
> it for a stump of wood, the fish is so cunning that, shutting its half-
> open mouth, it pulls them by their feet under the water.[8]

It says a lot about Champlain's presence of mind and temperament that, on the verge of battle with several hundred fearsome Mohawk warriors, he mused about a strange fish. It was most likely an alligator gar—a species no longer found in Canada.

As Champlain and his allies canoed south, he could see in the distance snow-capped peaks: the Adirondacks. He was told that these lofty mountains marked the territory of the Iroquois. As a precaution against ambush, they now switched to paddling at night and sleeping during the day.

At last, on the shores of the vast, beautiful lake with its strange fish and abundant waterfowl, they encountered an Iroquois war party, numbering some two hundred warriors of the Mohawk nation. At dawn, the two sides sent emissaries to negotiate with each other— which settled nothing other than that there would be a battle. The Iroquois had felled trees and fortified a position near the lakeshore. But, in a show of confidence, they left their defensive protection. Wearing wooden armour, they advanced in the open in tight formation, toward the coalition of Wendat and Algonquin warriors. Both sides were armed with bows and arrows, and some warriors carried shields. Champlain was clad in heavy plate armour—still standard in European warfare of the era—with his sword sheathed at his side and in his hands a heavy, unwieldly arquebus. He'd loaded it with four lead balls to inflict maximum damage—knowing that, once the fighting started, he might not get a chance to reload.

The Wendat and Algonquin chiefs had told Champlain that he must kill the Iroquois chiefs—there were three of them, each recognizable for his large stature, great feather plumes in his hair, and position in the lead. Champlain advanced ahead of the main party of warriors; now he was out in front all alone. When the onrushing Iroquois spotted this strange figure clad in shiny armour, they halted for a moment. Champlain took aim at the foremost chief and fired. The noise and thick plume of smoke startled the Iroquois, who'd never before encountered firearms. With that single shot, Champlain had managed to kill two of the chiefs and wound the third. The sight of their enemies in confusion and the chiefs dead roused the Wendat and Algonquin, who shouted furiously and began to unleash their arrows at the Iroquois. Meanwhile, Champlain's two French companions, concealed in the forest, opened fire with their arquebuses. Overwhelmed, the Iroquois turned and fled, but Champlain and the Wendat and Algonquin pursued them, "laying more of them low," as Champlain put it. About a dozen Iroquois were captured—the remainder escaped—while on the Wendat-Algonquin side, none had been killed and only about fifteen or sixteen wounded. It was a decisive victory.

Champlain, unusually for him, decided to name the lake where the battle had been fought after himself; with his astrolabe, he determined its latitude at 43 degrees and several minutes. Today, Lake Champlain straddles the international border between Quebec and Vermont. Although the Wendat and Algonquin were ecstatic with this triumph, little did they yet realize that it had only deepened their existing blood feud with the Iroquois—a feud that would last nearly a century, and by the end lay waste to much of their homelands as well as French Canada. The Mohawk would not soon forget the defeat they suffered that day.

After their victory, Champlain and his allies embarked in their canoes for the journey to Quebec. But once they were safely out of Iroquois territory, they halted to deal with their Mohawk captives. The Wendat taunted them by promising they would suffer the same agonies that the Iroquois inflicted on their own enemies. They singled one out and forced him to sing as they prepared to torture him. Champlain recorded:

> It was a very sad song to hear. Meanwhile our Indians kindled a fire, and when it was well lighted, each took a brand and burned this poor wretch a little at a time in order to make him suffer the greater torment. Sometimes they would leave off, throwing water on his back. Then they tore out his nails and applied fire to the ends of his fingers and to his *membrum virile*. Afterwards they scalped him and caused a certain kind of gum to drip very hot upon the crown of his head. Then they pierced his arms near the wrists and with sticks pulled and tore out the sinews by main force, and when they saw they could not get them out, they cut them off. This poor wretch uttered strange cries, and I felt pity at seeing him treated in this way . . . They begged me repeatedly to take fire and do like them.[9]

Champlain was eager to please his new allies, but he drew the line at torture and insisted that the captive be put out of his misery. Reluctantly, the Wendat allowed Champlain to kill the Iroquois with his arquebus. They then mutilated the corpse and forced the surviving captives to eat parts of it. After this macabre scene, the remaining captives had to continue the journey until they could later all be tortured in a similar manner.[10]

Back at Quebec, Champlain was greeted with a hero's welcome by the Montagnais and Algonquin—who celebrated when the scalps of the Iroquois were shown. A firm and lasting alliance had been forged in blood. The next two hundred years would increasingly bind the northern aboriginal groups and the French settlers together through shared ties and extensive intermarriage. As Champlain put it, by intermarriage they would become one people.

Champlain hoped that the battle would end hostilities and that he could now make a peace treaty with the Iroquois. Alas, this was not to be. The following summer, in 1610, the Mohawks, eager for revenge, invaded the St. Lawrence River Valley and fortified a position on the Iroquois River a short distance up from the St. Lawrence. The Algonquin and Montagnais—numbering several hundred warriors—attacked the Mohawk fort. Champlain had been journeying up the St. Lawrence when he learned of the ongoing battle; having promised to assist his allies, he hastened to the scene of action. As he charged into the fray, flying arrows ricocheted off his plate armour. But one Mohawk archer took more deliberate aim, and then unleashed an arrow straight at Champlain's unprotected face. The arrow, Champlain wrote, "split the tip of my ear and pierced my neck."[11] Champlain nevertheless kept fighting. The battle turned into a rout: all the Mohawks were killed, except fifteen who were taken prisoner—these unfortunate survivors were later slowly tortured to death.

The Iroquois were again defeated—and for a generation they would not venture to face French soldiers in battle again. Champlain brokered a shaky peace with the Mohawk and managed to keep it during his lifetime. But after his death, warfare with the Mohawk would resume on a vastly bloodier scale.

More immediately troubling were the four other nations of the Iroquois Confederacy, all of whom remained hostile to the Wendat, Algonquin, and other northern tribes. The Wendat and Algonquin still wanted Champlain's help in defending themselves from these formidable adversaries. Champlain agreed, and in order to further their alliance and encourage deeper understanding, both sides exchanged young men to live with each other. Champlain presented a Frenchman of about nineteen, Étienne Brûlé, to overwinter with the Wendat and Algonquin in their villages and in turn accepted several native youths.

Meanwhile, far away across the ocean in France, trouble was brewing. King Henri was assassinated by a religious fanatic, enraged at his tolerance toward Protestants. With his patron dead, Champlain's position in Canada was in jeopardy. He was, after all, only a fisherman's son—not a natural member of the French leadership class—and there were enemies in France as dangerous to him as any he could find among the Iroquois. Champlain hurried back to France to ensure ongoing support for his efforts in Canada. At first he was treated coolly by the new king and his advisers, but there was manifestly no one better qualified to lead French efforts in Canada. Champlain was thus allowed to return the next year, in the spring of 1611, to resume his grand project.

That year, he headed up the St. Lawrence in a small barque to explore more territory and to rendezvous with his native allies and Brûlé. At the island of Mont Royal (Montreal), Champlain halted to more thoroughly explore and map the area. The land around Mont Royal was an oasis of wildlife—Champlain noted that there were "so many herons that the air was completely filled with them."[12] But what particularly attracted his attention were the fearful whitewater rapids just above the island— the same rapids that had forced Cartier to turn back. Known as the

Lachine Rapids, this five-kilometre stretch of whitewater was for Champlain "the most fearful place. The roar is so loud that one would have said it was thunder, as the air rang with the sound of these cataracts."[13] One of Champlain's companions, a young Frenchman named Louis, along with two natives, attempted to paddle the rapids in a birchbark canoe. Champlain watched in horror as the canoe swamped and the three men disappeared in the wild, roaring cataracts. Only one managed to resurface below and swim to safety—the other two were lost. Champlain searched in vain for Louis's body, noting of the spot where he had disappeared, "my hair stood on an end to see so terrifying a place."[14]

Eventually, as prearranged, several hundred Wendat warriors arrived at the site along with Brûlé, who was dressed like a Wendat and had shown himself a quick learner in both the Iroquoian and Algonquin languages. All of them camped together and discussed their plans for the future—the need for an alliance against the Iroquois Confederacy, which the Wendat had been fighting for generations, and the mutual desire to have Champlain visit the Wendat villages. In the meantime, however, Champlain was needed back in France—so in his place he dispatched more of his young French companions to follow Brûlé's example and live with various native nations to learn their customs and languages. Among these interpreters was another Frenchman, Nicolas de Vignau, who was to live with the northern Algonquin tribes.

Despite his pledge to aid the Wendat and Algonquin in their battles with the Iroquois, Champlain's real interest remained exploration—not war. His energies for the next few years, however, were taken up with overseeing the growing fortress at Quebec and making almost annual ocean voyages back to France—adding to his growing fame as a navigator. In the frigid waters off Newfoundland he sometimes had to pilot his ship around huge mountains of icebergs, some taller than the masts of his ships. During this time he had with him a Wendat named

Savignon, who accompanied Champlain to France and learned French ways—just as several Frenchmen, the first "coureurs de bois," were in the process of doing with the Wendat, Algonquin, and Montagnais.

In the spring of 1613, Champlain finally had a renewed opportunity for exploration. That year he sailed back across the Atlantic to Quebec—where a small settlement clustered around the fort was struggling to survive—and headed back upriver. His goal was to head far inland, explore the interior, and see the immense lakes his native allies had told him about—perhaps even discover a route to Asia. At the Lachine Rapids, his party switched from their small ship to birch-bark canoes. From there they advanced—and with only four other Frenchmen, including Nicolas de Vignau and a native guide, it was a very small group to be travelling alone in dangerous territory.

They came to a large northern tributary of the St. Lawrence—the "River of Algonquins," which later became known as the Ottawa River. Champlain's scout, de Vignau, had claimed that during the time he spent with the Algonquin he'd gone up the river all the way to the northern sea, and that while there he'd seen an English shipwreck. Champlain didn't fully believe the story, but he went along. At the mouth of this new, unknown river, Champlain stood on shore with his astrolabe to gaze at the sun and work out the latitude—he put it at about 45 degrees, 18 minutes, an amazingly accurate estimate.

The journey up the Ottawa, against its swift current, proved extremely arduous. To make headway required alternating between hard paddling, dragging the canoes with ropes, wading through the swirling water, and in places where no other way was possible, portaging. In one particularly dangerous spot, Champlain was towing his canoe with a rope wrapped tightly around his hand when suddenly the canoe spun sideways in the current; the force was so strong that it nearly cut his hand off. At other times, the men were almost drowned by the fierce rapids they were attempting to fight their way up. And at night, because they knew there were marauding war parties of the Iroquois Confederacy around, they had to take turns keeping watch as the others slept near the overturned canoes. Wherever possible, Champlain selected island campsites that could be more easily defended in the event of an attack.

As they advanced deeper into the wilderness they encountered various bands of Algonquin nations, usually travelling in large groups for protection against their enemies. Many of them had already heard of Champlain's exploits, and the effect of seeing him now travel as they did, by canoe up a difficult waterway, won him further respect. Champlain was eager to make friends with all these tribes; to do so, he was asked to pledge support for them in their ongoing wars.

After passing through a wider, more tranquil part of the river—which the French later named Lac des Chats because of the mountain lions or bobcats in the area—Champlain decided, on the advice of his guide, to leave the river and strike overland to a chain of lakes. This would be easier, his guide believed, than continuing to fight against the fierce current.

The portage took them through forests of towering pines, cedars, birch, and balsam fir. Eventually they came upon a small lake where they could relaunch their canoes, paddling north until forced to portage again. Just beyond what is now known as Green Lake, portaging once more through dense brush and swatting relentless hordes of mosquitoes and blackflies, Champlain lost his astrolabe. Although he didn't need it to navigate—as a born sailor he could do that with the sun and stars—he did need it to accurately plot coordinates and chart territory. But Champlain evidently didn't realize that he'd dropped or misplaced it until it was too late. Over a quarter of a millennium later, in 1867, a local farm boy happened to unearth the strange brass instrument without knowing what it was. It now sits carefully preserved in the Museum of Canadian History, located on the banks of the river Champlain was mapping when he lost it. For the remainder of his journey upriver, he would have to make rough estimates of position rather than detailed calculations.

At what is now called Muskrat Lake, the party encountered another Algonquin encampment—where Champlain found that his reputation had preceded him. The chief, Nibachis, was in Champlain's words "astonished that we had been able to pass the rapids and bad trails," and remarked that "he did not know how we had been able to get through, when those who live in the country had great difficulty in coming along such difficult trails."[15] By imitating native methods of travel and sharing equally in the hard work of canoeing and portaging, Champlain was earning the respect of native nations. Seeing Champlain with his own eyes, Nibachis said that he "was everything the other Indians had told him."[16] Champlain and Nibachis shared a peace pipe and became friends—much as Champlain had previously done with many other chiefs. Afterward, Champlain and his little band pressed on farther still—portaging from Muskrat Lake back to the Ottawa River, having bypassed many of its worst rapids.

This section of the Ottawa River was much wider and full of forested islands, and here Champlain met with another Algonquin band led by a famed chief, Tessouat. Tessouat was impressed by Champlain and eager to make a pact; they smoked and feasted together. However, when Champlain informed him of his plan to continue upriver to meet with the Nipissing nation, Tessouat became alarmed. He told Champlain that it was too dangerous—that the Nipissings were a tribe of sorcerers who killed people through dark magic—and urged him not to attempt the journey. But Champlain was a man under the spell of the beyond, compelled by an irresistible urge to seek the unknown. Although he wasn't one to dismiss native tales of the supernatural (like most Europeans of his era, Champlain fully believed in witchcraft and supernatural powers), he was still eager to press on. He pointed out that his young companion, de Vignau, had told him that he'd already been there, and that it was only a short journey to the northern sea—which Champlain now wanted to see for himself.

At this, Tessouat and the other Algonquins suddenly erupted in fury. They shouted that de Vignau was a liar—that he'd never been north of their encampment. Champlain, who already had reasons to suspect de Vignau's honesty, turned on his companion and angrily demanded the truth. De Vignau withered under the pressure, confessing that he'd never seen the northern sea. Champlain was disgusted, but he rebuffed the Algonquins' offer to let them punish de Vignau. On the advice of the chief Tessouat, Champlain decided to defer his exploration farther north until a later date. In the meantime, they would head back to Quebec.

The return journey did nothing to improve Champlain's view of de Vignau. By the time they reached the Lachine Rapids, de Vignau had become withdrawn and despondent. He did not want to return to Quebec or France, preferring to remain among the Algonquin—but none of them wanted him. An outcast, de Vignau silently wandered off into the forest near Mont Royal, never to be seen again. Champlain wrote simply, "We left him in God's keeping."[17]

Despite the unfortunate affair with de Vignau, the other interpreters Champlain dispatched to live with various aboriginal nations worked out well—as did the various native youths who journeyed with Champlain to Quebec and France. Once again, exploration was a two-way street, with the Wendat and Algonquin exploring France just as the French were exploring Canada. What they made of France is difficult to say—certainly, much like the French who were exploring Canada, they found it a strange, alien, but fascinating place, perhaps a little too crowded, with enormous cathedrals, castles, and houses made of stone that seemed to reach the clouds. The land was full of bizarre animals, like a certain fat, hairless creature that the French kept in pens and sometimes ate. Strangest of all, the French kept some beasts inside houses! The horses, in particular, they seemed to like putting in special dwellings, with rows of compartments side by side, each home to one of these large antler-less animals. Even more mystifying was the oddity of men who came, once in a while it seemed, to torture the poor animals by hammering something into their hooves. Champlain had said it was to make the horses walk better, but this seemed doubtful.

While his Wendat and Algonquin companions were busy exploring these unusual surroundings, Champlain was lobbying for the continuation of his project in Canada at the French court—which remained ambivalent about the idea—and working on his masterful maps. He still yearned to see more of the New World. In particular, he wanted to visit the Wendat lands of the interior, as the Wendat were by far the most powerful of his allies.

✳

In the spring of 1615 Champlain embarked on his greatest journey of exploration. With a small party of some dozen men, he left his small ship behind at the island of Mont Royal and from there climbed into a birchbark canoe. They retraced his previous route up the Ottawa River, but this time pressed on to the Mattawa. The country around this turbulent, rapid-choked stream was, in Champlain's words, a "frightful and abandoned region."[18] The Mattawa led Champlain's band into the wide waters of Lake Nipissing. They traversed it without much trouble, and despite what he'd heard about evil sorcerers, the Nipissing tribe proved friendly enough.

Once they crossed the lake they reached a waterway later known as the French River. By this point their provisions were running low—they were reduced to a single meal a day. Fortunately, a profusion of wild blueberries and raspberries along the river helped save them from starvation. The hundred-kilometre-long river brought Champlain through alternating stretches of foaming whitewater and tranquil pools set beneath granite cliffs to the waters of a vast "freshwater sea."[19]

This immense inland sea was what we know as Lake Huron—Champlain called it "Lake Attigouautan" after a particular clan of the Wendat nation who lived near its shores. The astonishing fact that it was fresh water made Champlain realize that this mysterious land was larger than anyone had yet suspected—and that it couldn't be the western ocean that he and other French explorers had once conjectured. The lake itself was a source of wonder—Champlain noted that it "abounds in many kinds of excellent fish . . . principally trout which are of monstrous size; I have seen some that were as much as four and a half feet long . . . Also pike of like size, and a certain kind of sturgeon, a very large fish and marvellously good to eat."[20] At least the French wouldn't have to starve.

The party worked their way south along Georgian Bay, weaving through the Thirty Thousand Islands that dot the bay and provide shelter from its often dangerous storms. By midsummer they'd reached the country of the Wendat on Georgian Bay's southern shores. It was, to Champlain's amazement, utterly unlike anything he had yet seen in Canada. The Wendat lived south of the rocky uplands of the Canadian Shield, in the fertile and lushly forested lands of what is now the area around Midland and Barrie, Ontario. Here, they resided in heavily fortified villages, which in some cases were guarded by triple palisades up to four storeys high, moats, and watchtowers—testament to the warfare that plagued the area. The warriors were clad in wooden armour and carried shields; sentries were posted to keep an eye out for enemy war parties. Around the villages were fields of corn and other crops, sometimes covering up to a thousand acres. Well-trodden paths connected some dozen fortified Wendat villages—each home to several thousand people—scattered across several hundred square kilometres of a country Champlain called "Huronia." Overall, he estimated the population at about thirty thousand.

Champlain travelled to the different villages and met with as many of the Wendat as he could. He was well received—the natives perceived him as a man of great character—and his visit further cemented the friendly relations between the French and Wendat. He was told that the Iroquois Confederacy had been more aggressive than normal; they'd been making deadly raids into Wendat lands. The Wendat wanted revenge, and were planning a huge, full-scale invasion of Iroqouia. Champlain promised to fight alongside them. Other native allies also arrived to join the expedition—including many of the Algonquin chiefs Champlain had earlier befriended. Meanwhile, messengers were dispatched to nations that lived far to the south—roughly in what is now Pennsylvania—as these tribes were also at war with the mighty Iroquois Confederacy, and the Wendat needed as many allies as they could possibly muster for their invasion. When the force was ready, they marshalled over five hundred warriors, in addition to about a dozen French soldiers led by Champlain and the still-hoped-for reinforcements from the southern nations.

The war party headed south by canoe, travelling slowly given the immense size of the undertaking, until they reached the blue waters of another vast freshwater sea—what we know as Lake Ontario. It was too large a body of water to cross in open canoes, so the party had to paddle along the shoreline, eventually reaching the lake's southern shores. Here, they carefully concealed their canoes in thick brush, and then proceeded on foot into Iroquois territory. Should their canoes be discovered by the enemy, they would be cut off deep in hostile country.

Their target was a large Onondaga village located in the heart of the Iroquois Confederacy's territory: modern-day upstate New York. The Onondaga, one of the Confederacy's Five Nations, had been particularly active in their northward incursions into Wendat and Algonquin lands—and Champlain's allies had resolved to strike their blow against them. As they pushed on through lush deciduous forest southward from Lake Ontario, Champlain noted the abundance of chestnut trees and fed on their delicious nuts—another tree that, like so many others, has today been utterly devastated by invasive blight.

A few days of marching brought them to their objective: a large, heavily defended Onondaga village. Four huge palisades made of thick, interlocking timbers created impenetrable walls some ten metres high. On top of these walls were parapets that allowed Iroquois archers to unleash their arrows at any attackers while remaining protected behind a double row of wood timbers. Moreover, the fort was well supplied with water and had the means to extinguish any attempt to set it ablaze. Taking the town would require severe fighting and heavy losses.

The Wendat and the Algonquin did not lack for courage: upon their first sight of the fortress, they immediately rushed at a group of Onondaga warriors who were outside its walls. But the battle was a lopsided one—the Iroquois could rain arrows down from their high walls at the attacking warriors below, who were soon driven back. Champlain and his French companions came to the rescue with their arquebuses: the noise and smoke produced by their guns startled the Iroquois long enough for the Wendat and Algonquin to retreat.

Champlain and his Wendat and Algonquin allies regrouped in the woods at their encampment. Clearly, they would need a better strategy if they were to take the fort. Champlain had experience with sieges of European castles—and with sketches and hand gestures, he explained to his friends what had to be done if they were to take the town. They needed to construct a great movable tower—what in Europe was called a "siege tower," a platform on stilts protected by its own high walls and complete with loopholes for their arquebuses. It would have to be taller than the town's ten-metre walls, which would enable the French to fire over them. They would also need to construct large protective enclosures that could be carried forward by warriors to keep them safe while attempting to light the town's palisade on fire.

The Wendat and the Algonquin agreed, and together they began to build the siege tower and barricades described by Champlain. With amazing speed they completed the structures and once more readied themselves to attack the Onondaga fortress. Two hundred warriors pushed the siege tower forward toward the village walls, until they were no more than a spear length from the palisade. Two of Champlain's French companions climbed to the top of the siege engine and from there opened fire over the town's palisade. They killed many of the defenders—who were furiously unleashing a storm of arrows at their attackers below. Meanwhile, Champlain was on the ground with his native allies, carrying the protective barricades forward as arrows rained down upon them. The warriors piled kindling against the palisade and lit it on fire. But the wind was against them, and from above the Iroquois dumped water, extinguishing the flames.

The shower of arrows continued unabated—two Wendat chiefs were struck and fell wounded. Then Champlain took an arrow to the knee, followed by another to his leg, knocking him to the ground. With their leaders wounded and the plan to fire the village a failure, the Wendat and Algonquin retreated to the safety of the forest.

For Champlain, it was a bitter defeat. He wanted to try a second attempt to take the fort, but after several days of skirmishes in the woods with Iroquois warriors, who were now on the offensive, any thought of taking the fort had to be abandoned. They now needed to think of their own survival and a safe retreat. For Champlain and the other wounded, it was a horrible ordeal to get back to the canoes on Lake Ontario and then cross the lake. Champlain had to be carried, as did other injured warriors—all while the Iroquois pursued them. As they passed the St. Lawrence River's outlet near present-day Kingston, Champlain asked for a group to accompany him downriver to Quebec. But the Wendat refused, insisting that he spend the winter with them and help prepare for future battles with the Iroquois. He saw that he had no choice but to go along with this plan.

Champlain made the most of the opportunity, learning more about the Wendat—their language, culture, spiritual beliefs, hunting and farming methods, and politics. He was treated with great respect and honour, and was often asked to play a mediator role in disputes involving individual warriors. Champlain admired their courage, honesty, and the respect given to elders.

When his wounds had sufficiently healed, Champlain continued to explore by travelling to the different farming villages within Huronia as well as beyond to neighbouring nations. He also accompanied the Wendat on their deer hunts—which involved corralling hundreds of deer into great V-shaped pens, where they could then be slaughtered with spears.

Once, while off hunting alone in the forest, Champlain, curious as ever, spotted a strange bird. A new bird that he'd never seen before was exactly the kind of thing that appealed to him. Without another thought, he chased after it. It was, he wrote, "peculiar, with a beak almost like that of a parrot, as big as a hen, yellow all over, except for its red head and blue wings, and it made short successive flights like a partridge."[21] Champlain pursued the bird from tree to tree until he lost sight of it. When he stopped to look around him, he realized that he was lost. He had neither his compass nor his astrolabe, and the sky was dark and overcast. For three days he wandered alone in the vast forest, sleeping at night under trees and living off birds he killed. Finally, he found his way again and returned to the Wendat village— much to the relief of his anxiously waiting friends.

It remains a mystery what the strange bird was that Champlain described. Probably it was a species that is now extinct—most likely the Carolina parakeet, which was occasionally found in southern Ontario before its extinction in the late nineteenth century.

The following spring Champlain returned to Quebec, which remained a tiny outpost in the wilderness, home to only several dozen settlers. Not having heard from Champlain since the previous summer, the colonists had been convinced he was dead—but now here was their leader, emerging from the wilderness as if he were a ghost. They cheered at the sight of him.

Never again would Champlain have the chance to make journeys of exploration inland—exploration was a young man's game, and Champlain was now in his mid-forties. He would devote the remainder of his life to overseeing his settlement at Quebec: strengthening and improving the buildings and fortifications, experimenting with different crops, and maintaining good relations with the natives. He was also required to make regular voyages back to France to keep up the kingdom's interest in its tiny colony across the sea. Much of the French court remained indifferent to Canada, which, having failed as a supposed route to China, now seemed a faraway land of little importance.

The colony grew ever so slowly; the winters remained brutally harsh and the threat of war—despite Champlain's efforts to forge a lasting peace—could never be entirely extinguished. Champlain's desire for peace went so far that several times he even pardoned natives for killing French settlers—something that would have been inconceivable in the English colonies forming to the south, let alone in New Spain. But Champlain had always done things differently, and as he grew older, he was more determined than ever to achieve peace. He now rejected requests by his Algonquin friends to lead war raids into Iroquois territory, and instead sent peace emissaries, although they were tortured to death. In 1620, Champlain brought over to Canada for the first time his young wife—but, surprisingly enough, she found life in an isolated outpost in the wilderness less appealing than life at the French court, and returned to France after only a few years in the colony.

While Champlain could smooth over, at least temporarily, differences between the Algonquin and Mohawk, England remained a bigger problem. In 1628, when English privateers led by the three Kirke brothers arrived at the mouth of the St. Lawrence River, they pillaged and burned the French farmsteads there. They then turned their attention to Quebec itself, sending a messenger demanding that Champlain surrender the fort to them. The winter had been a particularly harsh one, and Champlain's band was running desperately low on food and gunpowder. But Champlain had devoted his life to founding Quebec, and he wasn't about to hand it over to a bunch of English pirates. He refused their demand.

The pirates weren't stupid—they knew it was better to starve out the French than fight them. They waited in their ships at the mouth of the St. Lawrence, keeping an eye out for the expected relief ships from France that would be carrying provisions and more settlers. When the sails of these French vessels loomed into sight, the English pirates opened fire with their cannons and quickly captured the unsuspecting, outgunned ships. In all, they captured over a dozen French ships and took some four hundred prisoners. Well satisfied with their prize, they left Quebec and sailed back to England.

This put Champlain and his settlers in a desperate plight. Already low on food, they would have to last another winter without any resupply— and were reduced to living off a tiny morsel of beans and peas rationed out per day, which they turned into a thin soup. Outside the fort's walls, they dug up roots and scrounged around for whatever berries they could find. They bartered for food with their Montagnais and other Algonquin friends—mostly eels and moose meat—but the natives themselves had precious little to spare. By the time the snows melted the next spring, the situation at Quebec was becoming horrendous. Their only hope was the arrival of French relief ships, but their hearts sank when they learned that the first sails spotted on the horizon were more English privateers—all five of the Kirke brothers this time. Their fleet had swelled to six heavily armed ships and some six hundred men, vastly outnumbering Champlain's little settlement.

Starving as they were, further resistance was futile. When faced with a renewed demand to surrender, Champlain grudgingly capitulated to the privateers. The Kirke brothers took the celebrated explorer on board their flagship as a worthy prize and planned to sail back to England with him. But in the waters off the Gaspé Peninsula the English encountered their own surprise—an incoming French ship. The English and French ships exchanged fire; one cannonball took the head clean off an English sailor. But the French ship, outnumbered and outgunned, soon surrendered.

The English sailed on to Tadoussac to pillage there and round up as many furs as they could lay their hands on. Here, Champlain met with a shock. His chief scout, Brûlé, whom he'd once looked upon almost as a son, treasonously agreed to help the English. The English were in need of Brûlé's skills—he'd now lived most of his life as a native, and was fluent in several native languages. Champlain denounced Brûlé and warned him that traitors got their just deserts. Brûlé ultimately met a fate worse than what Champlain probably had in mind—if the stories are to be believed, the Bear clan of the Wendat, knowing of Brûlé's treason, slowly tortured, killed, and cannibalized him.

Champlain was taken to London on board the Kirkes' flagship. But by the time they reached Europe, peace had been signed between England and France, which made Champlain a free man. Back in Paris, he argued strenuously in favour of Canada's long-term potential and pressed the French king to demand its return. It took three years, but finally, in 1632, the English crown agreed to give back Quebec to the French. Champlain was overjoyed, and as soon as he could he set sail for Canada.

He found it in need of much work, but with the energy that always characterized his actions, he threw himself into it. Champlain oversaw the building of new fortifications and buildings, dispatched more of his scouts to explore the interior and provide reports, and put in motion plans to establish habitations at Trois-Rivières and other strategic points along the St. Lawrence. But he was no longer the young, seemingly invincible explorer who had survived war wounds, Atlantic gales, scurvy, disease, frostbite, and whitewater rapids.

Champlain's health, as he turned sixty-five, declined rapidly. On Christmas Day 1635, he died in his bed—a rare achievement for a man of action in his era. His death was greatly mourned, not only by the French colonists, but also by dozens of northern native nations from the Wendat to the Mi'kmaq—who had seen in Champlain an honest and brave man, and a loyal friend. They would not soon see his like again. The founder of Quebec was buried inside the town's walls.

Champlain had successfully crossed the dangerous Atlantic some twenty-seven times, never once losing a ship. He travelled and explored widely, saw two great lakes, ran rapids in a canoe in a manner no European aside from Brûlé and a few of his other scouts had previously dared, fought in wars on two continents, and planted the first permanent seed of European colonies in Canada. He was, as French Canadians later named him, *le père du Canada*—"the Father of Canada."

His legacy is perhaps most fully told in the maps he left behind—maps many consider to be among the greatest ever made by any single explorer. Looking at Champlain's maps today, one is struck by their accuracy: they represent a great leap forward over all previous maps of North America. His masterful maps were the result of a complex, multi-layered approach that combined geographic data from many sources. First of all, Champlain had the maps of his predecessors to guide him—they were often crude and full of errors, but still provided a rudimentary base map. To these, Champlain could add his own detailed observations and corrections, the result of his many sea voyages to the waters off Newfoundland, Acadia, as far south as Cape Cod, and all through the Gulf of St. Lawrence, as well as his many canoe journeys. With his astrolabe and knack for celestial navigation, he recorded hundreds of sun and star observations that gave him his latitude. This helped fill in the details of his maps and correct previous errors. But most of his mapping remained essentially intuitive—sketching features that he saw from the deck of a ship or the bow of a canoe. It took a trained eye to pull that off with the degree of accuracy Champlain managed.

He had ventured far in his travels in the interior—all the way up the St. Lawrence from its mouth to the island of Mont Royal. He'd ranged southward to Lake Champlain and had seen the peaks of the Adirondacks; northward he had struggled up the Ottawa River and over the height of land to Lake Huron. He journeyed through much of what is now central Ontario, and across part of Lake Ontario and south into Iroquois territory. All these lands he mapped as he explored them—pausing whenever he could to take readings with his astrolabe. And what Champlain wasn't able to explore himself he dispatched his scouts—the coureurs de bois— to explore and report back on. He also incorporated into his maps the charts of other contemporary European explorers—like those of the English, who were busy exploring the Arctic regions in their quest for a northwest passage. Last, but certainly not least, Champlain drew from the knowledge of his aboriginal allies, whom he almost constantly asked about geographical matters. Several times he noted asking his native friends to draw birchbark maps for him. Undoubtedly, these maps filled in many of the final details on his charts.

Champlain was always revising his maps. His final version of his map of North America, published in 1632, shortly before his death, is a magnificent accomplishment. It reveals the outline of much of northeastern North America, from Baffin Island in the north to Chesapeake Bay in the south, and west to the Great Lakes. The Atlantic seaboard is charted in impressive detail; earlier errors are gone from his map, and we can see clearly now the Bay of Fundy, Cape Breton, Prince Edward Island, the Gaspé, Anticosti, and Newfoundland. The St. Lawrence River is mapped from its wide mouth all the way to its headwaters on Lake Ontario. The Ottawa is mapped northward, not only as far as Champlain made it, but also, on the basis of his aboriginal reports, beyond. Lake Huron and Superior—here labelled as "Mer douce" and "Grand Lac"—appear for the first time on a European map. They are large and not particularly well defined—since Champlain never saw Superior and only paddled Lake Huron's eastern shoreline through Georgian Bay's Thirty Thousand Islands. He didn't know about Lakes Michigan or Erie—but he conjectured, from his native reports and Brûlé, that Huron drained through some unknown watercourse eventually into Lake Ontario. Of particular note is how Champlain paid great attention to labelling the homelands of many different aboriginal nations—indicating their villages with drawings of their longhouses. And for a lifelong sailor, it's not surprising that Champlain liberally illustrated his map with sea creatures and ships under sail. On the technical side, he included an accurate scale and lines of latitude and longitude that correspond impressively to the measurements found on modern maps.

But although he set a new standard for accuracy, there remained much that Champlain didn't know—much in fact that no one really knew. What lay beyond the Great Lakes to the west was a complete mystery to Champlain—even the Wendat had been unable to tell him anything about these lands—and he still wondered whether there might yet prove to be a passage to China. The northern seas beyond James Bay were also unknown to Champlain. These were questions other explorers would have to answer.

The founder of Quebec—the consummate seafarer, explorer, soldier, and mapmaker that was Samuel de Champlain—had done his part by founding an enduring French colony in the wilderness of the New

World. To explore and map more of it would be a task taken up by the children and grandchildren of those first hardy settlers who managed to survive the winters—settlers who would, starting in the mid-1600s, refer to themselves increasingly as "Canadiens" and think of their country no longer as France, but as Canada.

{ 4 }

THE RISE AND FALL OF THE FRENCH EMPIRE: JACQUES-NICOLAS BELLIN'S MAP OF NORTH AMERICA

It is always the adventurers who do great things, not the sovereigns of great empires.

—MONTESQUIEU

It was a fine spring morning in 1652 when twelve-year-old Pierre-Esprit Radisson set off for some duck hunting with two friends. The youths had left their homes in nearby Trois-Rivières—an isolated frontier settlement—for some early-morning sport. But little did Radisson realize that he and his friends weren't the only ones hunting on the river that morning—nearby, silently stalking the young hunters, was an Iroquois raiding party. With lightning speed, the Iroquois sprang from the forest, killing Radisson's two friends and chopping their heads off as trophies. Radisson managed to fire a shot before he was overpowered. Perhaps because of his youth, or the bravery he showed in putting up a fight, Radisson's life was, for the moment at least, spared.

Radisson was taken as a captive back to the Iroquois villages. There he gradually won the favour of his "foster" family, who treated him more as an adopted son than a captive. During his years as a captive Radisson learned to speak Iroquoian fluently and accompanied the Mohawk on their war raids against tribes south of Lake Erie—in the process picking up skills that would prove valuable in his later career as an explorer and fur trader.

However, Radisson took the first opportunity to try to escape to the French settlements in Canada—only he didn't make it. The Iroquois recaptured him just before he could complete his escape. Since he had violated their trust by attempting to run away, Iroquois custom demanded that he be punished. Fortunately, it was only an ordinary bit of torture (a few ripped-out fingernails, burnt flesh, sticking a red-hot knife through his foot, and so on), after which his captors forgave him.

Radisson later managed to escape a second time. He made it to the Dutch settlements on the Hudson River—and from there eventually back to Canada. In 1659, hardened from his life with the Iroquois and now grown to manhood, Radisson joined up with his brother-in-law, Médard Chouart des Groseillers, to expand the French fur trade deeper into the interior. The two swashbucklers explored Lake Superior and learned from their Algonquin guides of a great saltwater sea some-where to the north—the same sea, as it happened, in which Henry Hudson had been cast adrift by his mutinous crew. But when the French authorities spurned Radisson and Groseillers for trading without a licence, they treasonously switched their allegiance to England and helped found the Hudson's Bay Company. So, the next time you're shopping at the Bay, just remember that it was founded by traitors.

In Radisson's account of his explorations, which must be taken with a grain of salt, he wrote of seeing unicorn-like animals and strange rep-tilian creatures; he imagined that he and Groseillers were "Caesars of the wilderness."[1] The unicorn was probably a flight of fancy helped by generous use of French brandy, but the reptilian creature perhaps wasn't an invention of Radisson's imagination—an actual species of giant salamander, the so-called hellbender, grows to a length of nearly two and a half feet and lives in mountain-fed streams in New York and Pennsylvania (where Radisson had been with the Iroquois).

Meanwhile, other explorers continued Champlain's work mapping the unknown reaches of the continent—and in the process, enlarging the empire claimed by the French kings. In 1668 Jean Peré was dispatched by the French colonial authorities to search for copper "north of Lake Ontario." The next year, he was joined by the Canadien Adrien Jolliet. The pair made it as far west as Lake Superior, where they did find copper deposits. Yet nothing was to come of the discovery, given the area's remoteness from Canada—a name that still referred only to what is today Quebec's St. Lawrence River corridor. Peré, however, pioneered a new route on his explorations when he journeyed back to Quebec through Lakes Erie and Ontario rather than the Ottawa-Mattawa-French system used by earlier explorers like Champlain.[2]

Increasingly, the pathfinders of New France were no longer Europeans but native-born Canadiens. The French colonists who managed to survive the brutal winters and Iroquois attacks rapidly developed their own strong sense of identity as a people distinct from their mother country. They called themselves Canadiens, and—given the scarcity of French women in the colony—many had at least some native blood. Reared in Canada, from childhood they learned by necessity to survive in the wilderness. Hunting, fishing, canoeing, and snowshoeing, as well as knowing the uses for different plants and trees, became second nature.

A French official in Canada, the army engineer Louis Franquet, noted the differences that had sprung up in just a few generations between the French and the Canadien settlers:

In wartime, the only people we can arm for the defence of the colony and send out to manhandle and harass the English are the *habitants*, because they alone can go forth in canoes in summer, and on snow-shoes in winter . . . they alone can make forced marches through the woods for three or six months at a time, stand up to the rigours of cold weather, and live out of the barrel of their gun, hunting and fishing as they go.[3]

Such skills, learned from childhood, made Canadiens not only formidable guerrilla soldiers in the wars against New England, but unrivalled as explorers.

The first of the great Canadien explorers was Adrien Jolliet's younger brother, Louis. Louis was born in 1645 on a frontier farmstead near the still tiny outpost of Quebec. His father died when he was five and his mother (women being scarce in the colony) soon remarried—only to lose her second husband when he drowned in the St. Lawrence. She married a third time shortly after.

The young Louis received a classical education at Quebec from the priests—who taught him Latin and Greek—and he learned to play the organ in church. With this firm scholastic background, he did the sensible thing and became a fur trader. After some initial trade journeys to the Great Lakes, Jolliet was hand-picked by the governor, the dashing Count Frontenac, to seek out a great river that, according to the native reports, was somewhere in the west. This was the Mississippi, North America's longest river, the upper reaches of which Jolliet reached in 1673 by birchbark canoe from Quebec, along with his Jesuit companion Jacques Marquette. The pair descended the wide river to within seven hundred kilometres of its mouth—turning back at the conflux with the Arkansas River. They mapped the route as they went and made trade contacts with numerous tribes who had never before encountered Europeans.

The challenge of following the Mississippi all the way to its mouth fell to the eccentric dreamer René-Robert Cavelier de La Salle. La Salle, a one-time priest in France who gave up his vocation because of "moral weaknesses," now lived on the remote and half-settled island of Mont Royal, deep in the wilderness. It was a hard and dangerous life. Iroquois attacks on the island—including the murder and scalping of settlers—remained commonplace. From his rough farmstead, La Salle dreamed of distant horizons, and especially of discovering a route through the wilderness to China—the same old dream that had haunted Cartier. Few of the other settlers on the island, used to a life of brutal hardship, took La Salle seriously. In mockery of La Salle's all-consuming obsession, they called his farmstead "La Chine."[4]

La Salle knew little of wilderness survival or native customs, and even less about canoeing or navigation. But what he lacked in competence he made up for in single-minded determination and unshakable confidence in his own destiny. Finally fed up with his fellow settlers' taunts, La Salle sold off his farmstead to raise the funds needed to mount his long-dreamed-of expedition. With the profit he made, he managed to outfit five canoes and recruit a crew of fourteen Canadiens and Algonquins to accompany him on his quixotic quest to find China.

They managed to make it as far as Lake Erie by cutting overland from the western tip of Lake Ontario. Erie then, as now, was a shallow, stormy lake—dangerous to watercraft of all sizes. La Salle, standing atop sandy dunes and gazing out across turbulent waters, was unsure how to proceed or which direction to take. His men sensed their leader's indecision, and questioned his competence. It was almost as if paddling a canoe to China might not be quite as easy as La Salle had led them to believe. Paralyzed by indecision and his men's unwillingness to follow him any farther, La Salle reluctantly turned back to Canada.

Failure, however, did little to dampen La Salle's conviction that he was destined for great things. One talent he did have in spades was self-promotion; returning to Quebec and then France, he was able to convince the French authorities of his worth and was soon back on the Great Lakes—where he established, on the governor's orders, new French outposts and strengthened existing ones. In 1675, at Lake Ontario's outlet on the St. Lawrence, La Salle rebuilt what had been a modest wooden fort into a more formidable stone fortress. This outpost, called Fort Frontenac after the governor, would extend French power deep into the Canadian interior. The fort would see heavy fighting both with the Iroquois and later in wars with the British colonies to the south—who eventually destroyed it. Two hundred years later, in the 1970s, archaeologists uncovered the ruins of Frontenac not far from where a Tim Hortons now stands in Kingston, Ontario.

Fort Frontenac functioned as a base of operations for La Salle as he continued to push inland to seek the Mississippi River. His plan was to build a chain of wilderness forts throughout the Great Lakes basin, thereby extending French control and facilitating his explorations. In 1678 he led a new expedition to seek the Mississippi, which he intended to follow wherever it might lead—hopefully Asia. Among his party on this new journey was the Dutch-born priest Louis Hennepin.

The party followed Lake Ontario's wooded shoreline until they reached the mouth of the turbulent Niagara River. Here, La Salle ordered the construction of another fort. Next he led his men partly up the Niagara River, and then, when the current proved too strong to navigate, overland along the edge of a spectacular, hundred-metre-high limestone gorge carved out over ten thousand years by the river's tremendous force. This gruelling portage through rattlesnake-infested forest brought La Salle and his followers to a spectacle that defied their wildest imaginations—the falls of Niagara. Hennepin, almost dumbstruck with wonder, described it as "a vast and prodigious cadence of water" that produced "a sound more terrible than that of thunder."[5] So immense was the volume of water roaring over the falls—among the largest of any waterfall in the world—that it produced a plume of mist visible from miles away. The perpetual mist bathing the plants and trees had created a microclimate of lush rainforest around the falls. To La Salle and his awestruck men, it must have seemed as if they'd strayed into some otherworldly dreamland.

But spectacular as the thundering falls were, they represented another serious obstacle in the quest for Asia. La Salle had earlier decided to forgo birchbark canoes—which had the advantage of being light enough to portage with relative ease—for much larger sailing vessels that could more easily handle the Great Lakes and hold much larger crews and supplies. Back at Fort Frontenac, La Salle had ordered his men to construct a small vessel that could be sailed across Lake Ontario—the first sailing ship ever to grace its waves. But that ship would never make it up the furious current of the Niagara River, let alone around the gorge and falls. Now La Salle needed a second vessel. So, once they'd bypassed the river's dangers, La Salle's men felled trees to build themselves a new ship. Christened the *Griffon* after the mythical bird featured on Frontenac's coat of arms, it was a barque of some forty-five tons armed with seven cannons that the French had laboriously hauled across the Niagara portage.

The *Griffon* took La Salle and his crew through Lakes Erie, Huron, and Michigan—waters that had never before seen a sailing ship. When they reached Lake Michigan's western shores, La Salle resolved to press on by canoe, sending the *Griffon* back to Niagara with a valuable cargo of furs. In the meantime, he began to lay the groundwork for his journey overland to the Mississippi—including preparations to establish another two forts that would serve as supply depots south of Lake Michigan. But with winter coming, La Salle grew alarmed when there was no word of the *Griffon*, which was supposed to have returned to rendezvous with the rest of the expedition. He never saw his ship again. After searching in vain for months, he learned from native reports that it had been lost in a fierce storm on Lake Michigan. Locating this long-lost wreck has haunted the dreams of many underwater archaeologists; despite numerous searches, to date the *Griffon* remains the most coveted undiscovered shipwreck on the Great Lakes.

His ship lost, two years would pass before La Salle at last continued Jolliet's earlier exploration: in 1682 he paddled the Mississippi all the way to the Gulf of Mexico, having left behind the sugar maples, birches, and white pines of Canada for the cypress swamps and alligators of the

Deep South. It was an impressive journey that would lead to French settlement in Louisiana—but once again, it wasn't the long-sought route to China.

Four years later, La Salle—his head still filled with dreams of greatness and wanting to outdo what Champlain had accomplished—set sail from France in command of a fleet of four ships to plant a colony at the mouth of the Mississippi. He lacked Champlain's navigational and leadership talents, however, and though his ships survived the crossing and reached the Gulf of Mexico, La Salle failed to find the Mississippi's mouth. He overshot the mark and ended up on the coast of what is now Texas. The expedition quickly fell apart: three of the four ships were lost; local tribes launched hostile attacks; and the colonists, lacking fresh water and with severe supply shortages, were struck down by malaria and other diseases. Many died, and disillusionment with La Salle's leadership was rife. Again history was repeating itself, but this time there was no one to warn La Salle of the mutiny brewing among his followers. He was shot in the head at point-blank range, probably never knowing what had happened. The mutineers stripped his body and left it to be devoured by wild animals. With La Salle dead, more infighting and murders followed until the colony completely disintegrated.

Exploring North America's wilderness was a dangerous business; Canada remained a volatile, turbulent country. A number of Jesuit missionaries were captured by the Iroquois, ritually tortured, and burned alive. Many of those who were lucky enough to escape bore the gruesome disfigurements of their torture: sliced-off ears and noses, scarred flesh, missing fingers—sometimes other missing parts. One such tragic figure was the Italian Jesuit Francesco Giuseppe Bressani, who had only one finger after the Iroquois sawed off his others. Yet, in 1657, he still managed to draw a remarkably beautiful map of Canada. Bressani's map shows in impressive detail the Great Lakes and principal canoe routes; it's richly illustrated with scenes of hunters on snowshoes and people canoeing, grinding corn into flour, and burning Jesuit priests alive.

What was unfolding in the forests of Canada was, basically, a replay of European history from a thousand years earlier when Christian missionaries ventured into the wilds of northern Europe to preach the gospel to Germanic tribes—who sometimes sliced off fingers and noses, and roasted these strange foreigners over bonfires. It took centuries, but eventually the Christian priests converted and "civilized" the northern barbarian tribes of Europe. The Jesuits, well aware of their own history, were determined to do the same in Canada.

Not everyone agreed with their aims—many young Frenchmen found Algonquin culture more to their liking than seventeenth-century French Catholicism. By the 1680s perhaps as many as eight hundred Canadien coureurs de bois were roaming the wilderness and, to the horror of Jesuits, assimilating into aboriginal cultures. The situation became sufficiently alarming that in 1665 Jean-Baptiste Colbert, the chief minister to the French king, outlawed the coureurs de bois by forbidding French settlers from leaving their farms along the St. Lawrence. The ban from distant France, however, proved impossible to enforce—the colony had no lack of adventurous young men who preferred the risks and uncertainties of life in the wilderness to farming along the St. Lawrence. They continued to leave the settlements and "go native." In doing so, they were inadvertently extending "Canada" beyond its geographic limits of the St. Lawrence.

Thomas Dongan, the English governor of New York from 1682 to 1688, declared that "It is intolerable to consider that wherever a Frenchman goes forth in America, it becomes part of Canada."[6] In opposition to French expansion, Dongan supplied arms to the Iroquois and encouraged war raids deep into Canada to terrorize the settlers. Massacres were a grim reality in the embattled colony; in 1689 a force of 1500 Iroquois warriors slaughtered twenty-four colonists at Lachine, captured a further seventy to be ritually tortured later, and burned the majority of the farmsteads to the ground. Earlier, in a 1660 battle that was to assume mythical proportions, a twenty-five-year-old professional soldier named Adam Dollard des Ormeaux had held out for five days in a small fort with just sixteen French companions and some Algonquin allies against an overwhelming attacking force of seven hundred Iroquois warriors. Dollard and his little band were all that stood between the Iroquois and Montreal. Before they'd left the settlement on their sacrificial mission, each man in Dollard's party had written out his last will and testament. In the end, they were all killed in battle—but like the Spartans at the pass of Thermopylae, they had sold their lives dearly. The heavy losses they inflicted on their attackers proved enough to avert any attack on Montreal. For this bloody last stand, the fallen Dollard was revered by Canadien colonists as the "Saviour of Canada."

The Iroquois terrorized French Canada for generations—killing and scalping numerous men, women, and children—and yet the Canadiens could be equally brutal in war. In 1690 a force of Canadien militia and their native allies inflicted utter devastation—including the murder of civilians—on the English frontier settlement of Schenectady in New York. Such terror raids—conducted by both Iroquois and Canadiens—were a horrifying but commonplace feature of North American frontier warfare.

Estimates suggest that around 10 percent of the Canadien population (i.e., the French colonists in Canada) died in the Iroquois Wars—an extremely high percentage, comparable to fatality rates in Germany during World War II.[7] Warriors like Dollard, the Algonquin chief Pieskaret, Pierre Le Moyne d'Iberville, and Madeleine de Verchères—the fourteen-year-old girl with the heart of a lion who almost single-handedly held off an Iroquois attack on a small fort—became the colony's folk heroes. The values of this war-plagued society were radically unlike our modern conception of Canadian values—instead of tolerance and diversity, the first Canadiens prized bravery in battle, hunting prowess, and skill with an axe or canoe (well, some might say the latter is still a Canadian value).

Besides the long-running Iroquois Wars that lasted nearly a century, the map of Canada was redrawn through the blood spilled in almost interminable imperial wars that pitted France against England. The first of these featured the Kirke brothers with their privateer fleet, pillaging and burning farms on the St. Lawrence and capturing Quebec. For three years after the Kirkes' triumph the English flag flew above Quebec, until diplomatic negotiations restored Canada to France. This conflict was followed by King William's War (1688–1697), in which Count Frontenac managed to hold off an English attempt to take the fortress of Quebec. Two years earlier, in 1686, the French soldier Des Troyes had led a force of Canadiens and French troops on a gruelling canoe journey from Montreal to James Bay to strike at the English forts there—capturing three of them. More conflicts followed: Queen Anne's War (1702–1713), King George's War (1744–1748), and the French and Indian War (1754–1763) were all bitter struggles that involved much fighting on Canadian soil and atrocities inflicted upon civilians. Innumerable raids, skirmishes, battles, and slayings simply became part of the rhythm of life in Canada and Acadia.

In terms of grand strategy, the French—after relinquishing any hope of discovering a direct route through the wilderness to China—had focused instead on carving out an empire stitched together with inland forts and alliances with diverse aboriginal nations. Forming a "crescent" along two great river systems, the St. Lawrence and the Mississippi, the empire claimed by France was designed to bottle up England's Thirteen Colonies on the eastern slopes of the Appalachians—an arrangement that suited aboriginal interests just fine and won France the support of numerous First Nations. Their support was critical given the lopsided populations of New France and Britain's American colonies.

Just as the southern agricultural nations belonging to the Iroquoian family had always greatly outnumbered the northern Algonquin peoples, the population of the English colonies vastly outnumbered the more northerly French ones—by a ratio of about 15 to 1. The reality was that it was simply impractical and reckless to try to support a larger population in a much harsher northern environment with limited food resources.

Thus, the only hope for French Canada in the regular wars with Britain's colonies was a ruthless strategy of guerrilla warfare; Canadiens and their native allies were highly adept at forest warfare, and they terrorized the frontier settlements of the English colonies. The strategy, however, proved unsustainable—especially given the superiority of England's Royal Navy, which prowled the seas from Hudson Bay to south of the equator. Gradually, in these repeated wars, the British Empire, aided by its powerful naval fleet, gained the upper hand—chipping away at New France's Atlantic possessions, which one by one fell to British control. When the French colonists in Atlantic Canada, the feisty Acadians, balked at swearing an oath of allegiance to the English king, they were rounded up and deported en masse to Louisiana, the French Caribbean, or back to Europe, many dying in the process.

In this vortex of war, cultures and territories were in a constant state of flux—including First Nations, who often had their own scores to settle. Nearly all the native nations in what is now southern Ontario were annihilated by the formidable and expansionist-minded Iroquois Confederacy of Five Nations. Despite being greatly outnumbered by their numerous adversaries, the Iroquois were master tacticians and reaped the benefits of a more centralized governing structure that allowed them to coordinate military strategy. At the height of their power in the mid-seventeenth century they could field some four thousand warriors, who were widely feared.[8]

Adding to the chaos and devastation of the 1600s were smallpox epidemics that ravaged First Nations populations, further weakening their ability to withstand European incursions and their own ongoing wars. Much like when the bubonic plague had struck Europe from Asia, the introduction of various Old World diseases to previously isolated New World populations proved utterly devastating. Thousands perished in epidemics for which traditional medicines had no treatment. Such widespread horror and death caused breakdowns in social orders; many of the Wendat—among the hardest hit by smallpox—in utter despair abandoned their old ways and converted to Catholicism, believing that would save them. In fact, it only made the Iroquois conquests easier. Estimates of the death toll caused by Old World diseases among aboriginal populations are difficult to make, but the latest genetic studies put the figure at a population decline of about 50 percent—the same as Europe's losses from the Black Death.[9]

By 1649 the Iroquois had triumphed over their ancient foes, the once mighty Wendat, whose villages were put to the torch; the few survivors who escaped annihilation fled to Canada. After eliminating the Wendat, the Confederacy launched all-out war on multiple fronts against numerous First Nations in the Great Lakes watershed and beyond. To the south they warred with the once powerful Susquehannock, and into Virginia against the Mannahoac. To the west they invaded the Ohio Valley, fighting the Shawnee, Illinois, Erie, and other tribes—pushing as far west in their raids as the Mississippi. In the northeast they struck hard against the Abenaki and Mohicans, and wiped out the Neutrals and Petun in what is now southern Ontario—while continuing to attack the northern Algonquin peoples, including the Odawa, Ojibwa, and Montagnais. When their foes were vanquished, the Iroquois claimed ownership over their lands by right of conquest, eventually ruling an empire from Lake Champlain to Lake Michigan. To replenish their losses in the widespread wars, the Iroquois, like the early Romans, incorporated choice members of vanquished tribes into their own nations—a policy that allowed them to continue their campaigns.

North of Lake Erie, in what is now southern Ontario, the Iroquois waged one of their most destructive campaigns against an agricultural people commonly known as the "Neutrals" owing to their neutrality in the wars between the Wendat and the Iroquois. Their own name for themselves was Chonnonton, meaning "People of the Deer." Because of their success as farmers, the Neutrals were able to develop communities that numbered in the thousands and were fortified by palisades. Estimates place their population at around forty thousand in the early 1600s—which would have made them the largest aboriginal nation in Canada. But, as is often the case, the Neutrals' decision not to take sides proved disastrous. Had they united with the Wendat, Algonquin, and other tribes fighting the Iroquois, they might have been able to hold them off. But on their own, even with their superior numbers and well-fortified villages, they were no match for the battle-hardened warriors of the Confederacy. Within just two years, in 1651 the Neutrals were conquered and wiped out as a distinct people.

European colonies were likewise being wiped from the map—New Holland, New Sweden, and New Scotland (in Latin, Nova Scotia) all disappeared as the Northeast came to be increasingly dominated by three major empires: French, British, and Iroquois. By 1701, war and disease had brought the once widely feared Iroquois to sign a Great Peace in Montreal—and thereafter their power continued to decline. That left New France and Britain's colonies as the sole remaining empires in northeastern North America.

＊

The French and English, in competition with each other, had by the dawn of the eighteenth century filled in the rough outlines of much of eastern North America—from Lake Superior and the Mississippi River southward down to the Gulf of Mexico, north to Hudson and James Bay, and east to the Atlantic Ocean. But what lay west of Lake Superior remained almost entirely unknown. On maps of the era it appears as one vast blank spot.

Long before Europeans reached the uncharted West, they heard second-hand reports from their native companions about the fearsome things that lurked there. While exploring the upper Great Lakes in the 1660s, Claude-Jean Allouez, a Jesuit missionary, reported that his native guide told him about "another nation, adjoining the Assinipoualac, who eat human beings, and live wholly on raw flesh; but these people, in turn, are eaten by bears of frightful size, all red, and with prodigiously long claws. It is deemed highly probable that they are lions."[10] This seems to be the first written account of a grizzly bear, though Allouez himself never saw one, and apparently didn't think the strange beasts were bears at all.

In 1690, the newly formed Hudson's Bay Company selected a young apprentice, Henry Kelsey, to explore inland to the west. It was said of Kelsey that he was "a very active Lad Delighting much in Indians Company, being never better pleased than when hee [sic] is Travelling amongst them."[11] Kelsey was sent alone to explore the interior with some Assiniboine hunters, thus making him the first European to set foot on the Great Plains in what is now Canada.

While travelling on the plains, Kelsey encountered the terrifying beast alluded to earlier by Allouez. In his August 20, 1691, journal entry, he noted without regard to English grammar: "To day we pitch to ye outermost Edge of ye woods this plain affords Nothing but short Round sticky grass & Buffillo & a great sort of Bear wch is Bigger than any white Bear & is Neither White nor Black But silver hair'd like our English Rabbit."[12] Kelsey naturally enough figured that if the fur-trading thing didn't work out, he could try his hand at poetry. In verse, he scribbled further details about this "great sort of Bear":

Thus it continues till you leave the woods behind
And then you have beast of several kind
The one is a Black a Buffillo great
Another is all Outgrown Bear well is good meat
His skin to gett I have used all ye ways I can
He is man's food and he makes food of men
His hide they would not me it Preserve
But said it was a god and they should starve[13]

Aside from Kelsey's brief foray into the lands of the man-eating bears, the North American interior remained for the next forty years entirely terra incognita to Europeans—a mysterious land on the edge of the known world, populated by fearsome beasts, tribes of cannibals, and other monsters—or so it was said. To probe these unknown regions was a challenge that ultimately fell to a remarkable family of Canadien explorers.

Of all the French explorers, it was the man known as Pierre Gaultier de Varennes et de La Vérendrye who did the most to extend geographic knowledge within what is now Canada. La Vérendrye ranks alongside Jolliet as among the greatest Canadian-born explorers of the French regime. His journals and letters are full of the stuff of legends—including tales of monsters and beasts, enchanted mountains, and tribes of dwarfs. Growing up from childhood around native people, La Vérendrye was also one of the first explorers to discuss at length aboriginal maps—which he asked his native guides and allies to sketch for him in the sand or snow, on birchbark, or whatever material was at hand.

Pierre was the youngest of eight surviving children, born in the wilderness of Trois-Rivières in 1685. Like other Canadiens, woodcraft and wilderness survival were an integral part of his upbringing; he had to learn to hunt, dress game, fish, start fires without matches, travel by canoe in the summer and snowshoes in the winter, and find his way in the forests. Also like most Canadiens reared in a time of constant war, he learned to fight. The king's law required all Canadien males to serve in the colony's militia from age sixteen through sixty. For the more adventurously inclined, there were full-time, professional regiments stationed in the colony. Pierre enlisted in one of these regiments when he was nineteen and soon saw action in New England and Newfoundland. Brave and full of energy, after these wars he crossed the ocean to France and fought in the War of Spanish Succession. When his older brother Louis was killed in action, he acquired his title: La Vérendrye. Pierre nearly shared his brother's fate—before the war was over he suffered a severe gunshot wound as well as eight sword cuts. He must have been remarkably strong and healthy to have survived such wounds in an era when medical treatment was often worse than useless—and especially to have eschewed a quiet life afterward in favour of the most gruelling lifestyle conceivable as an explorer in Canada's northern wilderness.

In 1712, La Vérendrye returned to his native Canada and married his long-waiting fiancée, Marie-Anne, to whom he had been engaged for five years. Their marriage, despite La Vérendrye's restless nature that drove him to make long journeys deep into the unmapped North American interior, was to be a happy and productive one. Together they had six children, many of whom would join their father on his exploring journeys. However, La Vérendrye's life was far from comfortable—despite his aristocratic-sounding title, he was not a member of the nobility and was struggling to make ends meet on his meagre thirty-eight-acre farm. Hunting, fishing, and fur trapping were a matter of necessity to keep food on the table and supplement the family income. It was a hard and dreary life that left La Vérendrye thirsting for something more.

As it happened, one of his surviving brothers was a fur trader operating far inland at Lake Superior, and it wasn't long before La Vérendrye left his farm on the St. Lawrence to join him in the fur trade. It was the kind of life—paddling birchbark canoes on an inland ocean, meeting with different aboriginal nations, surviving in the wilderness—that appealed to an adventurous Canadien. But the restless, ambitious spirit of La Vérendrye craved more than the ordinary goals of his fellow traders—he hungered after the truly unknown, and dreamed of pushing on beyond Lake Superior to lands no Frenchman had ever seen.

While on Superior, La Vérendrye befriended Ojibwa and Cree traders—both Algonquin nations on friendly terms with the French—who told him about lands to the west where the vast forests were said to thin out into wide grassy plains home to enormous herds of bison and antelope. Already middle-aged, La Vérendrye sought the distinction that had hitherto been denied him, and began to write letters from Superior to the governor in Quebec petitioning for an appointment to lead an expedition westward.

La Vérendrye's proposal was to seek the legendary "great river of the West," a river said to lead into the setting sun—meaning a route to the Pacific Ocean, and thereby of immense strategic importance to whichever empire should find and control it. For years fantastic rumours had swirled at French trading posts about this river. It was said to have a tributary with waters that flowed "red like vermillion," and that along its shores were "all kinds of wild beasts in abundance, and snakes of a prodigious size."[14] In a letter to New France's governor, La Vérendrye further explained that, reportedly, "On the same side of the river, but much lower down, there is a small mountain, the stones of which sparkle night and day. The Indians call it the Dwelling of the Spirit; no one ventures to go near it."[15]

La Vérendrye was told that near this mythical mountain with its eternally shining stones it first becomes possible "to notice a rise and fall of tide."[16] On the basis of reports provided by Cree chiefs, he believed the river to be an easy route to the "Western Sea," as it was said that "there are only two rapids requiring portages in the whole great river of the

West."[17] Incredibly, it seemed, the ocean was near at hand, for beyond Lake Winnipeg, the river "flows west a distance of ten days' journey, after which it turns a little west-north-west; and it is from that point that the rise and fall of the tides become perceptible."[18]

But there remained obstacles of a different sort. According to La Vérendrye's Cree reports, the river was home to "a tribe of dwarfs not over three feet or so in height, but numerous and very brave."[19] La Vérendrye figured they could handle the dwarfs, but, as his Cree partners explained to him, the real danger—besides all the giant snakes and beasts—were hostile tribes near the river's mouth. One of his Cree informants told him that "he did not think there was any man bold enough to pass by the different tribes that are to be found in great number lower down in order to make an exploration."[20] To his superior, the governor of New France, La Vérendrye recommended establishing a post on Lake Winnipeg that could be used as a basis for further exploration westward.

In the meantime, he remained in the region around Lake Superior and continued to gather whatever information he could about this fantastical river. Several Cree traders, as well as the Cree chief Auchagah, sketched maps for him showing the river. La Vérendrye explained to the governor:

> According to their map, which agrees with the one made by
> Auchagah, the lower portion of the river runs west-north-west.
> They state that there are whites at the mouth of the river, but that
> they do not know to what nation they belong, the length of the
> journey being such that none of them venture to go there; one
> would have to start from Lake of the Woods in the month of March
> in order to make the journey and could not hope to get back before
> November. What they report is founded on hearsay. What chiefly
> deters them from making the journey to the sea is that on a former

occasion, according to their story, two of their canoes were lost in the ice ten days' journey from Lake Winnipeg. Fear holds them back, and besides, as they can get all their wants supplied by the English of the near north, who are distant only twenty days' travel, what more would they go to seek at the Western Sea?[21]

Such information was, of course, inaccurate. La Vérendrye, and possibly the Cree for that matter, still had little idea of the true vastness of the continent, to say nothing of the formidable mountains that lay between them and the Pacific—unless (which is possible) something was lost in translation, and La Vérendrye had somehow confused Cree accounts of the rivers flowing into the northern sea, Hudson Bay, with the western ocean. This, however, seems unlikely, since La Vérendrye already knew about Hudson Bay and the English fur posts there; he noted that his Cree companions made canoe journeys to trade at those forts (and that it took them only twenty days to reach them). Whatever the explanation, La Vérendrye's intelligence about the nearness of the ocean and a river flowing almost directly there was wildly incorrect. But confidence springs from ignorance as often as it does from knowledge, and La Vérendrye was supremely confident that, within a year after establishing a base at Lake Winnipeg, he would reach the Western Sea. He urged in his letter that permission be granted for him to pursue these projects, lest, he warned, the English beat them to the discovery of the valuable route to the ocean.

Tales of rivers with red water, forbidden mountains of perpetually shimmering gems, fierce savages, and tribes of dwarfs seem like something straight out of the *Odyssey* or Sinbad the Sailor, but here we find it in the journals of actual explorers, in a world where almost anything still seemed possible. La Vérendrye's quest for a mythical river that would lead to the riches of the Pacific was reminiscent of Cartier's quest two hundred years earlier, when he too heard fabulous tales from his native guides of what lay just beyond the next river bend. The problem was that the French were putting too much faith in native reports; although the natives were masters of the geography of their homelands, they knew little about what lay beyond. In reality, the distances were so vast that asking Cree hunters about what lay in the far west was akin to asking clans of Scottish Highlanders about the geography of the Greek islands or Finnish fur traders about the Pyrenees Mountains.

But people generally believe what they want to hear, and La Vérendrye very much wanted to believe that there was an easy route to the Pacific. The French, as well as the English, had convinced themselves that a large saltwater gulf connected to the Pacific Ocean, comparable to Hudson Bay in the north and the Gulf of Mexico in the south, was waiting to be found somewhere in the west. La Vérendrye assumed that the "River of the West" would lead him without much difficulty to this gulf, and from there to the open Pacific. That the western tip of Lake Superior was a staggering 2500 kilometres as the crow flies from the Pacific coastline—and blocked by an immense chain of enormous, snow-capped mountains itself hundreds of kilometres wide—he had not the slightest idea.

Events, as it happened, led to French approval of La Vérendrye's quest. By the terms of the peace treaty concluded in 1713 that ended the War of Spanish Succession, the French monarchy had relinquished any claim to Hudson Bay—which was now firmly in English hands under their Company of Adventurers. This strategic blow to France left the French court eager to find new means to undercut their English foes in North America. Discovering a trade route to the Pacific from their settlements in Canada would fit the bill nicely.

In 1731, La Vérendrye got his wish and won official approval for an exploratory journey to the west under his command. For a major expedition to be led by a Canadien-born commoner rather than a member of the French elite was still a notable achievement. But after the fiasco with La Salle, it seemed that letting a Canadien take a crack at leadership couldn't hurt. On the other hand, La Vérendrye had promised a lot, and expectations were high that he would quickly succeed.

That spring, when the ice had thawed around Montreal, La Vérendrye set off with three of his sons and some fifty Canadiens and Algonquins manning his fleet of birchbark canoes. His official purpose was to search for the Western Sea, but La Vérendrye also intended to establish as many fur trade forts as he possibly could in strategic locations. This was a necessity, given that he lacked income to finance his ventures, and that the perennially cash-strapped colonial authorities in Quebec could offer him only minimal support. As has often been the case with exploration, official backing and prestigious-sounding titles masked a lack of money.

Over the next three years, La Vérendrye and his men constructed forts between Lake Superior and Lake Winnipeg. These posts would help create alliances with the tribes in the area—who were eager for French tools and other trade goods—as well as prove a much-needed source of income for the Canadiens. While overseeing the forts, La Vérendrye was busy compiling native reports on waterways and adding details to his maps of what lay beyond Lake Superior. He was wise enough to understand, as Champlain had, that plunging off into uncharted regions without the support of local aboriginal allies was bound to fail. For this reason, he did not attempt to initially venture west of Lake Winnipeg.

But when La Vérendrye finally returned to Canada in 1734 after three years of trading, exploring, and mapping, he found that the colonial authorities were less than impressed with him. He had failed to live up to his promise to discover the route to the Western Sea, and he was accused of having devoted too much attention to fur trading and not enough to exploration. Such criticisms no doubt stung. But like most successful explorers, La Vérendrye was tenacious and almost incapable of admitting defeat. He once more vowed to find the sea, whatever the cost, and in the spring of 1735—now fifty years old—he departed Montreal again to seek the far west.

It was not going to be an easy task. Virtual anarchy prevailed in the regions beyond Lake Superior, where aboriginal nations were waging war against each other. A coalition of Assiniboines, Crees, and Monsonis were busy warring against the Sioux and the Ojibwas, although alliances shifted easily and different bands sometimes pursued different policies. Like most French explorers, La Vérendrye tried to prevent warfare among the tribes, as this was contrary to the interests of the fur trade and impeded exploration. At a gathering of allied chiefs and warriors, La Vérendrye admonished them to end their wars, proclaiming that "The Saulteux and the Sioux are our allies and our children of the same Father. How can any man have so bad a heart as to want to kill his own relatives?"[22] But the complex web of tribal politics—often involving blood feuds that dated back generations—wasn't easily solved by outsiders. Attempting to impose peace on warring tribes proved easier said than done, and eventually La Vérendrye was forced to support at least some wars; otherwise, he would find himself without any allies.

To make matters worse, his talented nephew, Christophe, who'd been acting as his right-hand man, took sick and died. This was only the start of La Vérendrye's troubles. In the spring of 1736, his western forts were running low on provisions. His eldest son, Jean-Baptiste, set off across the island-studded, labyrinthine waters of Lake of the Woods with twenty-one other Canadiens to retrieve supplies from the Lake Superior forts. But while crossing the lake they were ambushed by a Sioux war party—who trapped them on a small island and massacred them to a man.

The murder of his son tore the heart out of La Vérendrye. Despite an offer from his allies among the Crees, Assiniboines, and Monsonis to attack the Sioux on his behalf, La Vérendrye refused. He knew that to retaliate against the Sioux would only spark more killings and put an end to any hope of pushing on across the plains into the far west. The sun had set on La Vérendrye's happiness: he was saddled with debt, and his hopes of fame and glory seemed a chimera. But still the spell of the unknown held him—he felt almost hypnotically compelled to carry on in his promise to find the Western Sea.

In the fall of 1738, La Vérendrye ventured up the Assiniboine River—halting near Portage la Prairie, west of what is now Winnipeg. At this strategic crossroads, he supervised the construction of a new French post, Fort La Reine, which the Canadiens rushed to complete before the onset of winter. They had more than just the plunging temperatures and hard winter to fear—they were deep in unknown territory, where many hostile bands, like the Sioux who had massacred their companions on Lake of the Woods, would gladly finish them off. A hastily constructed fort would at least offer them a redoubt from which to make a last stand, should it come to that.

La Vérendrye, however, was not one for idleness. He pushed on recklessly, even with the weather worsening. By December he'd made it to what is now North Dakota. It was to be the closest he ever came to the Western Sea—his farthest point inland. It was also farther than any French explorer had ever gone, but still a long way from the Pacific. After enduring the winter at his Fort La Reine, in the spring La Vérendrye returned to Montreal, leaving his surviving sons in the west to carry on exploring. They pressed northward to Lakes Winnipeg, Manitoba, and other large bodies of water, while to the west they made it as far as the Saskatchewan River. But the fabled "River of the West" was still nowhere to be found.

In the spring of 1742, after wintering in Fort La Reine, La Vérendrye's sons Louis-Joseph and François left the fort with instructions from their father to push as far west as possible. It was to be one final attempt to find the great Western Sea. All summer they travelled by canoe, working their way up snaking rivers and risking ambush by hostile tribes who might not appreciate foreigners trespassing on their lands. Mostly, however, the Canadiens were adept at making peaceful contacts—most interior nations had never before encountered whites and were eager to trade. Indeed, in contrast to the English and Spanish colonists—who had a tendency to fight anyone they came across—the Canadiens' success in establishing amicable relations with numerous and diverse aboriginal cultures was astonishing.

The brothers made it to the Missouri River and pushed on up it—even with the onset of winter they refused to give up. Instead, they discarded their canoes for snowshoes and continued on foot across the desolate, snowy plains. By January 1743 they'd reached the Yellowstone River and were confronted by a massive wall of stone, blocking any further progress. They had nearly reached the Rocky Mountains. Like Alexander the Great when he reached the mountains of the Hindu Kush on his quest to reach the "Outer Ocean," it now dawned on them that the continent was far larger than any of them had ever dreamed—if the Western Sea was out there, hidden beyond the mountains, there could be no easy route to it. Finally, the brothers turned back to report to their father what they had discovered.

That year, after listening to his sons' reports of their journeys, La Vérendrye, now fifty-eight years old, left the west for good. He resigned his post and returned to his farm in Canada. At first, his achievements were overlooked or discounted—he had failed to reach the Western Sea, and nothing else at the moment seemed to matter. But within several years, the colonial authorities and the French court back in Paris, thanks to the maps they now possessed, came to appreciate the scale of what La Vérendrye had accomplished in his explorations. He had established some eight new French forts west of Lake Superior, concluded numerous alliances with different tribes, mapped previously unknown water routes, set foot in places no European had ever seen, and added an immense tract of territory to the empire claimed by the

French crown. For this, in 1749 the king of France finally honoured La Vérendrye by awarding him the prestigious Croix de Saint-Louis.

Despite the recognition, at age sixty-four the old explorer once more felt the stir of adventure in his blood and the tug of faraway places, and made up his mind that he would again leave his farmstead for a final gruelling journey to the interior. The heart was willing, but his body, worn out by war wounds and years of hardships, was no longer up to the challenge. On December 5, 1749, while in Montreal preparing for his planned journey, La Vérendrye died.

Though they never reached the Pacific, La Vérendrye and his sons had gone farther west than any other French explorers in the history of New France. From Quebec to their farthest point inland, they had crossed in a round trip some seven thousand kilometres. In doing so, La Vérendrye and his sons brought French geographic knowledge of North America to its maximum extent before the British conquest of Canada in the Seven Years' War.

The geographical accomplishments of the French and their Canadien colonists are perhaps most fully told in the maps of the talented cartographer Jacques-Nicolas Bellin, a hydrographer in the French Royal Navy. Bellin was charged with compiling, revising, and creating the most accurate maps possible of France's far-flung empire. To do so, he relied upon the field maps made by explorers like La Vérendrye. Just four years before the Battle of the Plains of Abraham would seal Quebec's fate, Bellin unveiled a new map of North America that combined knowledge derived from generations of French explorers that included Cartier, Champlain, Jolliet, La Salle, and La Vérendrye—in short, the entire sum of French mapping and exploration in North America over two centuries. This mapping had, of course, been greatly aided by New France's close alliances with northern aboriginal nations, notably the Algonquin, Wendat, Ojibwa, Cree, and Montagnais.

Bellin's map shows numerous French wilderness forts and trading posts scattered throughout the French Empire's "crescent" from the Gulf of the St. Lawrence to the mouth of the Mississippi. Collectively, this vast domain represented "New France." Within the northern part of it, we see that "Canada" is now labelled as encompassing everything from Lake Michigan to northern Acadia. In other words, the often hazy sense of what qualified as Canada comprised—at least on Bellin's map—much of what is now the northeastern United States, including parts of the northern states of Michigan, Illinois, Ohio, Pennsylvania, New York, Vermont, New Hampshire, Massachusetts, and Maine. All these territories had become part of the domain of the Canadien traders and coureurs de bois—a fact that the governor of New York had found so irksome. At the same time, much of what is now western and northern Canada, as well as Newfoundland and Nova Scotia, was regarded as separate and distinct from Canada.

From Cartier's first voyage up the mysterious St. Lawrence through to the La Vérendrye family's push westward to the foothills of the Rockies, the French had explored an enormous swath of territory. They had encountered everything from polar bears to alligators, rattlesnakes to caribou. But in 1755, while Voltaire and Rousseau were publishing their philosophies and the Enlightenment was in full swing, over half of North America remained terra incognita to outsiders. It appears on Bellin's map as one immense blank space—labelled simply as "these parts entirely unknown." The westernmost details on the map are the ones supplied by La Vérendrye's sons; Bellin sketched lines of peaks representing the mysterious mountains that had blocked their path.

Bellin's maps—while an eloquent testament to the impressive achievements of more than two centuries of French exploration—reveal how little was still known of western and northern North America.

PETER POND'S MAP OF THE NORTHWEST

I can't say as ever I was lost, but I was bewildered once for three days.

—DANIEL BOONE (1734–1820)

L a Vérendrye had failed to discover the mythical "River of the West," but others still believed it was out there somewhere, beyond the known world. And in an age of competing empires, whichever one should find it first and take control of it would reap the rewards of a water route to the Pacific Ocean. By 1763 the once vast French Empire had been destroyed in North America—as had the empires of New Scotland, New Sweden, New Netherlands, and the Iroquois Confederacy. But the fate of the continent was far from settled. In 1776 a new and unexpected power arose to challenge the British Empire: the American Republic. And it too hungered for a pathway to the Pacific. Today, stashed away in the United States' Library of Congress, sits a curious, 227-year-old map made by an unlikely explorer of Canada's Northwest: the Yankee soldier Peter Pond. Pond believed that he'd finally found the gateway to the Western Sea, the long-sought River of the West—or at least, he thought he understood enough of the local aboriginal languages to figure out where such a river might be found—and he was confident enough that he marked it on the great map he presented to the newly minted United States Congress in 1790.

Pond's handing over his map to the U.S. government—a map that was, despite its many imperfections, the most detailed ever made of

territories at least nominally claimed by British fur trade companies—
was stirring the pot. The United States had just fought a successful war
for independence against the British Empire, and its national borders
remained a matter of serious contention. In an era when geographical
knowledge was limited, maps were essential to empire—after all, you
can't very well claim to rule a place that you can't find on a map. To
many Americans, the "new" lands Pond was mapping were simply
future territory for the United States. Pond's map brings into focus the
idea of Canada's boundaries—how in fact there is nothing inevitable
about them, and that if Thomas Jefferson and Pond had their way, most
of what is now Canada would have the Stars and Stripes flying over it.
Jefferson expressed the views of many of the American elite when, in
a letter to future president James Monroe, he wrote, "It is impossible
not to look forward to distant times when our rapid multiplication will
expand itself beyond those limits, and cover the whole northern, if not
the southern continent."[1]

Pond's background differed from most explorers of Canada's
Northwest in the eighteenth and nineteenth centuries. Most of the country's leading explorers were either born here or arrived at a young age
as apprentices in the fur trade. They tended to be serious, quiet types,
used to a life of solitude and isolation. As a rule they enjoyed excellent
relations with aboriginal peoples, and could normally speak at least one
or more native languages fluently—anyone who couldn't simply
wouldn't survive long in an environment where cooperation and respect
from aboriginal colleagues was vital.

Pond, on the other hand, was cut from a different cloth. He had a
reputation as a scoundrel, and was almost certainly a murderer, though
to his friends he was a dreamer and a man of incredible courage. He was
born in 1740 in Milford, Connecticut, in the days before the American
Revolution when Connecticut was still one of England's Thirteen
Colonies. According to Pond's own account of his family background,

"It is well known that from the fifth gineration downward we ware all waryers Ither by Sea or Land."[2] The young Pond was perhaps not likely to win many school spelling bees, but he felt certain that destiny had something great in store for him. Against the wishes of his parents, Pond wasted little time in enlisting in the army at the earliest opportunity; as a sixteen-year-old, in 1756 he joined a British colonial troop, the 1st Connecticut Regiment. Fortunately for men of martial inclinations, there was no shortage of wars at the time. The Seven Years' War, or "French and Indian War" as it was called in the Thirteen Colonies, had just broken out—a war that by its end would completely redraw the map of North America.

In Canada this conflict is primarily remembered for the Battle of the Plains of Abraham and the deaths of Generals Wolfe and Montcalm—but it was far more than just a war to settle the fate of Canada. It was the first truly world war, fought on four continents and three oceans and involving every major European state as well as most aboriginal nations in northeastern North America. This was the age of empire, when European monarchs treated maps as chessboards. Hundreds of petty kingdoms, duchies, and states then existed that could be conquered and reconquered or else traded in diplomacy; such, for example, was the fate of the Duchy of Parma, Silesia, and the island of Corsica, among many others.

Pond was swept up in this "Great War for Empire" when he rushed to enlist in the British colonial forces. But much to Pond's disappointment, his regiment did not see action and was dispersed later that same year. The war, however, was far from over, and Pond wasn't ready to return to the cobbler's workbench that his parents intended for him. In 1758, he again enlisted in the army. The following year, eager to find a regiment that would get him closest to the action, he transferred to the Suffolk County Regiment in New York and was promoted to sergeant, an unusual and impressive rank for a nineteen-year-old.

Pond's new regiment was dispatched to the New York frontier: the wilderness region around the Adirondack Mountains. This rough theatre of operations—a place of isolated forts, thundering waterfalls, and blue lakes; the haunt of mountain lions, black bears, and elk—inspired James Fenimore Cooper's subject matter in *The Last of the Mohicans*. In the shadow of the Adirondacks, fierce fighting raged as French regulars, Canadien militia, and Algonquin warriors ambushed and attacked British redcoats, colonial militia, and their Iroquois allies. The British had strength in numbers—and yet, under General Montcalm's leadership, the French and their aboriginal allies captured Fort William Henry on Lake George and inflicted severe losses on the British. Pond saw heavy fighting in these engagements. But he did not think much of his army's commanders, dismissing their plans as the "most ridicklas campane eaver hard of."[3]

After these battles, Pond found himself dispatched to the Niagara frontier to join a British force tasked with the capture of a French stronghold. This was Fort Niagara, the so-called "French castle"— a stone fortress that guarded the mouth of the Niagara River at the site where one of La Salle's wooden forts had once stood. After a hard-fought and bloody three-week siege, the fort fell to the British. Despite being in the thick of the action, Pond later recalled, "I Got But One Slite wound Dureing the Seage."[4]

The following year, Pond was commissioned an officer and joined the army under General Amherst that was massing in upstate New York for the invasion of Canada. The tide of war had turned, and the French— badly outnumbered in North America—were now on the defensive. A separate British army under General Wolfe had already captured Quebec City the previous September. The last remaining French stronghold in Canada was Montreal. Pond was serving there with his regiment when it surrendered on September 8, 1760—bringing an end to Champlain's dream.

Now that Canada was firmly in British hands, the outcome of the war in North America was a foregone conclusion; nonetheless, it would drag on for another three years before the Treaty of Paris in 1763 formally ended hostilities. During the peace negotiations, the British offered to return Canada to France in exchange for keeping their Caribbean conquests. But the French were indifferent—the colony had proven a financial burden, and very few French people had shown any interest in settling there. As Voltaire had quipped, Canada was no more than "a few acres of snow."[5] The French crown instead preferred to keep their most important Caribbean islands, which, owing to the sugar produced there, were worth far more than Canada. France also asked for two tiny islands off the coast of Newfoundland, St. Pierre and Miquelon, so that French fishermen could carry on the valuable cod fishery—which again was worth more than the entire fur trade in Canada. The map of Canada was thus redrawn: the old French Empire was erased, and in its place Britain now ruled an immense territory stretching from the Arctic Ocean down to the Spanish Empire in Florida. France retained only the inconspicuous little islands of St. Pierre and Miquelon, as it has to this day—giving Canada an easily forgotten international border with France.

Pond, however, felt that his thirst for adventure still hadn't been quenched, and with the war over, he had to find a new way to satisfy it. Like many adventurous souls before and since, he turned to the sea to find it—once back in his native New England, he promptly enlisted on a merchant vessel. He sailed to the West Indies, and intended to make seafaring his career, but when his ship returned to New England unwelcome news awaited him. Pond's father, facing poverty, had set off for the frontier to become a fur trader, and in his absence his mother had died of fever—leaving his numerous younger siblings with no one to care for them. Pond did the responsible thing and quit seafaring to take charge of his family. As he later wrote, the next three years he spent overseeing his siblings was the longest time he remained in one place between the age of sixteen and sixty.

By 1765, when Pond felt that his siblings were old enough to fend for themselves, he could no longer restrain his itch for more adventures. So he left to seek his fortune as a fur trader in the "Old Northwest" of the upper Great Lakes country. In that role he ranged over a wide area, from Montreal to Lake Superior, west to the Mississippi, and back to New York, rising steadily in prominence. This was turbulent territory, encompassing the homelands of diverse aboriginal nations, including the Odawa, Ojibwa, Potawatomi, Miami, Wea, Kickapoo, Mascouten, Piankashaw, Delaware, Shawnee, Wendat, and Mingo.

When the Seven Years' War ended and the Treaty of Paris redrew the map of North America, none of these tribes were consulted; European monarchs and diplomats simply ignored them. Smaller European nations were treated no better. The harsh reality was that, in the realm of European power politics, if a nation didn't command naval ships and cannons, it wasn't considered powerful enough to warrant a seat at the negotiating table. After the British conquest of Canada and the rest of the French Empire, the First Nations living in these territories were told by British "Indian agents" that they were now the subjects of a new ruler, His Majesty King George III—just as in 1768 the Corsicans were informed that they were now the subjects of His Majesty King Louis XV after he bought their country from the Genoese. In both instances, the takeover sparked armed uprisings. Maps, in other words, might be officially redrawn in the distant capitals of Europe, but realities on the ground could be a whole other matter.

If the map of northeastern North America were to be truly redrawn, it could only be through more bloodshed. Led by Pontiac, the charismatic and courageous Odawa chief, a native uprising began against the new British rulers of the Great Lakes watershed. Pontiac struck first at Fort Detroit, leading his warriors in a siege of the old French fort that was now in British hands. Inspired by Pontiac's actions, other tribes joined in the revolt. One after another, isolated and outnumbered British forts in the wilderness fell to aboriginal warriors—who believed their old ally France would soon renew the war and come to their aid. Although the French king was uninterested in restarting a war with England, some Canadiens did join Pontiac, as they too preferred the old fur trade alliances with aboriginal nations to British imperial rule.

But the old French Empire was not to be revived. At Detroit, the badly outnumbered British garrison managed to hold out, foiling Pontiac and forcing his warriors to lift the siege. Pontiac's leadership, while heroic, unintentionally alienated many traditional chiefs and elders. They looked upon Pontiac as an ambitious upstart who'd overstepped his authority in audaciously claiming to represent all native nations— and some even wanted him dead. Like many visionary leaders through- out history, in the end it was an assassin among his own ranks that proved Pontiac's undoing: he was struck down by a warrior sent by the Peorias tribe to kill him. With him died resistance—at least armed resistance— to the new British rulers of the Great Lakes.

Pond was not involved in these conflicts, but in his new role as a fur trader in the Detroit area he soon came to violence with some of his fel- low traders. A rival trader insulted and possibly cheated Pond; feeling his honour had been impinged, Pond coolly challenged the man to a duel. The next morning Pond calmly met his opponent over pistols. When the smoke from their flintlocks had cleared, Pond's adversary lay dead. Pond afterward freely confessed to the murder, but since duels were common in the lawless frontier regions, he never faced prosecution. And with his rival out of the way, for the next six years he prospered.

But there was something in Pond that made him restless; he was eager to seek beyond and push the boundaries. Not content with the fur trade in the Old Northwest—roughly the area of the upper Great Lakes west to the upper Mississippi—he wanted to push on much farther, deeper into the unmapped North American interior. His and his trade partners' logic was simple: undercut the Hudson's Bay Company's monopoly on the interior fur trade by bringing trade goods directly to interior peoples, sparing them from long canoe journeys to Company posts. These journeys could be fraught with dangers. Drowning in rapids, swamping in storms on large lakes and intertribal warfare remained a very real threat. The Cree, living closest to the Hudson Bay coast, enjoyed their roles as middlemen in the trade and often ambushed or waged war against other aboriginal nations that threatened their position. As a result, some interior nations gave up journeys to Hudson Bay altogether, and had to trade for their weapons and tools at greatly inflated prices—often many prime beaver pelts for a single rusty old musket and some shot.

Pond played the unlikely role of peacemaker in some of this warfare. In 1774 renewed war erupted between the Sioux and Ojibway, traditional enemies, which threatened the fur trade between Lakes Michigan and Superior and the upper reaches of the Mississippi. The head trader at Fort Michilimackinac—a key post situated on the strait between Lake Michigan and Lake Huron—tasked Pond with acting as a peace emissary to the Sioux. Carrying a wampum belt that had been specially made for the purpose, Pond met with eleven different Sioux chiefs and invited them to a peace council at Michilimackinac. Fortunately for all involved, at the fort a peace treaty was brokered between the Ojibwa and Sioux that was to last for a decade and allow normal trading to resume.

After this, Pond drifted farther west. By the mid-1770s he was operating as a fur trader in the Lake Winnipeg watershed and westward into Saskatchewan. This was well within the fur trade territory of the Hudson's Bay Company, and competition between trade rivals could be intense, with occasional violence. By 1777, Pond was chosen by his partners in Montreal to push on farther still—far into the northwest to the little-known Athabasca country, rumoured to be rich in furs. It was exactly the kind of challenge that appealed to Pond, although it would be a mistake to romanticize the task required of him. He would have to live in extreme isolation, hundreds of kilometres from the nearest frontier town—alone in a small cabin for long and brutal winters, with few contacts with the outside world, a monotonous diet, and scant luxuries or entertainments.

But the business logic was sound: Cree and Dene (Chipewyan) trappers were happy to trade with Pond rather than make a longer journey to the Hudson's Bay Company forts. After two years in the wilderness, Pond returned with his canoes laden with all the furs they could carry. In fact, he had so many furs—about 8400 beaver pelts in all—he had to build huts for them since he couldn't take them all on one journey to the trading posts at Lake Superior.

For good or ill, Pond's reputation was fast becoming legend. The fur trader Alexander Henry called him "a trader of some celebrity in the northwest," while fellow trader Roderick McKenzie wrote of Pond that "he thought himself a philosopher, and was odd in his manners."[6] More shrewdly, the mapmaker David Thompson described Pond as "a person of industrious habits, a good common education, but of a violent temper and unprincipled character."[7] Just how violent and unprincipled was soon to become clear.

By 1781 Pond had returned to what is now northern Saskatchewan; he spent the winter of 1782 in the woods at Lac La Ronge, where he found himself faced with unwelcome competition from a fellow trader, a Swiss ex-soldier named Jean-Étienne Waddens. Waddens and Pond were of different temperaments and didn't get along—a fact not helped by the trade competition between them. By February, in the depths of a long, bitter north Saskatchewan winter, Pond and Waddens fought. The details are hazy; we don't know if it was a fist fight, a duel, or just a shouting match. At any rate, a month later, in March, after a tense dinner shared by Waddens, Pond, and a third fur trade clerk, Waddens was found mortally wounded in the thigh by a gunshot. He died soon after from loss of blood.

Suspicion immediately fell on Pond, who had apparently quarrelled with Waddens again that night. In such an isolated location, there was no court of law, no magistrates, and no police. It was not uncommon for explorers or traders to disappear or meet with fatal accidents—and duels to settle differences were a fact of life. But rumours circulated and word spread, and back in Montreal Waddens's widow petitioned the British governor of Quebec to bring charges against Pond for her husband's murder. When Pond eventually returned to Montreal, he was questioned over the murder. But with scant evidence and the difficulty of securing a conviction for a crime committed on the edge of the known world, the charges against Pond were dropped—though suspicions lingered.

With his rival dead, Pond pushed on farther north, seeking new trade routes and wanting to explore more of the unknown. By the spring of 1783 he'd reached the previously unmapped Athabasca River and found it a promising source of new furs. Meanwhile, in his absence, the Scottish fur merchants who'd settled in Montreal since the British conquest had agreed to set aside their differences and form the North West Company as a rival to the Hudson's Bay Company. Pond, given his unique talents, was allotted a share in the new company and tasked to act on its behalf as the trader farthest inland. He began to map and explore the country around Lake Athabasca—an immense lake covering some 7850 square kilometres and with towering sand dunes on its southern shores. Here, Pond learned of rivers draining northward— and from his aboriginal guides and companions, who undoubtedly provided him with sketch maps, he learned the approximate locations of Great Slave and Great Bear lakes. As far as cartography went, this was all new geographical information unknown to outsiders, and Pond was eager to get credit for exploring it. In 1784 he returned to the settled East and began to work on the map that was to earn him a modest reputation. How he was able to make such a relatively accurate map without evidently much formal schooling in mathematics—which is necessary in order to take the careful astronomical observations needed to establish latitude and longitude—has long baffled historians.[8] In Montreal, over the course of the winter of 1784–85, Pond drew his map; it would be the first to hint at the existence of a large river draining northward to the Arctic Ocean.

But what Pond did next with his completed map—a valuable thing to possess, geographical knowledge being at a premium before the days of easily available printed atlases—is even more important. He presented his map to the United States Congress, which had just emerged victorious from its Revolutionary War. Tensions between the newly formed United States and the British Empire remained high— especially in the hazy and still contested fur trade territories and border regions; there were many forts here that remained in British hands but which the Americans claimed as their own. Border clashes and renewed war were distinct possibilities. Many of the leaders of the American government were not circumspect in expressing their territorial ambitions for the new Republic. Thomas Jefferson, in particular, had an insatiable thirst for explorers' maps to satisfy his desire to know about the rest of the North American continent. He dreamed of greatly enlarging the United States and talked openly of conquering Canada. Tensions remained high and memories of the late war were still fresh and bitter—especially in Canada, where some thirty thousand Loyalists had just arrived to escape persecution in the United States.[9] So what was Pond up to in giving the most detailed map ever made of the Northwest to the United States government? Particularly after it had just fought a war with Britain?

Pond might have claimed that he was merely a disinterested promoter of geographic knowledge. In April 1785 he had, after all, presented another copy of his new map to the lieutenant-governor of Quebec, although as a subject living in British territory, he could hardly have done otherwise. But this was an era of plots and intrigues, and not everyone trusted Pond's motives. Alexander Dalrymple, a cartographer with the East India Company, questioned Pond's loyalty to the British crown. Many of his fur trade companions also suspected that this Connecticut Yankee's loyalty to Britain was driven solely by temporary self-interest arising from the fur trade.

At any rate, once the snows had melted in the spring of 1785, Pond climbed into a birchbark canoe with a few French-Canadian voyageurs and once again set out from Montreal for the uncharted regions of the Northwest. He was headed back to the Athabasca watershed to trade on behalf of the North West Company—in which he was a shareholder—and took several clerks and voyageurs with him. There was also, to Pond's displeasure, new competition. Another trader, John Ross, had recently arrived in the Athabasca district to compete directly against him. But as others had discovered to their peril, trying to compete against Pond could be a dangerous undertaking.

Over the next two years, Pond continued to explore northward toward the Peace River, gathering more information from his aboriginal contacts for his ever-expanding map. But over the winter of 1786–87, competition from Ross became more serious. In a scuffle with Pond's men, Ross was shot and killed. When they returned to Canada, two of Pond's men were apprehended for the murder and brought to Quebec to stand trial—but again, evidence was hard to come by for a crime committed over three thousand kilometres away, and they were acquitted. Many, however, suspected Pond's hand in the murder. It was alleged that he'd ordered the murder and dispatched one of his voyageurs, Péché, to carry it out. The trader Peter Fidler believed as much—in his journal in 1791 he wrote, "Mr. Ross was shot by one Peshe [Péché], a Canadian, by order of Pond."[10]

Although Pond could not be convicted, the pattern of bad things happening to men who crossed him was now obvious to everyone, and Ross's death made it difficult for Pond to continue in the fur trade. His old companions shunned him; he was forced to retire, and in 1788 he left the Northwest for good. Back in the settlements of the East, Pond continued to work on his maps, revising and adding more details based on his own first-hand observations, on what he'd learned from local aboriginal people, notably the Cree and Dene (Chipewyan), and on the published reports of other explorers. His maps were an impressive achievement: they were the first to show the lands west of Hudson Bay in substantial detail, including Great Slave Lake and Lake Athabasca. But because Pond wasn't able to accurately estimate longitude on his travels—something that required meticulous astronomical observations as well as a chronometer—he mistakenly guessed that these giant lakes were much closer to the Pacific Ocean than was the case. Once again, the true size of the North American landmass had been underestimated.

Pond ended up substantially revising his map based on what he learned from the reports of Captain James Cook—who, anchored in his ship off the Pacific coast of Alaska, mistakenly believed that the inlet now known as "Cook Inlet" was the mouth of a major river flowing from the east. Pond hastily jumped to the conclusion that this must be the mouth of the mythical "River of the West," and with conjecture begetting conjecture, he concluded that this river must drain the huge Great Slave Lake he'd learned of from his aboriginal trade partners, and accordingly drew it onto his map. From Great Slave (a lake Pond himself had never seen), one could then paddle, he reasoned, straight to the Pacific Ocean. This assumption proved a major error—but it would not be recognized as such until Alexander Mackenzie set out to explore Pond's hypothetical river. Despite these errors, Pond's maps were in the 1780s the most detailed ones in existence for the vast lands of the Northwest.

Pond still craved recognition for his explorations, and he even began to prepare a copy of his map to send to the empress of Russia, Catherine the Great. He wanted his young trade partner, Alexander Mackenzie, to carry the map with him on his explorations; Pond assured him that if he followed the river marked on his new map it would take him straight to Russia. The Russians, meanwhile, had been slowly expanding eastward into Siberia; the land beyond that remained the greatest uncharted expanse of territory in the northern hemisphere. On maps of the eighteenth and early nineteenth centuries it appears as one giant blank space, typically labelled as "these parts entirely unknown." The most learned authorities speculated that it might be home to woolly mammoths, mastodons, and other strange beasts—much like how today we imagine creatures on distant planets. As for Pond, on his map of these mysterious regions he marked that there were "falls said to be the largest in the known world." There may, in fact, have been a kernel of truth to this claim. Pond may have heard, in native languages he could only partially understand, of the enormous falls on the Nahanni River in what is now the Northwest Territories—an actual waterfall nearly twice the height of Niagara Falls. Given the rough location of where he marked the waterfall on his map, this seems likely. But what exactly Pond hoped to accomplish by sharing his half-fanciful map with the Russians is uncertain.

On a more practical level, Pond returned to the United States to seek new employment there. The U.S. government recognized Pond's particular talents and his experience in dealing with aboriginal nations, and in 1792 he was sent by their secretary of war as an emissary to the Miami nation, which had been fighting with American settlers on the frontier. This seems to have been Pond's last adventure; afterward he returned to his native Connecticut and settled down to write his memoirs. He had ranged over an immense expanse—from the warm seas of the Caribbean as a merchant sailor to the harsh wilderness of the subarctic as a fur trader. Whatever his character, Pond's maps must rank highly in any consideration of historic North American maps; they helped fill in many blank spaces and significantly advanced geographic knowledge of the continent. Their merits were mostly the result of what Pond learned from his Cree guides and fur trade partners, while their defects stemmed from his overactive imagination and his zeal for exaggerating the extent of what he really knew. Pond's maps were the first to hint at the existence of Canada's longest river, which would become known as the Mackenzie after Pond's successor; Mackenzie himself, however, called it the "Disappointment River" after it led him not to the Pacific, as Pond promised him it would, but to the dreary wastes of the Arctic. In pushing on deeper into the Northwest than any white trader had ever gone before, Pond also expanded the realm of the empire—though just which empire remained a matter of contention. Fame and fortune, however, eluded Pond, and he died impoverished in 1807. If not for his maps, he might have been entirely forgotten.

{ 6 }

SAMUEL HEARNE'S MAP
OF THE COPPERMINE RIVER

He displayed such instances of personal courage and magnanimity, as are
rarely to be found.

—SAMUEL HEARNE, DESCRIBING MATONABBEE

I n 1769 a young English sailor, Samuel Hearne, stood atop the wind-swept battlements of a massive stone fortress and gazed out on what to him was the edge of the known world—the bleak, inhospitable coast of western Hudson Bay. As far as Hearne could see, stretching to the distant horizon was a wild, savage land of stunted trees and low-lying tundra, home to polar bears, packs of wolves, and tribes he as yet knew little about. Hearne was to be sent off into this uncharted wilderness to search for copper deposits rumoured to exist at the mouth of a great river. Untold sufferings and hardships awaited him; his chances of survival were slim; and if he succeeded, he could expect scant reward.

But then Samuel Hearne was a man accustomed to adversity.

His childhood in England was pretty much nonexistent—his father died when he was three, and by eleven he was serving on a warship in the Royal Navy. Britain's navy was the finest in the world, but professionalism in naval warfare came at a high price. Naval discipline was by modern standards almost inconceivably harsh. The slightest infraction typically called for lashes with the "cat-o'nine-tails" until the offender's back was reduced to a bloody pulp. Other punishments included being forced to walk the gauntlet—when shipmates on board the crowded vessels would whale away at the offender with knotted rope or other implements, often knocking him unconscious. Half-rations, bad food, surgical amputations, drowning, and death in battle were all standard fare. The punishment for desertion, cowardice, challenging a superior, "failure to do his utmost," and much else was death. Even officers of the highest ranks couldn't evade punishment. Admiral John Byng, for his failure to defeat the French at the outset of the Seven Years' War, was court-martialled, sentenced to death, and executed by firing squad. Samuel Johnson likened the navy to being in prison—only worse, since it included the chance of drowning.

It was this harsh, brutal world that the eleven-year-old Hearne was thrown into. Almost immediately he saw action in the Seven Years' War when his ship took part in an attack on French ports. There was nowhere to hide on board a ship—above or below deck sailors were maimed and killed. Cannonballs, grapeshot, and flying splinters from ship's decks and masts were just some of the ways to die. The thunder of cannons, the screams of the wounded amid the thick, suffocating smoke, the sulphuric smell of gunpowder, and decks that became slick with blood as ships pitched about, firing away at each other, all became part of Hearne's boyhood.

There was little time for leisure. Naval officers had to be rigorously trained from childhood in order to master the science of navigation and the command of a warship that was expected to sail on any of the world's oceans. They needed to be individuals of high cognitive abilities, with a strong grasp of the mathematics required for navigation and artillery use; they also needed exceptional physical and mental toughness to endure the hardships of life at sea. Hearne certainly had the grit for life in the navy—but he was too much the free-spirited, restless wanderer for the rigid discipline a naval career required. When the Seven Years' War ended in 1763 the Royal Navy had to downsize, and Hearne, now eighteen and with seven years of naval service to his credit, was happy to leave. But since sailing was the only trade he knew, he soon signed on board the merchant ship *Churchill*, a Hudson's Bay Company sloop.

For almost a century the Company had been trading in furs with Cree, Dene, and Inuit trappers in exchange for iron tools and other European-made goods. Hearne's ship was tasked with resupplying the lonely forts on Hudson Bay's windswept coast. For the next two years, sailing past icebergs, walruses, polar bears, and beluga and bowhead whales in frigid Arctic waters became Hearne's life. The Arctic seas were fraught with hazards; the Company had lost several of its ships in storms on Hudson Bay, and there could be few less hospitable places on earth to be shipwrecked than on its bleak Arctic shores—where polar bears might make a meal of any marooned sailors.

In 1719 two Company ships had been lost with all hands during an expedition led by the veteran fur trader James Knight. Knight had been probing the still-uncharted waters of western Hudson Bay, hoping to discover the Northwest Passage to Asia as well as gold and copper deposits that reports claimed existed somewhere in the western Arctic. The two ships under Knight's command had headed north of 64 degrees latitude—but after that, Knight and his ships vanished. Rumours spread among the trading posts on Hudson Bay's southern shores that Knight and his crews had been shipwrecked and massacred by Inuit.

Half a century later, it was Hearne who solved the mystery of what happened to Knight's expedition. The Hudson's Bay Company had been experimenting with whaling on the bay. Hearne, a mate on board one of the ships, while harpooning whales, visited a large, desolate rock island lying about thirteen kilometres off the northwestern coast. In the Arctic sun the uninhabited island gleamed eerily white, a strange mirage rising above the dark waters. The sailors named it "Marble Island" after the shining white boulders covering its landmass, although the boulders were actually quartzite. As they approached the barren outcrop—the haunt of polar bears, seals, and walrus—they suddenly spotted two shipwrecks lying in about five fathoms of water. The remains of Knight's two ships had been found.

The captain of Hearne's sloop decided to put to shore on the strange island. On shore, Hearne started to piece together what had happened to Knight. Scattered about the eastern end of the island were guns, anchors, cables, bricks, an anvil, and various other relics. There were also two sun-bleached human skulls and some scattered bones. Nearby was part of what had been a makeshift dwelling. The house, Hearne recorded, had been "pulled to pieces" by the Inuit for its wood and iron, but there was no clear sign of violence.[1] Evidently the survivors from the shipwrecks had lived on the island for at least a time. Not far from the dwelling Hearne found a great number of oak shavings and chips—which he deduced were left by the carpenters attempting to lengthen their ship's longboat as a means of escape from the island.

Hearne returned to the island on whale-hunting excursions over the next few summers. On these trips, he encountered several old Inuit hunters and asked them about the details of what had happened to Knight and his crews. The Inuit told Hearne that about fifty men had been shipwrecked on the island and had built a dwelling to survive the winter. By the spring, however, many had perished from starvation and scurvy. Trapped on the island, the survivors numbered only about twenty by the onset of the second winter. The next summer, at least five were still alive until they too died that year.

Hearne accepted these Inuit oral histories as the correct version of what had happened to Knight and his men, dismissing the rumours that they'd been massacred. Throughout his life, Hearne would show an unusual willingness to put his faith in aboriginal oral history over European sources. He eventually learned to speak both the Athabaskan and Algonquin languages fluently, and even made a dictionary of the former. It was Hearne's willingness to embrace aboriginal knowledge, expertise, and methods of travel that was to prove the secret of his success as an explorer.

In the 1760s the Hudson's Bay Company had been facing considerable criticism for its lacklustre approach to exploration. In London, politicians criticized the Company's special privileges, especially its fur trade monopoly, and argued that it had done little to deserve it. The Company had failed to discover a Northwest Passage and had lately shown little interest in sending explorers inland from the seacoast. Such criticisms from afar, however, overlooked the difficulties of probing the harsh lands west of Hudson Bay, where sub-zero temperatures lasted from September through May. In mid-winter there were only six hours of daylight; temperatures typically plunged to a bone-chilling minus 40 degrees Celsius. Anyone who ventured out in such conditions risked losing their fingers and toes to frostbite—if not their lives. The brief summers brought intense swarms of blood-sucking insects that numbered in the millions and included blackflies, mosquitoes, sandflies, deerflies, and horseflies, which could drive people and animals mad. Finally, because of the scarcity of food resources in the subarctic forest and Arctic barrens, famine was unavoidable at least some of the time—even the most skilled native hunters accepted it as a normal part of life. In harsh times, especially during the ice breakup in the spring, nearly every hunting band lost people to starvation. Given the food scarcities, violence was common; stronger hunting bands regularly attacked and robbed weaker bands. For all these reasons, the English and Scottish fur traders much preferred to remain holed up in their forts on Hudson Bay—letting the natives who could manage the journey bring furs to them.

To the extent that there was exploration, it was entrusted to "leading men" among the Dene and Cree who were on friendly terms with the Hudson's Bay Company. In 1762, the commander at Prince of Wales's Fort, Moses Norton, received a report and a map made by two intrepid

Dene explorers, Idotlyazee and Matonabbee. They had journeyed deep into the interior, beyond the ordinary hunting grounds of the Dene, and discovered a distant river flowing into the sea, near which were rich deposits of copper. As proof, they brought with them a chunk of copper ore. This finding prompted Norton to set sail for England to persuade the Company's London Committee to support an expedition to more thoroughly explore the river and its copper deposits, and crucially, to map the route. It might, after all, prove a navigable river that could serve as a shortcut through the continent—perhaps even lead to the discovery of the Northwest Passage to Asia.[2] The London Committee was sufficiently intrigued that they agreed to support the expedition.

The question was who to entrust with such a difficult, dangerous undertaking. It would have to be someone who was not only strong and healthy enough to endure the rigours of an extreme journey, but also had the surveying knowledge necessary to map the territory. Equally important would be finding someone who got along well with the Dene and was skilled in overcoming cultural barriers; earning the respect and goodwill of the natives would be critical. Norton, after careful consideration, recommended the young sailor Samuel Hearne—much to the latter's own surprise.

Hearne had spent the previous winter at Prince of Wales's Fort studying celestial navigation and surveying with the astronomer William Wales, and practising how to use a quadrant—a navigation instrument that was an improvement over earlier astrolabes. He was young, healthy, and apparently good on snowshoes. He was also an experienced seaman inured to deprivations and hardships, and he'd already shown an ability to communicate with the Inuit when he helped solve the mystery of what had happened to Knight's lost expedition. The London Committee agreed with Norton's choice and approved the expedition.

Norton, however, given his long years of experience as a trader on Hudson Bay and his role as commander of Princes of Wales's Fort, insisted upon planning the expedition for Hearne. He appointed the Dene hunter Chawchinahaw as his guide and assigned two common sailors from the Company to go with him. Also included in the party were several "homeguard Indians," a term used for the local Cree who grew up at Hudson Bay posts and were on close terms with the traders.

Norton's choice of guide proved less than auspicious—once a safe distance from the fort, Chawchinahaw balked at the idea of trying to reach some far-flung river he'd never seen before, and promptly robbed and abandoned Hearne and the Cree. Despite this misfortune, Hearne remained committed to the enterprise, and almost immediately upon his return to the fort a month later—in a ragged and half-starving state—he wanted to leave on a second attempt. This time, however, he determined that he should be the sole European in the party, as his two English sailor companions hadn't been respected by the Dene and were therefore a liability.

Norton agreed, and appointed a new Dene guide, Conneequese, to lead Hearne and his "homeguard" Cree companions. They left the fort in late February on snowshoes, heading for the northwest interior. Blizzards often forced the party to hole up in their little moosehide tents for two or three days at a stretch before it was safe to continue. This time they wandered for months before Conneequese confessed that he was lost and didn't know the way to the so-called "Far Off Metal River."[3] History repeated itself; Hearne and his Cree friends were once more robbed and abandoned. To make matters worse, Hearne's quadrant broke—rendering any attempt at accurate mapping impossible. Eight months after leaving, Hearne was back at Prince of Wales's Fort in November 1770. Amazingly, he remained undaunted by the failures and hardships he had thus far encountered and was more determined than ever to find the river.

What gave Hearne confidence that he could succeed was a fortuitous encounter during his retreat to the fort, when he had happened to cross paths with a remarkable man who was to exert a powerful influence on his life: the Dene leader Matonabbee. Matonabbee had been leading a gang of his followers—including his seven wives—on a trading trip to Prince of Wales's Fort when he encountered Hearne's party. Hearne recorded the auspicious moment: "The courteous behaviour of this stranger struck me very sensibly. As soon as he was acquainted with our distress, he got such skins as we had with us dressed [by his wives] . . . and furnished me with a good warm suit of otter and other skins."[4] Matonabbee further helped Hearne and his "homeguard" Cree friends— who were out of their element on the Arctic barrens—by telling them where they could find a clump of dwarf trees to make snowshoes. Best of all, Matonabbee entertained them with a "grand feast" that came as a welcome relief to Hearne and his two companions.

That night as they sat around a crackling campfire, with Matonabbee's wives dancing and singing and the men and children feasting on caribou and fish, Matonabbee earnestly asked Hearne if he intended to make a third attempt to reach the Coppermine. Hearne replied that he would, provided he could find better guides than the ones he'd thus far been relying upon. Hearing this, Matonabbee offered his services— assuming that the governor at the fort agreed. Unlike Hearne's previous guides, Matonabbee had actually been to the river.

To Hearne, a young man who lived a hard and lonely life, Matonabbee became more than just a friend and guide; he was Hearne's hero, a larger-than-life figure whom Hearne lionized in his account of their shared journey. Matonabbee was about thirty-three or thirty-four— making him eight or nine years older than Hearne. He was the son of a Dene father and one of his Cree slaves. Like Hearne, Matonabbee's father died while he was young. Fatherless, he was informally "adopted" by the governor of Prince of Wales's Fort, Richard Norton (the father of Moses Norton). However, Norton soon left for England, and his successor showed no interest in Matonabbee. He was returned to his father's Dene relatives, whom Matonabbee accompanied on their wandering hunts. He proved extremely talented in that regard, and was later employed by the Company as one of their "homeguard Indians" who helped supply the post with fresh meat and other vitals.

Highly intelligent and a natural leader, Matonabbee could speak both Athabaskan (the language of his Dene father) and Algonquin (the language of his Cree mother). He had also learned a few English words—though not enough to converse. Given Matonabbee's pedigree and talents, the Company had relied upon him as a peace emissary to the inland Cree and Dene, who were frequently at war with each other. Such wars were a hindrance to the Company, given that war meant less trapping and therefore less profit. Matonabbee was eventually successful in his peace efforts, which helped add to the respect and prestige he commanded.

Certainly anyone crossing paths with Matonabbee would be struck by his appearance. Hearne wrote of him:

> In stature, Matonabbee was above the common size, being nearly six feet high . . . he was one of the finest and best proportioned men I ever saw . . . His features were regular and agreeable, and yet so strongly marked and expressive, that they formed a complex index of his mind; which, as he never intended to deceive or dissemble, he never wished to conceal. In conversation, he was easy, lively, and agreeable, but exceedingly modest.[5]

Hearne further described Matonabbee as brave, loyal, and kind—a superb leader who in Hearne's words exhibited "universal humanity to all the human race."[6] His only fault, Hearne thought, was a tendency to jealousy regarding his wives.

Matonabbee attributed the failure of Hearne's two previous attempts at reaching the Coppermine not only to the incompetence or treachery of his guides, but more crucially to the lack of women in his party. This explanation baffled Hearne—until Matonabbee explained that the women could carry everything while the men remained unencumbered by heavy loads, and therefore free to hunt. Moreover, women were needed to make and mend clothing, pitch tents, start fires, and, Matonabbee added, keep men warm at night. Plus, they didn't require as much food as men did—at least according to Matonabbee's estimation. Hearne accepted Matonabbee's explanation and trusted in his experience.[7]

Back at the fort, Norton agreed with Hearne's new plan to seek the Coppermine with Matonabbee as his guide. But Hearne upset Norton by refusing to take any of the homeguard Cree—who, he said, didn't know the territory beyond the treeline and weren't respected by the Dene, their ancestral enemies. Norton reluctantly agreed with Hearne's insistence that the party consist solely of the Dene and himself. To map the territory they were to cover, Hearne prepared a base map on parchment showing what he already knew of the Hudson Bay coast and the rivers draining into it. That way, he could simply add fresh details to the map as they advanced.

It speaks volumes about Hearne's temperament and grit that after enduring nearly a year's worth of living in the open on the Arctic tundra and suffering severe deprivations—including long periods of fasting that made subsequent eating extremely painful—he departed on a new journey after only twelve days recuperating back at the fort. Hearne fully expected the journey to take about two years—two years in which he'd see no other Englishman or European, and during which he'd communicate only in what had become his second and third languages, Athapaskan and Algonquin, just as he'd been doing for most of the past year. To have any chance of success, he would have to live as a Dene: hunting, fishing, and constantly travelling.

On December 7, 1770, Hearne and Matonabbee, along with the latter's wives and several male followers, left the fort on snowshoes to seek the Coppermine. Although Matonabbee inspired much greater confidence than had Hearne's previous guides, things still got off to a rocky start. Matonabbee had expected to come across a cache of provisions he'd stored before arriving at the fort, but just over a week into their journey he discovered that his cache had been raided and plundered by other Dene. This left the party destitute of provisions until they could find success hunting, which might take days. Hearne marvelled at their response: "This disappointment and loss was borne with the greatest fortitude; and I did not hear one of them breathe the least hint of revenge in case they should discover the offenders; the only effect it had on them was, that of making them put the best foot foremost."[8] Such stoic resignation and forbearance in the face of adversity greatly impressed Hearne—himself no stranger to adversity.

All through their winter journey northward, the party alternately feasted on caribou when they were fortunate enough to kill any and starved for days when they had no luck hunting. Hearne felt he could never have endured the travails of these recurring fasts if not for the example set by his Dene companions, who somehow remained upbeat and light-hearted even after days with no food. Fortunately, with Matonabbee's skills, it seemed there would be less fasting than on Hearne's previous trips—during which his party had been reduced to eating burnt bones, scraps of old leather, lichens, and anything else they could find. Before his adventures were over, Hearne would be able to discourse on such delicacies as tundra swans, Canada geese, partridges, gulls, beavers, porcupines, caribou, muskox, numerous species of fish, and much else that he and his companions had subsisted on.

For weeks after leaving the fort, they wandered through an uninhabited no man's land where animals were scarce and the country too harsh to support any population—though in other, more favourable locales, they would often cross paths with Dene families. Matonabbee kept to the treeline, following a northwesterly course so as to avoid the hardships and difficulties of surviving on the open, windswept Arctic tundra, where there were no trees to shelter them from the chilling winds and no wood for fires. When forced to cross immense frozen lakes, the wind would cut into them mercilessly—during one such crossing, one of Matonabbee's wives suffered severe frostbite.

The more time Hearne spent with the Dene, the more his perspective began to change. He started to think the fur trade did little to improve their lives besides supplying them with iron tools. He reflected that "those who have the least intercourse with the Factories, are by far the happiest."[9] Hearne made a habit of recording the Dene names for lakes and rivers when they had them and translating them into English—it was never his style to name anything himself, aside from perhaps the Coppermine River, although that seems to have been a rough translation of the Dene name.

By mid-April, with the ice melting, Matonabbee began preparations for leaving the shelter of the subarctic forest and pushing out onto the tundra—where the caribou herds would be headed to graze. To this end, the party gathered the materials they would need to fashion birchbark canoes, which could be carried with them until the time came to assemble the canoes for fording rivers. Hearne, a talented artist, drew sketches illustrating the construction process of a birchbark canoe, which he found ingenious. He noted with admiration:

> All the tools used by an Indian in making his canoe, as well as in making his snow-shoes, and every other kind of wood-work, consist of a hatchet, a knife, a file, and an awl; in the use of which they are so dextrous, that every thing they make is executed with a neatness not to be excelled by the most expert mechanic, assisted with every tool he could wish.[10]

The Dene's canoes were smaller and lighter than ones made farther south—in part because birch trees in the subarctic were much smaller, but also because the Dene preferred to travel mainly on foot and use their canoes only to cross rivers and lakes. This meant canoes had to be small and light enough to be carried long distances.

While these canoe preparations were ongoing, Hearne's group encountered another band of Dene hunters who were also preparing to follow the seasonal caribou migration onto the tundra. From this group Matonabbee purchased a new wife, who was to become his eighth. One of his other wives was heavily pregnant, and gave birth just as they were about to set off on foot across the tundra. Hearne was amazed that the woman—who'd been in labour for fifty-two hours—was able, almost immediately afterward, to keep up with the others, carrying her infant and everything else required of her.

They covered about twenty kilometres a day on foot. Gradually the black spruce, tamarack, and clumps of trembling aspens thinned out until they were walking on the vast, treeless plains of the Arctic tundra. Several fierce thunderstorms forced them to huddle up for a day at a time—and even in late May temperatures plunged below freezing. In severe weather, Matonabbee preferred that they remain inside their tents rather than expose themselves to the elements. Shortly after enduring one of these storms, he discovered that one of his wives, as well as the wife of another man in the party, had gone missing. Hearne recorded:

> It was supposed they went off to the Eastward, in order to meet their
> former husbands, from whom they had been taken by force. This
> affair made more noise and bustle than I could have supposed; and
> Matonabbee seemed entirely disconcerted, and quite inconsolable for
> the loss of his wife. She was certainly by far the handsomest of his
> flock . . . She had not, however, appeared happy in her late situation;

and chose rather to be the sole wife of a sprightly young fellow of no note . . . than to have the seventh or eighth share of the affection of the greatest man in the country. I am sorry to mention the incident which happened while we were building canoes . . . and which by no means does honour to Matonabbee: it is no less a crime than that of having actually stabbed the husband of the above-mentioned girl in three places . . . for no other reason than because the poor man had spoken disrespectfully of him for having taken his wife away by force. The cool deliberation with which Matonabbee committed this bloody action, convinced me it had long been premeditated design; for he no sooner heard of the man's arrival, than he opened one of his wives' bundles, and, with the greatest composure, took out a new long box-handled knife, went into the man's tent, and, without any preface whatever, took him by the collar, and began to execute his horrid design. The poor man anticipating his danger, fell on his face, and called for assistance; but before any could be had, he received three wounds in his back. Fortunately for him, they all happened on the shoulder-blade, so that his life was spared. When Matonabbee returned to his tent, after committing this horrid deed, he sat down as composedly as if nothing had happened, called for water to wash his bloody hands and knife, smoked his pipe as usual, seemed perfectly at ease, and asked if I did not think he had done right?[11]

Although Hearne was horrified by these actions, it didn't change his view of Matonabbee as a man of exceptional "courage, magnanimity, and humanity."[12] This might seem odd to modern readers, but Hearne, having grown up in a harsh and brutal world, adopted a kind of cultural relativism that led him to see Matonabbee's actions in a different light. Hearne accepted them as consistent with Dene cultural norms, in which women were often fought over in single combat between two men—a practice not exactly unknown in Europe (the fatal duel between Romeo and Paris over Juliet is one example). Among the Dene, like the ancient Macedonians, the greater and stronger the man, the more wives he acquired. Poor hunters and weaker individuals had no wives at all—and no children. Hearne witnessed many of these contests throughout his time with the Dene:

> It was very unpleasant to me, to see the object of the contest sitting in
> pensive silence watching her fate, while her husband and his rival were
> contending for the prize. I have indeed not only felt pity for those
> poor wretched victims, but the utmost indignation, when I have seen
> them won, perhaps, by a man whom they mortally hated. On those
> occasions their grief and reluctance to follow their new lord has been
> so great, that the business has often ended in the greatest brutality; for,
> in the struggle, I have seen the poor girls stripped quite naked, and
> carried by main force to their new lodgings.[13]

Even Matonabbee, although strong and agile, was not immune to losing his wives in these contests. Hearne reported that while they were hunting on the edge of the tundra, he was challenged by a much stronger man for one of his wives. Knowing that if he accepted the challenge he would lose the fight, and therefore one of his favourite wives, Matonabbee attempted to buy the other man off with gifts of gunpowder, shot, a kettle, and other items. The incident was all the more galling to Matonabbee as the wife in question was the one he'd just purchased the previous month. Such an affront to his honour, like that suffered by Achilles when Agamemnon took from him the slave girl Briseis, caused Matonabbee to become withdrawn and sullen to the point where he wanted to abandon the journey to the Coppermine. Hearne, alarmed by this turn of events, was able to console Matonabbee by pointing out to him that the honour and renown he'd win by reaching the distant Coppermine would far exceed that lost to his rival.

Encouraged by this thought, Matonabbee now resolved to push on with all haste to the Coppermine. To this end, he decided to leave behind the majority of his wives and children and to travel as light as possible, with only the bare essentials—a few guns, some ammunition, a couple of kettles, flints, and spare hides for clothing. Of his wives, he selected two with no children to accompany them; the rest were to stay behind and rendezvous with the main party later. The other men in the group with multiple wives did the same.

Meanwhile, when some of the other Dene hunters in the area learned of Matonabbee's plan to penetrate far into the country of the Inuit—their ancestral enemies—they were eager to come along. They used the last bit of subarctic forest to prepare wooden shields, as they fully intended to fight any of the Inuit they encountered. Altogether, Matonabbee's followers now numbered about sixty warriors.

These war preparations alarmed Hearne. However, his attempts to dissuade the Dene from seeking to attack the Inuit—or "Eskimo" as the Dene called them—were met with ridicule. The Dene accused Hearne of cowardice. Hearne replied that he wasn't afraid of the Inuit and if it came to a fight he wouldn't hesitate to defend himself or his friends, but that he thought it imprudent to aggressively seek out and kill Inuit who'd never done anything to him. Hearne noted:

> This declaration was received with great satisfaction; and I never
> afterwards ventured to interfere with any of their war-plans.
> Indeed, when I came to consider seriously, I saw evidently
> that it was the highest folly for an individual like me, and in
> my situation, to attempt to turn the current of a national prejudice
> which had subsisted between these two nations from the earliest
> periods, or at least as long as they had been acquainted with
> the existence of each other.[14]

By the first of June the party was advancing north on foot as fast as they could travel, usually covering about thirty-five kilometres a day. Though the days were warm, many lakes still remained sufficiently frozen that they could safely walk across the ice. About three weeks after leaving the majority of women and children, the party came to a large, ice-free river. Here they met a large number of Dene, who were killing caribou from canoes as the animals attempted to swim across the swollen river.

These natives, living far inland from Hudson Bay, had never before encountered a European, although they had acquired some European tools from trade with other Dene. Hearne recorded the surprise his appearance occasioned:

As I was the first European whom they had ever seen . . . it was
curious to see how they flocked about me, and expressed as much
desire to examine me from top to toe, as an European Naturalist would
a non-descript animal. They, however, found and pronounced me to
be a perfect human being, except in the colour of my hair and eyes: the
former, they said, was like the stained hair of a buffaloe's tail, and the
latter, being light, were like those of a gull. The whiteness of my skin
also was, in their opinion, no ornament, as they said it resembled meat
which had been sodden in water till all the blood was extracted. On the
whole, I was viewed as so great a curiosity in this part of the world,
that during my stay there, whenever I combed my head, some or other
of them would ask for the hairs that came off, which they carefully
wrapped up.[15]

A few of these Dene hunters agreed to escort the party northward, as they were more familiar with the country.

The party was now nearing the upper reaches of the Coppermine River; Matonabbee decided at this point to now leave all the women behind. Several days were spent hunting caribou and drying the meat in the sun so that the remaining women would have enough food while the men went ahead. Hearne, meanwhile, used his quadrant to take observations of the sun and work out the latitude—although he didn't have Champlain's talents in that regard, and his estimates weren't particularly accurate.

When the party began heading north again, despite it being July, they were plagued by bad weather, including sleet and snow. At night, under the midnight sun, they huddled in the crevices of rocks or the lee side of boulders to escape the chilling wind and freezing rains. They'd reached a bleak, desolate moonscape that the Dene called the "Stony Mountains," a ridge of low-lying, but steep and precarious, rock hills. The overcast skies and steady mix of sleet, snow, and rain added to the grimness of the landscape. The northern Dene they'd met led the party across the mountains; at times the going was so rough and steep that Hearne and his companions were reduced to crawling on their hands and knees. At night, chilled to the bone and with their garments soaked through by the freezing rain, they huddled in small caves or beneath boulders. The lack of wood and wetness made starting fires impossible, so they ate their venison raw, having run out of all dried provisions. In the morning, fifteen members of their party, unnerved by the difficulties, decided to abandon the journey and head back to the encampment with the women.

To make matters worse, a freak snowstorm struck that saw so much snow accumulated that even the oldest member of their party said he'd never seen anything like it. The snow fell heavily for nine uninterrupted hours, to the point where, as Hearne put it, "we were in danger of being smothered in our caves."[16] Still, they pressed on as the snow melted in the midday sun, encountering large herds of muskox grazing on the tundra. On the bank of a small creek they found enough dwarf willow to make a fire and cook some caribou meat—the first warm meal they'd had in a week.

Near where they camped that night was a large marsh, in the middle of which were a number of low hills. These hills, Hearne learned, were the homes of grizzly bears that dug caves into them for dens. Hearne was astonished at the strength of grizzlies; in their quest for their principal prey, arctic ground squirrel, they would frequently overturn enormous boulders.

The days suddenly became hot and windless, causing Hearne and the Dene to suffer much from thick clouds of mosquitoes. But after two weeks of wandering, and some uncertainty over where they were, the party at last reached the banks of a fast-flowing river: the Coppermine. It was not, Hearne quickly perceived, the large river native reports had originally made it out to be. Instead, it was laced with rocks and rapids, and "no less than three falls were in sight at first view."[17] The river flowed between large and mostly barren hills—what trees existed had largely been scarred by fires.

Three hunters were sent ahead as scouts to see whether any Inuit were camped farther downriver, while the remainder of the party shot muskox and caribou and dried the meat. This way, Matonabbee explained to Hearne, they wouldn't have to hunt downriver, as firing guns there would alert the Inuit of their presence. Hearne, meanwhile, worked on mapping the river, which was so full of waterfalls and rapids that he quickly concluded it would never serve as a navigable route.

In a few days the three scouts returned. They had discovered five tents of Inuit on the west side of the river, in a place that was ideal for an ambush. Hearne protested that they should continue mapping the river, but he was ignored. Instead, all preparations were now devoted to attacking the Inuit. To accomplish this, Matonabbee and the others resolved to cross the river immediately; there was a tranquil enough stretch that would allow for paddling in their canoes. Then, once they'd ferried the party across, the warriors painted their shields and prepared themselves for battle.

They advanced cautiously and silently, sometimes wading across mudflats and swamps rather than along the tops of hills or the river's high cliff banks, where they might be spotted. Hearne was amazed by the transformation among his companions—who seemed bent on complete annihilation of the Inuit. He'd told them that he would "not have any hand in the murder they were about to commit, unless I found it necessary for my own safety. The Indians were not displeased at this proposal; one of them immediately fixed me a spear, and another lent me a broad bayonet for my protection."[18]

Under the midnight sun, as the Inuit lay sleeping in their tents, the Dene crept ever closer to their camp. A huge thundering waterfall nearby helped conceal their approach. All of sudden, the Dene rushed on the tents. Hearne recorded what happened next:

In a few seconds the horrible scene commenced; it was shocking beyond description; the poor unhappy victims were surprised in the midst of their sleep, and had neither time nor power to make any resistance; men, women, and children in all upward of twenty, ran out of their tents stark naked, and endeavoured to make their escape; but the Indians having possession of all the landside, to no place could they fly for shelter . . .

The shrieks and groans of the poor expiring wretches were truly dreadful; and my horror was much increased at seeing a young girl, seemingly about eighteen years of age, killed so near me, that when the first spear was stuck into her side she fell down at my feet, and twisted round my legs, so that it was with difficulty that I could disengage myself from her dying grasps. As two Indian men pursued this unfortunate victim, I solicited very hard for her life; but the murderers made no reply till they had stuck both their spears through her body, and transfixed her to the ground. They looked me sternly in the face, and began to ridicule me, by asking if I wanted an Esquimaux wife; and paid not the smallest regard to the shrieks and agony of the poor wretch, who was twining round their spears like an eel![19]

Hearne begged that they end the girl's torture and put her out of misery:

On this request being made, one of the Indians hastily drew his spear from the place where it was first lodged, and pierced it through her breast near the heart . . . My situation and the terror of my mind at beholding this butchery, cannot easily be conceived, much less described . . . even at this hour I cannot reflect on the transactions of that horrid day without shedding tears.[20]

The horror was not yet over. There were, they discovered, seven more tents of Inuit on the opposite side of the river, concealed beneath a hill. Hearne noted:

Our canoes and baggage had been left at a little distance up the river, so that they [the Dene] had no way of crossing to get at them. The river at this part being little more than eighty yards wide, they began firing at them from the West side. The poor Esquimaux on the opposite shore, though all up in arms . . . were so unacquainted with the use of fire-arms, that when the bullets struck the ground, they ran in crowds to see what was sent them, and seemed anxious to examine all the pieces of lead which they found flattened against the rocks. At length one of the Esquimaux men was shot in the calf of his leg, which put them in great confusion. They all immediately embarked in their little canoes, and paddled to a shoal in the middle of the river, which being somewhat more than a gunshot from any part of the shore, put them out of reach.[21]

With the Inuit having fled to the island, the Dene began to loot the tents of everything they could find: food, hatchets, knives, copper utensils. After the plundering, they climbed atop a nearby hill and shouted insults and derision at the bereaved Inuit still cowering on the island. Then they headed back upriver to fetch their own canoes so that they could cross the river and plunder the tents on the other side. It was while retracing their steps that the Dene happened upon an old Inuit woman who'd been separated from the others:

> We saw an old woman by the side of the water, killing salmon, which lay at the foot of the fall as thick as a shoal of herrings. Whether from the noise of the fall, or a natural defect of the old woman's hearing, it is hard to determine, but certain it is, she had no knowledge of the tragical scene which had been so lately transacted at the tents . . . When we first perceived her, she seemed perfectly at ease, and was entirely surrounded with the produce of her labour. From the manner of her behaviour, and the appearance of her eyes, which were as red as blood, it is more than probable that her sight was not very good; for she scarcely discerned that the Indians were enemies, till they were within twice the length of their spears of her. It was in vain that she attempted to fly, for the wretches of my crew transfixed her to the ground in a few seconds, and butchered her in the most savage manner. There was scarcely a man among them who had not a thrust at her with his spear; and many in doing this, aimed at torture, rather than immediate death, as they not only poked out her eyes, but stabbed her in many parts very remote from those which are vital.[22]

The Dene similarly speared to death another old Inuit man whom they found alone. They then proceeded to the remaining seven tents on the east side of the river. Hearne reported what followed:

> When the Indians had plundered the seven tents of all the copper utensils, which seemed the only thing worth their notice, they threw

all the tents and tent-poles into the river, destroyed a vast quantity
of dried salmon, musk-oxen flesh, and other provisions; broke all
the stone kettles; and, in fact, did all the mischief they possibly could
to distress the poor creatures they could not murder, and who were
standing on the shoal before mentioned, obliged to be woeful spectators of their great, or perhaps irreparable loss.[23]

Modern readers will likely find Hearne's description of the massacre shocking. But it has been supported by modern archaeological
findings, and we must remember that there is absolutely nothing in it
that can't also be found in accounts from ancient Greece and Rome,
the Vikings (for example, when Freydis slaughtered half the Vinland
settlement in cold blood), or for that matter, contemporary conflict
zones.[24] After the Dene had finished their destruction of the Inuit
camp, the party enjoyed a meal of fresh salmon in celebration of their
victory. It was the best meal they'd had in a long while. Hearne's
companions now happily offered to assist him in finishing the survey
of the river.

Hearne was reeling with shock from the massacre he'd just witnessed, yet he had little choice but to finish his exploration. He followed
the river with some of his Dene companions toward where it emptied
into the sea. Though they didn't taste any salt water, likely because the
tide was out, Hearne was certain that they'd reached the Arctic Ocean
and not just another large lake: seals could be seen resting on offshore
ice floes, and along the gravelly shoreline were scattered whalebones.
Any hope of it being of any value to the Hudson's Bay Company was
immediately dispelled.

Matonabbee, Hearne, and the others retraced their steps up the river
and later went to search for the supposedly rich copper mines. This,
too, turned out to be a decided exaggeration. The so-called mine was
in reality a "jumble of rocks and gravel, which has been rent many

ways by an earthquake."[25] For four hours they searched the area for copper, but in the end they could find only a single piece of any considerable size, which weighed about four pounds. Hearne took it with him to show his superiors—it now sits in a museum in London, England.

The return journey to Prince of Wales's Fort took nearly a year of wandering back across the tundra and along the subarctic forest, following the seasonal migrations of caribou and muskox. They finally arrived at the fort on June 30, 1772. Hearne had been gone for eighteen months and twenty-three days. He'd spent, in total, nearly three years on his quest.

In a certain sense, it was on this long, laborious return journey that Hearne made his real contributions to exploration. As a mapmaker, he was indifferent. His latitude and longitude observations were frequently off—sometimes by significant margins. He estimated the mouth of the Coppermine, for instance, at two hundred miles farther north than it actually is. Compared with his contemporaries like David Thompson and Peter Fidler, Hearne was not much of a surveyor. But his contributions to exploration as a naturalist and ethnologist were beyond compare.

Hearne made extensive and often incredibly detailed notes about the different animals he encountered both on his journeys and in his later years as a fur trader. He discussed not only the "principal Quadrupeds" that inhabit the "high Northern latitudes" but also birds, fish, frogs, insects, molluscs, whales, and walrus.[26] His lengthy discussion of the life habits of the beaver is still considered among the most authoritative ever written, and he discussed muskox, wood bison, and other species in a similarly detailed fashion. In doing so, Hearne made significant contributions to the emerging field of zoology, as he identified and described birds and animals previously unknown in Europe. His first-hand observations of the life history of various animals were eagerly read and incorporated into scientific treatises by naturalists, such as the Swedish classifier Carl Linnaeus—who invented the system of taxonomic classification for plants and animals still used today. Hearne was also one of the earliest writers to treat the grizzly bear with something like scientific curiosity, and his observations were later cited by Charles Darwin in his seminal *On the Origin of Species*, which established the theory of evolution by natural selection.[27]

Equally impressive were Hearne's accounts of aboriginal cultures. Unlike some other European explorers who had little interest in native culture, Hearne was profoundly interested in understanding the lives, beliefs, and cultural practices of his native companions, and he mastered two very different aboriginal languages, even creating a dictionary of one. His writings on northern native cultures are still considered among the most valuable anthropology studies ever made.

In 1776, after more years deep in the interior with the Cree, Hearne was named commander at Prince of Wales's Fort. By this point, the long years he'd spent living as a native in the interior, isolated from other Europeans, had firmly marked him out in his contemporaries' minds as something of an eccentric. Hearne wasn't exactly a typical fur trader—he kept tame beavers as pets, openly rejected Christianity in favour of agnosticism, adopted native modes of travel that entailed living alone for years in Dene society, enjoyed painting landscapes around the fort, and was an avid reader of Voltaire.

In the summer of 1782, a faraway war unexpectedly reached Hearne's post on Hudson Bay. In the distant colonies to the south, the American Revolution was redrawing the map of North America—and France, eager to strike a blow against its British rival, had declared war and intervened on the rebels' side. Now, as Hearne stood on the massive stone ramparts of his fort gazing out across the waters with his telescope, he could scarcely believe what he was seeing—three French warships approaching. The French squadron had almost three hundred men under arms and over a hundred cannons. The odds were hopeless:

to defend the fort Hearne had only thirty-nine civilians under his command. He wisely chose to surrender without a shot rather than spill unnecessary blood. Hearne and the others were taken prisoner on board the French ships and transported to Europe.

Although Matonabbee and Hearne might not be anywhere near as famous as Lewis and Clark, they ought to warrant serious consideration as rival claimants to the title of the greatest exploring duo in North American history. Their shared journey was well over four thousand kilometres in an environment far harsher and more difficult than the lands traversed by Lewis and Clark. Matonabbee and Hearne accomplished nearly all of this on foot—only occasionally using canoes to cross rivers and lakes. And, however imperfectly, they mapped an immense tract of territory that had previously been entirely unknown to outsiders.

But there was no happy ending for Hearne or Matonabbee. Matonabbee committed suicide after the surrender and destruction of Prince of Wales's Fort; his life and prestige had been connected to the fort since childhood. That winter, with no one to provide for them, several of his wives and children starved. As for Hearne, saddened by the loss of his great friend, he returned to the fort after the peace terms restored it to Britain. For several more years, he lived a lonely life there. His reputation as an explorer was attacked by armchair critics, notably the geographer Alexander Dalrymple, who refused to believe Hearne's assertion that there was no river leading from Hudson Bay to the Pacific Ocean. Although Hearne was correct on this essential point, he would not live to see himself vindicated. In 1787, his health failing, he returned to England. He died, impoverished, five years later from an apparent kidney or liver disease. He was forty-seven, unmarried, and with no children. Five years after his death, Hearne's remarkable manuscript of his journey to the Coppermine was finally published. Though he would have been surprised by its success, Hearne's *A Journey from Prince of*

Wales's Fort in Hudson's Bay, to the Northern Ocean remains one of the greatest works of exploration literature—an eloquent testimony to his remarkable friend Matonabbee and their shared journey to the coast of the Arctic Ocean and back again.

FIRST ACROSS NORTH AMERICA: ALEXANDER MACKENZIE'S QUEST

He has made a journey which is the most astonishing that has ever been undertaken, having crossed the whole breadth of the immense continent of North America.

—POLISH DIPLOMAT JULIAN NIEMCEWICZ,

REPORTING ON ALEXANDER MACKENZIE, 1798

Alexander Mackenzie could almost feel the salt air . . . the sea had to be close. To the west, beyond the banks of the river they'd been following, were snow-capped mountains. To the east lay flat ground covered by dwarf spruces and tamaracks. Mackenzie had led his band of men deep into uncharted territory to find the Pacific Ocean. And now, after months of wandering, they had at last reached the ocean—*only there was a problem.* Instead of finding the Pacific, as Mackenzie had intended, they had apparently arrived at the frigid shores of the Arctic Ocean. For days Mackenzie had had nagging doubts about whether they were on the right course. The great river had been taking them northward instead of west—and the longer they followed it, the harder it was to believe that it would lead to the Pacific. The nearby icebergs, whalebones, and Eskimo pretty much seemed to confirm their worst fears.

Despite this initial failure, Alexander Mackenzie ranks as one of Canada's—and indeed the world's—greatest explorers. In a couple of thousand years, when history has mingled with legend, Mackenzie might become to Canada what Odysseus is to Greece. He made not one but two epic journeys off the edge of the map. Thirteen years before Lewis and Clark crossed North America to the Pacific Ocean, Mackenzie did it with fewer resources, less fanfare, and over a more difficult route; he remains the first known person to have traversed the continent from the Atlantic to the Pacific north of Mexico.

Mackenzie certainly looked the part of the hero. He was physically imposing: tall, strong, and strikingly handsome. A contemporary described him as "blond, strong, and well built." Nature had given him, in his own words, "a constitution and frame of body equal to the most arduous undertakings." The only surviving portrait shows a smooth-shaven man with blue eyes, tousled blond hair, and a cleft in his chin. Upper Canada's governor, John Graves Simcoe, called Mackenzie "as intelligent as he is adventurous."[1]

Fittingly for an explorer, Alexander Mackenzie had been born on the wild and forlorn Isle of Lewis in the Outer Hebrides, a chain of windswept islands lying off the northern coast of Scotland. The Gaelic-speaking islanders traced their ancestry back to Vikings who had colonized the isolated islands in the ninth century. The islands ever since had famously bred tough, hardscrabble seafarers, fishermen, and hunters; it was from this adventurous stock that the Hudson's Bay Company did much of its recruiting for the fur trade. Mackenzie was one of four children, and like most explorers who left their mark in Canada's wilderness, he became acquainted with loss and adversity early. His mother died while he was a child and his only brother "followed the sea, and was lost on the coast of Halifax," as the family's record put it.[2] When Alexander was ten his father decided they would sail to Britain's Thirteen Colonies in search of better prospects, with his two sisters left behind in Scotland to be raised by relations.

Tensions had been mounting for years in the American colonies, and shortly after the Mackenzies' arrival, rebellion erupted against the

British crown. The Mackenzie clan was no stranger to violence; they'd fought in many a war in Scotland against both the English and other Scots. But Alexander's father was a Loyalist, and he and his brother, who had earlier migrated to the colonies, enlisted in Loyalist regiments to fight the rebels. Meanwhile, young Alexander was sent north with two of his aunts to live in the Mohawk Valley of northern New York. But when the valley was overrun in 1778 by rebels who pillaged and burned Loyalists' lands, the boy Mackenzie was sent to safety in Montreal.

Montreal at the time was a small cluster of stone houses, churches, and wood dwellings on the edge of the wilderness; black bears, moose, and timber wolves roamed the nearby forests. The majority of the residents were Canadiens, with a small minority of English and Scottish settlers. Alexander briefly attended school there, but by age fifteen he had to earn a living. He found a job as a clerk in the fur trade. In 1780 word came that his father had died—apparently of scurvy—leaving Alexander on his own. For the next five years he worked for the firm of John Gregory, one of the town's independent fur merchants. These experiences as a clerk probably helped Mackenzie improve his handwriting, and he likely also picked up some French during this time—useful for communicating with the Canadien voyageurs who were to be his future exploring companions.

When Mackenzie turned twenty in 1784, Gregory sent him inland to the fur post of Detroit. This was Mackenzie's first taste of wilderness travel, and he evidently enjoyed it. Times were changing; with the conclusion of the American Revolution, the map of North America was to be redrawn—and that meant the fur territories southwest of the Great Lakes would soon be under American control. Fur traders loyal to Britain would find themselves excluded. Accordingly, in 1785 Mackenzie's superiors redirected him to the far west to carry on the trade there. This was his first experience of prolonged wilderness living and the dangers of a trade in which violent scuffles were not infrequent. In 1787, partly in an attempt to prevent bloodshed between rivals, the firm Mackenzie worked for was absorbed by the larger North West Company—a partnership of Montreal-based traders that intended to compete head on with the powerful Hudson's Bay Company.

As part of the merger, Mackenzie was assigned to winter deep in the wilderness of Athabasca with one of the North West Company's most experienced men—the eccentric trader Peter Pond. Pond, a Yankee, had an unfortunate propensity to shoot people he disagreed with. But other than that, he was not a bad fellow. Mackenzie would have to spend the winter with him in an isolated cabin. Fortunately, Pond took a liking to his new young partner. All that winter, by the light of their fire, Pond regaled Mackenzie with tales of his adventures. He explained that he'd almost single-handedly discovered—or nearly discovered—or at any rate conjectured—that there was a river flowing out of a giant lake, Great Slave, that led straight to the Pacific Ocean. Pond even claimed that he'd nearly reached the shores of the Pacific—he'd been within mere days of the ocean when he was forced to turn back, or so he said. Naturally, he would have liked to have had the distinction of following the river to the sea and meeting the Russians who traded there, except that he was now nearly fifty and planning on retiring. But, so Pond told Mackenzie, he saw in him the spirit and grit needed to carry on his explorations. He would lend Mackenzie his maps so that he could be the first to reach the Pacific—and, far more importantly, vindicate to posterity Pond's status as the world's greatest geographer.

The stories of this strange man stirred adventure in Mackenzie's blood; he succumbed to the itch to explore. "The practicability of penetrating across the continent of America," he later wrote, became the "favourite project of my own ambition."[3] In the depths of that long winter, he set off on snowshoes to visit his cousin and closest friend, Roderick McKenzie, who was a trader at his own isolated post in northern Saskatchewan. Mackenzie wanted to discuss with Roderick what

Pond had told him about a route to the Pacific. Roderick—who by fur trader standards was more a scholar than an adventurer—was happy to help his ambitious cousin. Mackenzie would need Roderick's assistance, not only in overseeing the fur-trading posts in his absence, but in establishing a new base of operations farther north, on the shores of the vast Lake Athabasca. With his cousin's help, the new post, named Fort Chipewyan, was built in the summer of 1788. Twenty-five-year-old Mackenzie intended to leave the fort the following spring to seek the Pacific.

For his expedition Mackenzie recruited four tough Canadian voyageurs: Joseph Landry, Charles Ducette, François Barrieau, and Pierre de Lorme. He'd formed a high opinion of voyageurs' skill with birch-bark canoes, once remarking that a "European on seeing one of these slender vessels thus laden, heaped up, and sunk with her gunwale within six inches of the water, would think his fate inevitable . . . but the Canadians are so expert that few accidents happen."[4] Two of the voyageurs were joined by their Cree wives. Mackenzie also recruited a Dene chief, Aw-gee-nah, who was nicknamed "the English chief" owing to his earlier role with the Hudson's Bay Company, where he'd been a follower of Matonabbee. Aw-gee-nah was accompanied by his two wives as well as a couple of his Dene companions and their followers. For good measure, the party also included a stray German, John Steinbruck. Steinbruck's presence in the far west is something of a mystery; he may have come to North America as one of the Hessian mercenaries fighting in the American Revolution and afterward drifted into the fur trade. At any rate, he wound up at Fort Chipewyan at the right time. For the first stage of the journey to Great Slave Lake the expedition was to be accompanied by Laurent Leroux, an experienced Canadian trader who'd been to Great Slave on a trading mission three years earlier. The plan was to have the party split up once they reached the lake, with Leroux remaining behind to establish a trading post there.

The Skálholt Map, made in 1590 by the Icelandic scholar Sigurd Stefánsson, survives in a 1690 copy preserved in Denmark's Royal Library. It is the oldest map that incorporates knowledge of the Vikings' Vinland voyages.

ENTILLES:

DE CANCER:

MER OCCEANE:

MER DESPAIGNE:

MER DE FRANCE:

TIQVE:

Terre du Laborador.

This portion of Pierre Desceliers's huge 1550 world map shows "CANADA" and features unicorns, ostriches, and strange beehive-like dwellings. South is oriented at the top of the map; to make sense of the geography, turn the map

upside down. Jacques Cartier is the bearded figure near the St. Lawrence River.

Samuel de Champlain's masterful map of New France (1632), the result of twenty-five years of collaborative exploration with First Nations and his coureurs de bois, represented a great leap forward in accuracy over all previous maps of Canada.

Jacques-Nicolas Bellin's 1755 map of New France represented the cumulative efforts of more than two centuries of French exploration. Most of the continent's north and west, however, remained *terra incognita* to outsiders.

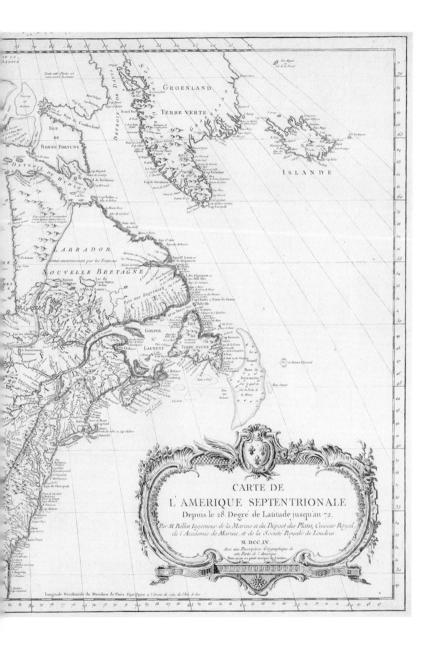

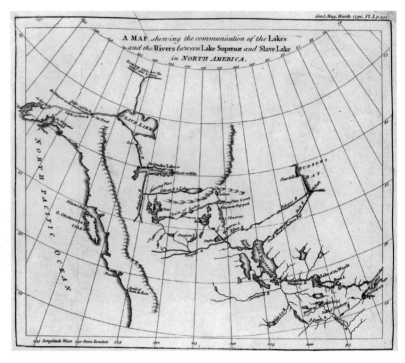

Peter Pond's final revisions to his map of the Northwest (1790) included a nonexistent river flowing from Great Slave Lake to the Pacific Ocean. The river, according to the map, has "Falls said to be the largest in the known world."

Source: Library of Congress Geography and Map Division, Washington, D.C., 20540-4650 USA dcu.

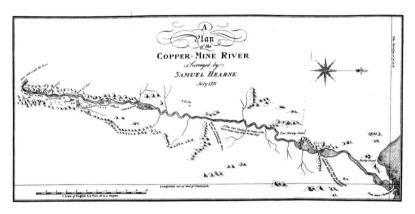

Samuel Hearne's map of the Coppermine River, while pleasing to the eye and fairly accurate in its details of the river, was off by over three hundred kilometres from its true latitude. Regardless, Hearne's journey disproved the idea of a water route from Hudson Bay to the Pacific. This section of Hearne's map shows the Coppermine River meeting the Arctic Ocean (lower right).

Source: Samuel Hearne, *A Journey to the Northern Ocean . . .* (London: A. Strahan and T. Cadell, 1795).

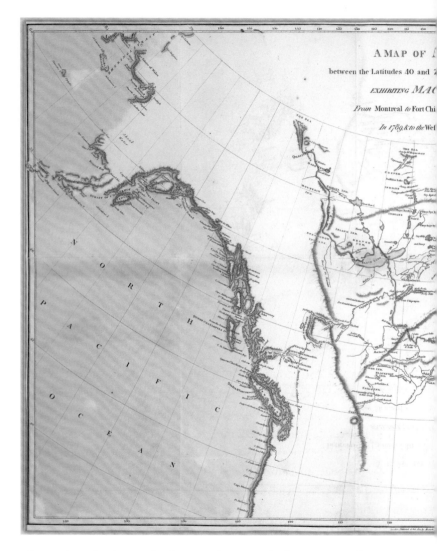

The continent begins to take shape on this map, which accompanied
Alexander Mackenzie's published account of his voyages (1801).
Mackenzie's routes to the Arctic and Pacific oceans are labelled in red
and yellow, respectively. His two epic journeys added fresh details to
maps, but much remained uncharted, and "Canada" still referred only
to the lands east of Lake Superior.

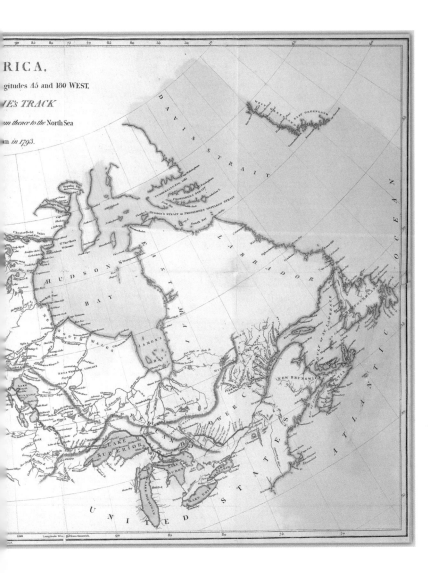

RICA,

gitudes 45 and 180 WEST,

IE'S TRACK

n thence to the North Sea

n in 1793.

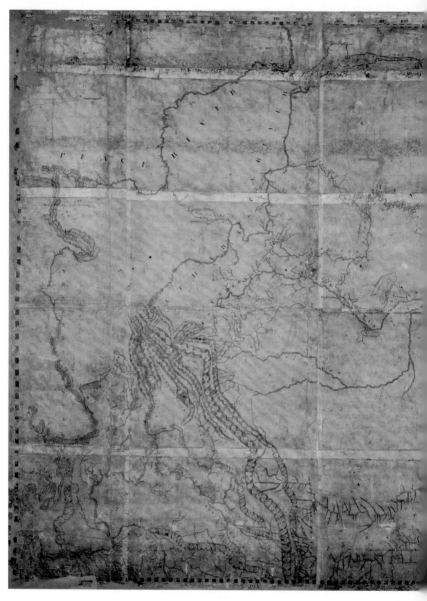

David Thompson's life work found expression in his giant five-by-three-metre map of the Northwest (1814). Lake Superior appears in the lower right; the Pacific coast is at the far left, and Hudson Bay in the upper right. The map is now preserved in Ontario's provincial archives in Toronto.

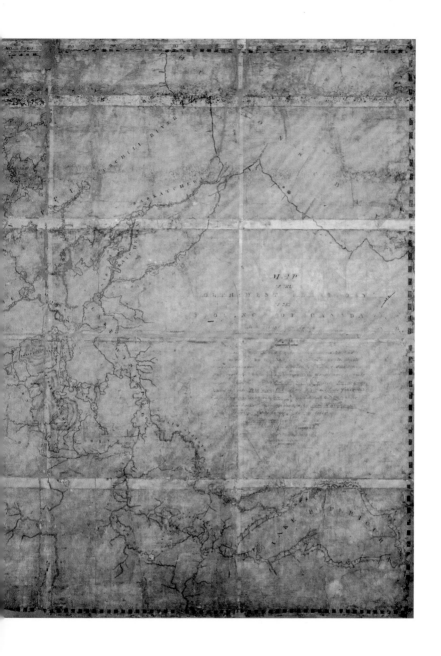

This torn map of Canada's bloodiest border point shows the siege lines and fortifications that witnessed intense combat in the summer of 1814. The map is an 1815 copy of one made by Captain Samuel Romilly and Lieutenant George Philpotts of the British Army's Royal Engineers. South is oriented at the top of the map.

Source: Library and Archives Canada, NMC 22340.

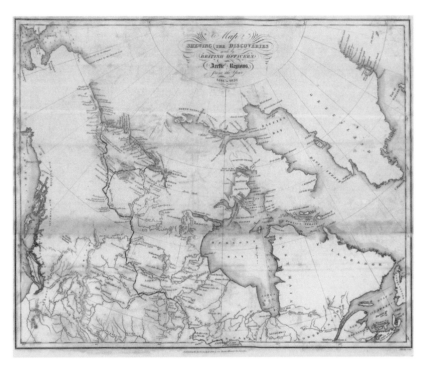

Canada's western and eastern seacoasts had been charted by the 1820s, leaving only the Arctic shores shrouded in mystery. This 1828 map, which accompanied John Franklin's published account of his second overland Arctic expedition, shows his party's route through the Arctic wilderness. Although Franklin's ill-fated party mapped a significant section of the Arctic seacoast, much of the High Arctic remained uncharted until the twentieth century.

Source: Osher Map Library, University of Southern Maine.

While much has changed in the century and half since Confederation, we are lucky that here in Canada many of the forests and rivers that First Nations and explorers trekked through look much the same today as they did when European kings claimed these lands on their maps, and when bears outnumbered humans in what would one day be called "Canada." I just hope we manage to preserve them over the next 150 years.

With the ice freshly melted, on June 3, 1789, the party climbed into their birchbark canoes and set off along the waters of Lake Athabasca. For all of them, it was to become a journey into the unknown—even the Dene guides had never been to the lands they were seeking beyond Great Slave Lake. On the bright side, at least they had Pond's map, which would surely lead them to the Pacific Ocean.

On the second day the group reached the large Slave River, which drains Athabasca northward. The river, however, was full of hazardous rapids, meaning they were often forced to endure long portages. At the head of one such dangerous rapid, a canoe under the care of one of Aw-gee-nah's wives got caught in the current. In desperation, she jumped from the canoe and managed to swim to safety just before the birchbark vessel vanished over a thundering waterfall.

Soon after these dangers, the party arrived at the encouragingly named "Rapids of the Drowned," where three years earlier two canoes had been lost and five men drowned on a voyage organized by Cuthbert Grant, another North West Company trader. Leroux, who'd been part of that voyage, could testify to how powerful the rapids were. The gruelling portages demanded full stomachs; to supplement their bland pemmican rations, the party fished and hunted geese, ducks, and beavers.

Six days into their journey Mackenzie's crew reached the vast, ice-covered waters of Great Slave Lake—an immense freshwater sea larger than Lake Ontario or Erie. The weather had turned bitterly cold, with strong headwinds and freezing rains. When paddling against the biting winds they had to wear their winter mittens to keep their hands from freezing. The cold, however, did have one advantage—it brought relief from the bugs.

The still-frozen lake forced the party to wait until enough open water appeared along the edges to continue. During this time they lived off bird eggs, beavers, wild berries, fish, waterfowl, and one unfortunate sandhill crane. For weeks they had to gingerly navigate in their birchbark canoes through shifting mazes of ice, occasionally becoming trapped for days on islands when the channels through the ice became blocked. At times Mackenzie and his Canadians would split up from the Dene, only to rejoin them every few days in the maze of ice. When more water opened up, Mackenzie ordered his men to raise sails on the canoes. This allowed them to travel much faster, although sailing such shallow, narrow vessels can be extremely hazardous; without the most expert precision, a wave can easily swamp a canoe. When some waves did inevitably spill in, the group would rely on their teakettles to bail out the accumulating water.

As they travelled, Mackenzie took careful notes—working out their latitude from the sun with his sextant, noting the magnetic declination with his compass, and sounding the mysterious depths of the lake: the deepest in North America. After three weeks the party split up, with Leroux and some of the Dene remaining behind on Great Slave while Mackenzie led the rest to find the great river Pond had marked on his map as leading to the Pacific.

While camping on some islands, Mackenzie was surprised to find deserted old campsites and lodges. Aw-gee-nah explained that the tribe of Dene who once lived in the area had been driven away by attacks from their Cree enemies, who lived to the south. Now only a few Dene remained on the lake—and these, though eager to trade with Mackenzie and to assist him, knew little about the great river he was seeking beyond its entrance. Since they lived off the lake's bounty, they had little need to undertake a hazardous journey down a giant river.

As it happened, Aw-gee-nah was also struggling to remember where the river was; he hadn't visited in years, and the labyrinth of ice and islands made locating it difficult. One of the locals they met agreed to escort the party to the start of the river—but when he, too, got confused in the islands and ice, Aw-gee-nah "wanted to shoot him for having undertaken to guide us in a Road he did not know."[5] Mackenzie felt this was a tad harsh. Fortunately for all concerned, the next day, June 29, they at last found the start of the river.

It was a vast, wide waterway unlike any Mackenzie or the voyageurs had ever seen. Nearly four kilometres across, it had a swift current, with different channels around numerous islands. Its high, sandy banks were crowned with forests of aspen, spruce, and poplar; in the distance were mountains whose summits were hidden in the clouds. Beyond these, so Mackenzie hoped, lay the ocean. Their guide, meanwhile, told them that he'd never been beyond this point in the river, and could be of no further help.

What lay before them was, even to a strong, confident young man like Mackenzie, an unsettling prospect. To add to their uneasiness in paddling down an immense river none of them knew anything about, the weather turned against them—the skies darkened as huge bursts of thunder shook the land. For days they suffered rain, fog, and recurring lightning storms. But they pressed on, passing forested islands and occasionally shooting caribou for food. Not knowing what might lie ahead, and given their earlier accident on the Slave River, the party remained on edge. In his journal Mackenzie noted: "We went on very cautiously here expecting every moment that we would come to some great Rapid or Fall. We were so full of this that every person in his turn thought he heard a Noise & the falling of water." [6] And yet, despite Pond's claim that the river contained the largest falls in the known world, they found none.

At night, when they camped beside the river, Mackenzie made a habit of scaling some of the nearby mountains in order to scout out the surrounding lands. Since they were so far north they had ample daylight for these climbing excursions; the sun didn't set until ten p.m., and it rose before two a.m.

Mackenzie, like Shackleton, had a gift for leadership. He knew exactly how to motivate his men to give him their all, and with his iron constitution and remarkable stamina, he expected much from them. Typically he would wake his exhausted companions at three or four a.m. With muscles aching, they'd travel for some fifteen or sixteen hours, sometimes longer if Mackenzie felt the occasion demanded it. And if there were no obstacles like rapids or stormy weather, they would often cover over 140 kilometres a day.

It wasn't until they'd canoed over seven hundred kilometres down the huge river that they encountered any people on it. Smoke rising from the distant bank had attracted their attention, and as they neared the shore, several campfires and small shelters came into view. These natives, it turned out, were a northern branch of the Dene, and had never seen Europeans. Their tools were made of stone and bone; their only garments were animal skins. Mackenzie noted that they had facial tattoos and goose quills pierced through their noses, and that they were armed with clubs, spears, bows, and daggers made from antlers. When his fleet of canoes approached the shore, the alarmed natives fled. Mackenzie ordered his men to keep their distance and allow Aw-gee-nah to try to communicate with them. After much tense discussion, Aw-gee-nah was able to persuade the natives that they came in peace. To show that their intentions were friendly, Mackenzie presented them with a gift of knives, awls, axes, fire steels, flints, rings, and beads.

Fortunately, the language they spoke was a dialect of Athabaskan (the Dene language), and thus they could communicate without difficulty with Aw-gee-nah and his wives and companions. Mackenzie, always interested in learning languages, was himself making strides in Athabaskan as well as Algonquin (the language of the Cree)—in addition to the Gaelic, English, and French he already spoke. Years later, he would attempt to create dictionaries of Athabaskan and Algonquin.

Once the natives had calmed down enough to communicate, they warned against trying to head downriver. Mackenzie noted:

Suffice it to say that they would wish to make us believe that we would be several Winters in getting to the Sea, and that we all should be old Men by the time we would return. That we would have to encounter many Monsters . . . Tho' I put no faith in those Stories, they had a different Effect upon the English Chief [Aw-gee-nah], and his young Men . . . It was their Opinion and wish that we should absolutely return, adding to the above Reasons many others—that they were informed that there were very few Animals below this, and the farther we went the fewer there would be . . . that we should Starve, even if no other accident befell us.[7]

Mackenzie was able to allay these fears and convince his Dene companions to push on. For the next several days a ridge of snowy mountains remained in sight to their west. Mackenzie and one of the young hunters attempted to scale a rocky hill near the river to gain a better view, but the swarms of mosquitoes were so intense that they turned back without reaching the summit. It wasn't the first time, nor would it be the last, that hordes of mosquitoes have foiled an explorer.

Continuing downriver at a rapid pace, they encountered more small bands of Athabaskan-speaking natives along its shores—who tended to flee at their approach. As he'd done before, Mackenzie gave them presents to show that they came in peace. In exchange, the natives offered them fish and arctic hare meat as well as information about what lay downriver. They warned of the people who were said to live at the river's mouth; many told tales of past attacks from these violent strangers. They also spoke of monsters. Some of the natives accompanied Mackenzie's party in their own canoes for a day or two, but generally they were unwilling to go any farther than a few days' travel from the safety of their own camps. The farther they went, the more difficult it became for Mackenzie's Dene companions to understand the local languages as the dialects were increasingly different from their own.

Mackenzie dismissed any concerns about monsters and hostile war parties. But there were plenty of hazards that did alarm him and his Canadian voyageurs. On July 7, the river, which had been an incredible four kilometres wide, suddenly narrowed all the way down to a few hundred metres as it squeezed into a limestone canyon. The sight of this high-walled canyon, with whatever dangers it might hide, "did not at all please us," as Mackenzie laconically noted in his journal.

Mackenzie's band had reached what would later be named the Ramparts, a ten-kilometre-long canyon with imposing cliffs averaging some forty metres high. But after some of the local natives had gone ahead in their canoe, they figured it was safe to follow. Fortunately, they encountered only small rapids in the canyon, which they navigated without trouble.

Three days later the party came upon another twisting canyon, this time with limestone walls that towered nearly a hundred metres. Still flying along with the current and covering well over a hundred kilometres a day, they were nearing the river's vast, labyrinthine delta where the waterway splits into hundreds of different channels around low-lying islands. When Mackenzie took a reading with his sextant, he discovered that they were farther north than he'd expected. In his journal, he confided, "I am much at a loss here how to act being certain that my going further in this Direction will not answer the Purpose of which the Voyage was intended, as it is evident these Waters must empty themselves into the Northern Ocean."[8] Knowing now that they weren't going to reach the Pacific, and despite the hardships and danger, still Mackenzie pushed on. As he put it, "I determined to go to the discharge of those Waters, as it would satisfy Peoples Curiosity tho' not their Intentions."[9]

His Dene companions, however, didn't want to press on. They worried, with good reason, that they'd never make it back upriver before the winter set in; and more than that, there were the Inuit to fear. Mackenzie was able to placate them by promising that they'd continue for only seven more days: after that, regardless of whether they'd reached the ocean, they would turn back.

That night the party camped on one of the delta's hundreds of islands. "I sat up last Night," Mackenzie wrote, "to observe at what time the Sun would set, but found that he did not set at all."[10] This bewildering sight could only mean that they'd passed north of the Arctic Circle and were now in the land of the midnight sun—where, for at least part of the summer, the sun never sinks below the horizon. An amazed Mackenzie woke one of the voyageurs "to see what he never saw before."[11] The half-asleep Canadian, seeing the sun shining and thinking it was time to depart for the day, set about to break camp and rouse the others. Mackenzie could scarcely persuade him that it was still barely past midnight.

They continued paddling through the maze-like delta, snaking between islands. On shore Mackenzie and his companions found evidence of Inuit camps, but no Inuit. The Dene were apprehensive of an ambush. In some places, fresh tracks could be seen in the sand from where the Inuit had apparently been fishing. By now the forests had thinned out and almost completely disappeared. On one island, Mackenzie and his voyageurs discovered two enormous, bizarre skulls with fearsome teeth, evidently from some sort of creature they'd never before imagined. Even Aw-gee-nah and the Dene didn't recognize the strange, unsettling skulls. Maybe these were from the monsters they'd been warned about? Mackenzie, however, eventually concluded that the skulls must be from the beasts known as "Sea Horses," or what we know as walruses. They all agreed that they'd arrived in a very strange place.

Meanwhile, even the guide who'd joined the party from one of the last encampments they'd encountered was at a loss as to how to navigate through the delta. The fleet of canoes passed more islands, and then at last came to a large expanse of water, which the guide claimed to be a lake. Mackenzie decided to camp on the largest island in sight.

While the others set nets to fish, he and Aw-gee-nah hiked to the island's highest point to try to make sense of where they were. In the distance they could see ice floes, and to the south, just barely visible, a chain of mountains. On the hike back to the others Mackenzie noted that they saw many "partridges," snowy owls, and "very beautiful Plovers, the nest of one of those I found with 4 Eggs," as well as an Inuit grave beside which lay a bow, a spear, and a kayak paddle. There were also, rather alarmingly, "Many Bones of white Bears."[12]

It seemed that this vast, ice-choked lake was to be the end of their travels. They had failed to reach the Pacific, and whether they'd reached the Arctic Ocean was unclear, since the guide had insisted it was just a giant lake. Mackenzie wrote:

> My men express much sorrow that they are obliged to return without
> seeing the Sea, in which I believe them sincere for we marched exceed-
> ing hard coming down the River, and I never heard them grumble; but
> on the contrary in good Spirits, and in hopes every day that the next
> would bring them to the *Mer d'Ouest*, and declare themselves now and
> at any time ready to go with me wherever I choose to lead them.[13]

But Mackenzie and his voyageurs, as well as the Dene, were in for a surprise. In his July 13 journal entry he recorded:

> Soon after we went to Bed last Night (if I may use that expression,
> in a country where the sun never sinks beneath the horizon) some
> of them were obliged to get up and move the Baggage on account of
> the water rising.[14]

The tide was coming in—this was no lake, it was the Arctic Ocean! They had reached the sea after all.

Mackenzie and his men devoted the next three days to exploring the barren island and surrounding waters. With their nets they caught a variety of fish, including ones they'd never seen before. There were other surprises, too: one of the voyageurs spotted something bobbing in the distant sea. The Canadians, accustomed to a life spent in the woods and unfamiliar with the sea, thought they were chunks of ice— but then Mackenzie recognized the "ice" as submerging whales. Excitedly, he and the others pushed off in their canoes to pursue them. But thick fog made it difficult to see, and they were unable to get close. Perhaps these whales were the "monsters" the natives upriver had warned about. That Mackenzie and his voyageurs would risk chasing after whales on the frigid, icy waters of the Arctic Ocean in a mere birchbark canoe, when all it would take to drown them was a flick of a whale's tail, might seem reckless. But these men made their living by taking risks; they were seasoned adventurers seldom deterred by danger. If they hadn't been, they never would have set off deep into uncharted territory.

When the fog started to clear, Mackenzie, still overcome by curiosity, ordered his men to prepare the canoes; he wanted to investigate the pack ice. They paddled out, unable to see much through the lingering fog as their canoe bobbed with the ocean swells. Suddenly a hard northeast wind arose. Waves began to lap over the canoe, forcing two men to bail while the others paddled hard for the shore. They barely escaped disaster. The Dene, meanwhile, had an even narrower escape when their canoe filled with water; fortunately, the wind drove their swamped canoe onto an island.

After this adventure on what is now called the Beaufort Sea, Mackenzie decided to stick to the leeward of the islands as they continued to explore. He hoped to encounter Inuit who might be able to tell him more about the surrounding territory. But, despite plenty of evidence of past encampments, no people were to be found. So on July 16, once they'd measured the tides on the island and killed some swans, cranes, and a luckless snowy owl for food, the party began their gruel-ling journey back upriver.

It would be a race against time to get back to their fort before the onset of winter. The swift current made paddling in many places impossible; to make headway, they had to track their canoes upstream with rope while hiking on shore. It was exhausting work, not helped by the hordes of blood-sucking insects and recurring storms. But Mackenzie kept his men motivated, and given that they still had to find time to hunt and fish, they maintained an almost superhuman pace— averaging approximately forty-five kilometres a day upriver.

Ten days into their return journey, the party encountered another small group of Dene. From them Mackenzie heard some intriguing news: on the other side of the mountains lay an even larger river. This river, they said, was home to people who "are Big and very wicked [and] kill Common Men with their Eyes." These bizarre people, the natives claimed, "make Canoes larger than Ours" and hunted "a kind of a large Beaver the Skin of which is almost Red."[15] Such fantastic stories, likely passed down through many intermediaries and embel-lished with each retelling, were nevertheless of sensational interest to Mackenzie. It seemed to be a clue that there was, after all, a route to the Pacific. The "canoes larger than ours" might refer to the huge dugout canoes of the west coast, and the large beaver with almost-red skin might be the Pacific sea otter.

Mackenzie was keen to get as much information as he could about what lay beyond the mountains. It was still his ambition to find a way across the continent. When on the following day he asked the natives more about these stories, and especially the river said to lie on the other side of the mountains, they told him "they knew nothing about it but hearsay, that none of them were further than the Mountains on the other side of the River, that they were told it was a much larger River than this, that it ran towards the Midday Sun."[16] Mackenzie offered a gift of trade beads to anyone who could draw him a map. One man traced a long waterway, though he'd only heard stories about it. Mackenzie assumed that this was his ticket to the Pacific—that the river he was looking at in the sand led to the inlet Captain Cook had seen when mapping the Pacific coastline from his ship. Mackenzie asked if the mapmaker would go with him across the mountains to find the river, but "this he would by no means consent to, alledging [sic] that he did not know the Road."[17] If Mackenzie wanted to reach the Pacific, he'd have to find his own way.

On August 22, thirty-seven days after leaving the Arctic Ocean, the party arrived back at the waters of Great Slave Lake. Crossing Great Slave—amid fierce winds, huge waves, and storms—was fraught with danger. Some days they were completely windbound. Mackenzie and his voyageurs often took terrible risks, traversing many miles of open lake with their canoes under sail whenever they could. The canoes would at times become separated from each other and take on water that had to be frantically bailed out. Even modern canoeists, equipped with spray covers, lifejackets, and GPS, would almost never attempt such a hazardous crossing. But Mackenzie was racing against time. By September 3, they had escaped the dangers of the open lake and arrived back on the Slave River. From there it was another nine days to their isolated fort on Lake Athabasca, concluding a journey of 102 days in which they'd covered over four thousand kilometres.

Though he couldn't have known it at the time, the river Mackenzie and his companions had explored is the longest waterway in all of Canada, and the thirteenth longest in the world. Its immense drainage basin represents a fifth of Canada's landmass. But Mackenzie felt more a sense of failure than of accomplishment. In a letter, he called it the "River Disappointment" since it hadn't led him to the Pacific as Pond had claimed it would. He noted dryly, "It proved that Mr. Pond's Assertion was nothing but conjecture."[18] Today, of course, it's known as the Mackenzie River, but Mackenzie himself never called it that. In his journal, he simply referred to it as the great or grand river—a translation of the Dene name. His journey to the shores of the Arctic Ocean had once again proven, as Hearne's had, that there was no mythical Northwest Passage that led straight from Hudson Bay west to the Pacific—a fact that armchair geographers in Europe were having a hard time accepting.

Mackenzie spent the winter at his Fort Chipewyan, giving him plenty of time to mull over his voyage, the maps he'd made of it, and the errors on Pond's charts. Although he'd just led one of the great journeys in exploration history, he was not at all satisfied. He still dreamed of finding a route to the Pacific.

✳

When the ice melted, Mackenzie would have to make the long journey all the way to Lake Superior to meet with the other North West Company partners and report to them about what he had learned. That spring, while making his way there, Mackenzie crossed paths at a trading post with one of the rival Hudson's Bay Company surveyors, Philip Turnor. Turnor, who'd been trained in the latest surveying instruments, seems to have made Mackenzie self-conscious about his own lack of cartographic training. Indeed, Mackenzie was a bit sensitive on this subject. In what must have been an agonizing decision for a man of action under the spell of exploration, he decided that he had no choice but to pry himself away from the Northwest and journey to England that winter to improve his mapmaking abilities. For his second attempt to cross the continent, Mackenzie was determined to be better prepared.

Mackenzie had never been to England—to him it was as much un-explored territory as the Arctic tundra. Now, after a long sea voyage across the Atlantic, he arrived for the first time in the bustling metrop-olis of London—surely a cultural shock for a Canadian fur trader.

This was the London of Jane Austen and Edmund Burke. Across the channel, revolutionary fervour had led the French to imprison their king and queen and proclaim a republic. Mackenzie, accustomed to a life spent around campfires in the wilderness, eating caribou and beaver, must have felt out of place. Over the winter he spent in London, he tried to make himself inconspicuous and avoid socializing—remaining almost obsessively focused on his mission. He purchased the surveying tools he would need to determine longitude—something that had previously been impossible—and learned to use them. When the spring of 1792 arrived, he wasted no time in boarding a ship bound for Canada.

Mackenzie's plan was to cross the length and breadth of North America from the Atlantic all the way to the Pacific coastline, a distance of well over four thousand kilometres as the crow flies. Of course, in practice the route was much longer, given all the snaking rivers, lakeshores, portages, mountains, and other detours that stood in the way. And yet despite Mackenzie's new tools and rigorous preparations, he still wasn't particularly well equipped for the monumental task that lay before him: mapping a route across the mountains to the distant ocean. Ideally, expeditions of Mackenzie's era ought to have included the following equipment if they were to successfully measure latitude and longitude: "a transit instrument, a timepiece, a refracting telescope powerful enough to observe Jupiter's satellites, a thermometer, barometer, and an azimuth-theodolite."[19] Mackenzie had only a simple compass, an old sextant, a basic chronometer for tracking time, and a telescope. Still, although none of his gear was cutting edge, it was an improvement over the bare-bones instruments he'd had on his first journey.

In 1792 Mackenzie was back at his fort on Lake Athabasca, a place that—at nearly three thousand kilometres from the settlements of Upper Canada—was by most people's standards already off the edge of the map. Mackenzie's new expedition was to be even smaller than his first, consisting of a mere ten men. In contrast, the Lewis and Clark expedition that set off in 1804 from the United States to seek the Pacific Ocean numbered thirty-three people. And a proposal from a British Army officer, made the same year as Mackenzie left on his quest, called for a hundred-man strong party, backed up by supply ships, to round the Horn to the Pacific coastline and chart a path across the continent—a proposal that was quietly dropped after learning of Mackenzie's audacious undertaking.

In the wilderness of Athabasca, the pool of expedition applicants wasn't large—but they were all, by necessity, experienced in the wilderness. As his second-in-command, Mackenzie selected his fellow trader Alexander Mackay, who became his close friend. Mackay, as it happened, was to marry the daughter of Jean-Étienne Waddens, the Swiss ex-soldier whom Peter Pond had murdered. That unfortunate woman, like her mother, would also lose her husband to violence: in 1811 Mackay was serving on board the merchant ship *Tonquin* on the Pacific coast when he and the rest of the crew were massacred by a Nootka war party. Mackenzie also chose six Canadian voyageurs—two who'd gone with him on his first journey, Joseph Landry and Charles Ducette, and four new faces: François Courtois, Baptist Bisson, Jacques Beauchamp, and François Beaulieux. Besides the voyageurs, Mackenzie had two young Dene natives from the Beaver tribe who lived in what is now northern Alberta, one named Cancre and the other whose name is not known. Last but not least, the party included Mackenzie's large, faithful dog.

On October 10, 1793, "having made every necessary preparation," Mackenzie and his party set off from Fort Chipewyan to seek the Pacific Ocean.[20] The first leg of their journey was through relatively familiar territory; they crossed Lake Athabasca to the mouth of the Peace River and then worked their way upstream. Mackenzie had made preparations for them to overwinter on the Peace so that when the snows melted in the spring they'd have the best possible chance of making it over the formidable Rocky Mountains, down to the Pacific, and back again before freeze-up. No one had any idea—not even Mackenzie's two Dene companions—about what they might encounter in the mountains.

Ten days into their journey, already facing early snows and freezing temperatures, Mackenzie's band arrived at a small North West Company outpost on the Peace River—the last one they would see. This post was under the care of Mackenzie's friend John Finlay. Mackenzie had wanted to include Finlay in the expedition, but ultimately ruled him out, since privately, he felt "he is too weak a constitution."[21] Mackenzie and his crew spent a few days at Finlay's post before setting off again. By the end of October, with the weather worsening, they'd reached the forks of the Peace River. Mackenzie's party took the western fork, and then, a short distance up, halted to build a fort that would serve as their winter quarters.

A few months earlier, Mackenzie had sent two Canadians ahead with instructions to begin building a fort on the site—to clear trees and square timbers for buildings and to fell logs for a palisade. Now all hands were set to work finishing the log cabins before the weather worsened. Meanwhile, about seventy members of the Dene tribe that hunted and trapped in the area had come to meet Mackenzie. Mackenzie, who by now was well-known throughout the district for his travels and his standing in the fur trade, was greeted with much celebration and smoking of peace pipes. These Dene, known as the "Beaver Indians" to the Canadians, hunted the territories around the Peace River and so were unable to tell Mackenzie much about the far side of the mountains. They were, in fact, relatively recent arrivals in the area, having been driven westward in warfare with more powerful Cree tribes that lived to the east.

By Christmas Mackenzie was able to move from his tent into one of the finished log dwellings, and soon the other buildings were complete. They christened their little establishment on the edge of the known

world "Fort Fork." Over the winter the group passed their time chopping firewood, hunting, and in Mackenzie's case, taking notes on the
birds that overwintered. He also worked on his astronomical observations of Jupiter's moons, part of the complicated process needed to
determine longitude. His observations were generally impressive—
checked against modern scientific measurements, Mackenzie's recorded
coordinates were usually only slightly off.

Mackenzie was also busy acting as a self-taught doctor and surgeon
to both his men and the local Dene, who would occasionally show up at
the fort with various injuries. He treated these as best as he could. One
native had come to the fort with a severely injured hand from the burst-
ing of a gun; Mackenzie carefully dressed his wound three times a day
until it healed, winning the man's lasting respect and friendship.

Much of the winter was grim and monotonous. In one of his journal
entries Mackenzie noted, "On the 22nd a wolf was so bold as to venture
among the Indian lodges, and was very near carrying off a child."[22]
Sometimes Mackenzie and his men would hear of internal quarrels
among their neighbours, the Beaver tribe. In one incident, a man was
stabbed to death in an argument about a woman. By April, the snows
had melted; Mackenzie wrote in his journal, "Mr. Mackay brought me
a bunch of flowers of pink colour, and a yellow button, encircled with
six leaves of a light purple."[23]

With the snows melting, the birds returning, and Mr. Mackay picking wildflowers—they could only mean one thing: the time had come
to head into the mountains. Mackenzie ordered that final preparations
be made. The birchbark canoes were freshly sealed with spruce and
pine resin and loaded up with the winter's supply of furs, which would
have to be taken to the eastern trading posts; Mackenzie assigned two
voyageurs not included in the expedition to transport them. As for his
own party, they were to travel west in a single large canoe, measuring
some twenty-five feet long and nearly five feet wide. They loaded it

with three thousand pounds of provisions, including arms, ammunition, tents, tools, kettles, and presents for the various tribes they expected to encounter. Then Mackenzie, his six Canadian voyageurs, two Dene youths, his friend Alexander Mackay, and his dog climbed into the canoe. As they pushed off from the bank, Mackenzie noted: "My winter interpreter . . . whom I left here to take care of the fort . . . shed tears on the reflection of those dangers which we might encounter in our expedition, while my own people offered up their prayers that we might return in safety."[24]

Mackenzie pushed his men to their utmost on the journey, often starting the hard day of paddling, poling, and lining the canoe upriver at four a.m. Their heavily laden canoe had to be repaired regularly to deal with leaks. For food, they hunted elk and bison. Five days after leaving the fort, Mackenzie noted finding the tracks of a large, unfamiliar animal:

> We perceived along the river tracks of large bears, some of which were nine inches wide, and of a proportionate length. We saw one of their dens, or winter quarters, called *watee*, in an island, which was ten feet deep, five feet high, and six feet wide; but we had not yet seen one of those animals. The Indians entertain great apprehension of this kind of bear, which is called the grisly bear, and they never venture to attack it but in a party of at least three or four.[25]

A few days later Mackenzie wrote in his journal, "We this day saw two grisly and hideous bears."[26] On these "hideous" bears Mackenzie made no further comment.

Mackenzie's two Dene companions had never ventured this far upriver—but they had once been part of a war party that went into the mountains to attack the tribes that lived there, and warned that these people might prove hostile. Nine days into their expedition, after they'd passed numerous islands and tributary streams, the snow-capped peaks of the towering Rocky Mountains suddenly loomed into sight. Despite the formidable barrier they represented, Mackenzie recorded that "they formed a very agreeable object to every person in the canoe, as we attained the view of them much sooner than we expected."[27]

Over the following days the mountains loomed ever larger as they fought their way up the river's swift current. Frequently, the canoe was damaged by rocks in the water and had to be repaired. There were hazards above water, too: Mackenzie noted that canoeing near the river's high banks "was rendered very dangerous, from the continual falling of large stones, from the upper parts of them."[28] To lighten the canoe's load over difficult stretches, Mackenzie, Mackay, the two Dene hunters, and Mackenzie's dog travelled on foot. In his journal, Mackenzie gave few details about his canine companion, but it was most likely a type of sled dog; at any rate, it was clearly a large, strong breed, for he noted that when coming upon a herd of bison, he "sent our dog after the herd, and a calf was soon secured by him."[29]

When the party returned with the skinned bison calf for dinner, they found the river running through a steep canyon full of furious whitewater rapids, rock islands, and waterfalls. Mackenzie and the voyageurs, after scouting out the situation, felt that their best chance of making headway was to cut across to the far side of the river and then line the canoe with ropes up the rocky shore of one of the islands. They managed to do so, though not without damaging the canoe on some rocks. The voyageurs, however, were so expert at quickly repairing canoes that they were soon underway again. They lined the canoe farther up the canyon, bypassing waterfalls, until they were confronted with violent rapids that blocked their path. There was no choice but to recross the river back to the other side. Mackenzie wrote that "the traverse was rendered extremely dangerous, not only from the strength of the current, but by cascades just below us . . . Mr. Mackay, and the

Indians, who observed our manoeuvres from the top of a rock, were in continual alarm for our safety."[30]

Although they managed to make it across, the far side was little better than what they'd just escaped from—more furious whitewater blocked their path. To make headway, the voyageurs had to scramble along the rocky banks as they pulled the canoe up the rapids with rope. Meanwhile, Mackenzie climbed up the bank to join the others. Watching from atop the cliff, he couldn't help noting that "one false step of those who were attached to the line, or the breaking of the line itself, would have consigned the canoe, and every thing it contained, to instant destruction."[31] Fortunately, the rope held, and they made it out of the immediate rapids, avoiding the occasional rocks that kept crashing down the steep banks—any one of which might have flattened them.

The next day they pushed deeper into the wild canyon, encountering obstacles even more difficult than what they had so far faced. In places, the canyon's vertical walls and furious current forced them to edge precariously along the cliff face, loose stones toppling at their footsteps into the deadly rapids below. The men slowly shuffled sideways along the cliff edge, backs to the canyon wall, until finally they reached an opening where they could stand freely and together heave on a rope to tow the canoe toward them. As they were hauling it upriver, the canoe was badly smashed on some rocks. Fortunately, they'd packed enough birchbark and pine resin to repair it; but knowing that further damage was inevitable, Mackenzie dispatched two men to climb the cliff and gather more birchbark.

As it was, their progress upriver had slowed to a crawl because of the endless rapids and other obstacles in the hellish canyon. They were repeatedly forced to unload the canoe, portage, line, pole, and furiously paddle across to the opposite side of the canyon, and try whatever they could to make their way up it. In many places, the current nearly dashed the canoe to pieces against the rocks.

After several days, there was still no end in sight. The river ahead, as far as they could make out, was blocked by violent rapids. Around their fire at night Mackenzie heard his men begin to grumble for the first time. "It began to be murmured on all sides," he wrote, "that there was no alternative but to return."[32]

Such concerns were perfectly understandable—raging mountain rivers were never meant to be canoed *upstream*. But Mackenzie had already met with failure once on his quest for the Pacific, and he would not, under any circumstance it seemed, consider giving up. He resolved to climb out of the canyon and go ahead on foot to scout a way forward—an arduous trek that revealed no end to the cascades and rapids. Their only hope, Mackenzie concluded, was to try to cut overland, portaging the canoe and all their provisions, until the river became less dangerous.

Portaging their canoe, provisions, and themselves over the mountain proved to be a gruelling undertaking. They had to first cut a path through the woods, clearing away the undergrowth and something aptly called "devil's club"—a tall shrub with sharp spines that when brushed against leaves a painful, itchy rash. This wasn't the only surprise the mountains had in store. Mackay, while scouting ahead on the stony mountain slopes, discovered "several chasms in the earth that emitted heat and smoke."[33] In this distant land, these mysterious chasms must have seemed like something out of an old legend about monsters and orcs. They were, most likely, natural smouldering coal seams, some of which can still be found in the Rockies.

At night, while the others slept, Mackenzie would stay up to take observations of Jupiter's moons and work out their longitude; during the day he'd gaze at the sun with his sextant to determine their latitude. Their journey was, after all, about expanding the map beyond the known world.

After four days of hauling their canoe and provisions over the mountain, they at last reached a spot where it looked like the river might allow for navigation. The voyageurs cut long poles to push the canoe upstream; then, on May 25, they relaunched it in the river beneath towering, snow-crowned mountains that rose to heights of some two thousand metres. Frigid gusts of mountain air chilled the party; they took to wearing their blankets to keep warm. As they struggled onward the mountains seemed to close in around them, blocking out the sun and leaving them shivering as they paddled and poled their canoe in the shadows.

One morning, after a stormy night, Mackenzie was awoken by the barking of his dog, who was running back and forth in an agitated state. At first it seemed that nothing was amiss; the party packed up and began their toils upriver. The dog, however, continued to bark, until at last they spotted what was causing the alarm—a large wolf was following them along a ridge overlooking the river. The wolf had apparently been attracted by the scent of fresh meat from an elk they'd killed.

After portaging around more waterfalls, they soon came to a fork in the river. The western branch looked more promising. But Mackenzie recalled a warning he'd heard from an old Dene hunter back at their fort: don't be deceived by the forks. Many winters ago, as a young man, the hunter told him, he'd gone into the mountains, finding that the western fork was "soon lost in various branches among the mountains." But the northern one, he said, led to a portage that would take them to a large river.[34] It was this river that Mackenzie wanted to find— he hoped it would drain into the Pacific—and he trusted the old man's story. He ordered his voyageurs to paddle for the northern fork.

To lighten their load, Mackay and the two Dene members of the party hiked overland while Mackenzie and the voyageurs guided the canoe along. That night, when the two groups met back up at their campfire, Mackay and the Dene arrived in a state of panic—during their overland trek they swore they heard gunshots, which, they assumed, could only come from Cree war parties. This news put Mackenzie's men on edge; they extinguished their fire, loaded their muskets, and kept their daggers close. The party fanned out across the island they'd camped on, each taking cover behind the foot of a tree. On guard, they "passed an uneasy and restless night" until dawn.[35]

The next day, as they continued upriver, Mackenzie noted a spot where two large trees had recently crashed into the river from the erosion of the banks. These, he concluded, were the "gunshots" Mackay and the others had heard.

As they penetrated deeper into the mountains, Mackenzie took Mackay and the Dene with him to scale a small peak and see what lay ahead. But from its summit all that was visible were unbroken chains of snow-capped peaks in all directions. Returning somewhat downcast, they were surprised to find that the voyageurs were nowhere in sight. Alarmed, they fired their guns—but the only reply was the eerie echo of the gunshots through the surrounding mountains. They split up, with two men searching upriver and two downriver, but still there was no sign of the missing voyageurs. Horrible thoughts about what might have happened began to form in their minds. As darkness descended they made a makeshift bed of evergreen boughs and prepared to spend the night under the stars. With the canoe gone, they were stranded in the mountains.

Just as they began contemplating how to build a raft to escape from the mountains, Mackay found the voyageurs. The canoe, it turned out, had been severely damaged in a rapid, delaying them for hours. Immensely relieved to be reunited, the party celebrated their deliverance with a draught of rum each. Two days later, after enduring more hardships, they were rewarded with a delicacy for dinner—roast porcupine. In addition to their dried pemmican, they lived off wild rice and parsnips, various berries, and the animals they hunted.

On June 9, with the river narrowing as they worked their way farther and farther up, the party encountered two natives, armed with bows and spears, on the banks. At first they were hostile, conveying with shouts and gestures that Mackenzie and his men weren't welcome. But the dialect they spoke was understood by Mackenzie's Dene companions, who were able to explain that they weren't looking to fight. After some hesitation the men welcomed the explorers ashore; then out from hiding emerged another man, two women, and some children— the whole of their hunting band. Although they'd heard of white people, they'd never met any, and certainly didn't expect to encounter any high up in the mountains. The strangeness of Mackenzie and his men's appearance caused no end of wonder.

That night, as they camped together, Mackenzie through his interpreters asked the natives about the surrounding territory. In this he was disappointed, as the natives knew little about what lay beyond the vast mountains. Their iron tools, which showed they had some indirect contact with Europeans, were traded from other interior tribes, who in turn got them from still more remote tribes, all the way out to the vast "Stinking Lake," a phrase Mackenzie took to mean the sea. At this place, it was said, came "vessels as big as islands."[36] The small band lived up in the mountains for fear of hostile tribes, and would not, no matter what Mackenzie promised, agree to accompany them westward.

This was discouraging news. But by now Mackenzie was a practised veteran in dealing with strangers, and he knew that he might have more luck once they became better acquainted. As they sat feasting on trout and chatting around a shared fire, he continued to communicate through his interpreters—occasionally making out some of the words himself, as he'd picked up quite a bit of Athabaskan.

Mackenzie knew enough of the language to recognize that one of the local men had said something about a great river—and pressed him to tell him more about it. The man explained that it flowed toward the midday sun, and that a branch of it could be reached by portages through various lakes, starting from the river they now camped on. But the inhabitants near this large river, he warned, were a warlike people who'd kill anyone they met. Unlike the tribes east of the Rockies, they lived in big houses on islands. Mackenzie, excited by this news, snatched up a sheet of birchbark and some charcoal from the edge of the fire. Could he draw them a map?

This the man happily and quickly did. Staring at the completed birchbark map, Mackenzie felt a new sense of optimism—*this could be their route to the Pacific*. Hopefully, it would prove a better map than Pond's. The next morning, before they got underway, Mackenzie thanked the man with gifts of tools, pemmican, trade beads, and other items.

Another day's travel brought the party, just as the map indicated, to the source of the Peace River. The fishing in this beautiful, lonely lake was spectacular. Near its placid waters Mackenzie saw many birds— including a "beautiful humming-bird," swans, and geese—as well as beavers and moose.[37] In the surrounding mountains were strange animals that he and the Canadians had never seen before: majestic bighorn sheep, white mountain goats, and whistling marmots. As they left the lake, carrying their heavy loads and the birchbark canoe, Mackenzie's band were crossing the Continental Divide—to the east, all waters drained to the Arctic, to the west, the Pacific. With this portage finished, for the first time Mackenzie's party would finally get a chance to travel downstream.

Alas, it was not that simple. They found their progress out of the lake blocked by logjams and fallen trees across a small stream they intended to follow; they had to clear a way through with their axes. Then, after they'd pushed through these obstacles, the creek began to grow rapidly bigger from all the mountain streams, swollen with the spring runoff, feeding into it. Soon they could hear the bone-chilling roar of whitewater waiting downriver. Mackay, the two Dene hunters, and the dog prudently went ahead on foot while Mackenzie and the Canadians prepared to run the rapids.

Despite their skill, the frail birchbark canoe was no match for the thunderous rapids; almost immediately they struck a rock, causing water to gush in. The fierce current spun them sideways, throwing the canoe with tremendous violence against more rocks and all but destroying it. Mackenzie and the voyageurs were flung into the raging mountain river, where they struggled to keep their heads above water. They clung for dear life to the wreckage of the canoe as the current sucked them down through wild cataracts. At last, the current carried them to a small eddy. Mackay and the others, who'd been racing along the rocky banks, horrified by the unfolding scene, now rushed to their aid, wading into the swift water and trying to save as much of their gear as they could. Mackenzie, meanwhile, held on to the ruined canoe until everything was transported to shore. Then he too staggered out of the icy water, his body numb from hypothermia as he collapsed on the riverbank.

The men made a large fire to warm themselves, and then contemplated their situation. They'd lost all their musket balls, which they depended on for hunting, as well as various other items. And with their canoe utterly wrecked, it seemed they had no choice but to turn back. Mackenzie sat by the fire and said nothing.

After they'd finished their meal, along with a few rounds of rum, Mackenzie finally spoke. He had no intention of turning back. He urged them to think of "the honour of conquering disasters, and the disgrace that would attend them on their return home" without having reached their goal. He further reminded them of "the courage and resolution which was the peculiar boast of the North men."[38] As for the lost bullets, Mackenzie said they had buckshot that could be melted down to make new ones. Once again, this iron-willed explorer demonstrated his gift for inspiring others to follow him. It was heartily agreed that they would push on.

The next day half the party went to search the woods for birchbark to rebuild the canoe while the rest hiked along the river to scout out what lay ahead. When the all-important bark was gathered, the voyageurs set to work on the canoe. The scouts returned the next day, their clothes tattered and their faces cut from hacking through dense forest, to report that as far as they could see the river was an endless succession of falls and rapids. It appeared as if they would have to portage a great distance.

Mackenzie divided the party: some would clear a trail through the forest and haul their provisions, and the rest would gingerly guide the canoe downriver—which, they hoped, would be safer now that the canoe wasn't heavily loaded. It was painstakingly slow going. Those blazing a trail were tormented by sandflies and mosquitoes; much of their portage took them through a morass of swamp, which they sank into under the weight of their loads. Meanwhile, the canoe was again punctured and had to be repaired. Several waterfalls blocked all progress by water, forcing them to carry the canoe across the swamps. And at one point, their faithful dog fell into the river and was swept under a logjam—but to the relief of all, Mackay and the hunters managed to save him.

It took five terrible days of almost unceasing effort, struggle, and hardship, but at last Mackenzie's party made it through their portages and emerged on the banks of a larger, more navigable river—the river marked on their birchbark map. Their plan was to relaunch the canoe, and with luck, drift downriver all the way to the ocean.

Over the following days they paddled downriver—passing through canyons, running rapids, portaging where necessary, and coming across the abandoned remains of cedar houses unlike anything they'd seen east of the Rockies. At one point, when smoke was spotted rising from the forest, Mackenzie's two Dene companions went to investigate. They found two unfriendly natives who spoke a language they couldn't understand. Alarmed by the sight of these strangers, the natives fired arrows; fortunately the Dene were able to take cover behind some trees, and made it back to the canoe without further trouble.

Eventually they encountered more natives. These strangers, doubtless surprised and alarmed by their appearance, almost immediately fired arrows at them. Mackenzie's party assumed this meant that they weren't welcome. They managed to paddle outside their range, keeping to the opposite riverbank for safety. Here, they disembarked. But rather than flee, Mackenzie wanted to show that their intentions were peaceful. He had his men stay put while he rather riskily wandered alone down the riverbank, figuring the natives might be more willing to talk if he was alone (but just to be safe, he tucked a couple of flintlock pistols in his belt, along with the sword he always wore). Once he was separated from the others, Mackenzie used hand gestures to try to persuade two of the natives to cross the river. They were hesitant at first, remaining offshore in their canoe with weapons close at hand. Mackenzie laid out beads, looking glasses, and other gifts as a sign of friendship. After a short while, the natives came ashore and accepted the gifts.

They had never encountered Canadians or Europeans before. But as it turned out, they spoke a dialect of Athabaskan, and thus could be understood by Mackenzie's Dene companions. When their apprehension had subsided, the Canadians invited the strangers to come across to their camp. The other members of their band were nervous at first, but Mackenzie offered more gifts as a token of friendship.

The rest of the day and the night were spent camping with the natives. Meanwhile, the voyageurs worked on repairing their canoe and searching for more birch trees, since the natives had warned them that there were no birch downriver. As for the river itself, they said it did flow to the sea, but that numerous dangerous rapids and falls made the route unnavigable by canoe. Even more alarming, they said that the tribes downriver would kill anyone who approached. These violent tribes, they told Mackenzie, lived in underground houses—which may sound far-fetched, but is an accurate description of the dwellings made by the Shuswap tribe of central British Columbia.

Two of these natives agreed to accompany the party as guides. Mackay volunteered to go with one in a small canoe, while the other rode in the large canoe with Mackenzie and the others. Downriver, they soon met with various people, all of whom reacted with similar alarm at first sight of their canoes, but became friendly after presents were offered and their peaceful intentions explained. From an old man at one of these encampments, Mackenzie learned more about the great river they were now following: it was very long and perilous, and along it were many different tribes that spoke a variety of languages and were often at war with one another. The old man drew Mackenzie a map on birchbark, although he'd never gone all the way down the river, which was considered too dangerous a journey to be undertaken. Instead, Mackenzie learned, their custom was to travel overland through the mountains to the seacoast. Apparently it could be reached more easily that way than by following the river's long, tortuous course, which led far to the south. And the tribes that lived on the sea immediately to the west, they said, traded with white people who came in large "canoes"; it was from these tribes that they themselves traded for iron, copper, and other European goods.

Paddling down an unknown river full of lethal rapids and waterfalls and inhabited by tribes that might want to kill them didn't sound all that appealing to Mackenzie's men. He noted, "My people had listened with great attention to the relation which had been given me, and it seemed to be their opinion, that it would be absolute madness to attempt a passage through so many savage and barbarous nations."[39] To add to their difficulties, they were running low on ammunition; and even if they did make it down the river, getting back up it would be a daunting prospect. Mackenzie weighed his options. Their best course, he decided, was to abandon the river and strike overland westward. But in explaining his decision to his companions—and the obstacles and dangers they were sure to face in going on foot through the mountains—Mackenzie, in his own words, made clear that, "I would not abandon my design of reaching the sea, if I made the attempt alone, and that I did not despair of returning in safety to my friends."[40] Upon hearing this resolution, the assembled party, Mackenzie recorded, "unanimously assured me, that they were as willing now as they had ever been, to abide by my resolutions, whatever they might be, and to follow me whenever I should go."[41] The dangers and hardships they'd shared had forged a strong bond, and now, with the sea so close, no one could think of giving up.

In order to take the overland route, the party had to first return to where the path through the mountains began. While Mackenzie and the voyageurs laboured at transporting the canoe back upriver, one of the natives agreed to escort Mackay and the Dene hunters on foot. But when Mackenzie's party met up with Mackay and the Dene a few days later, they found them in a state of panic. Their guide, they said, had run off after they'd encountered a hostile group who were armed with bows and spears. Abandoned and alone, Mackay and his friends had holed up in a deserted lodge, prepared to fight if need be.

This news alarmed the voyageurs. Mackenzie made preparations for their defence: in addition to their daggers and axes they loaded their muskets and pistols; they would camp within an old lodge, as it offered the best protection. Lookouts were appointed to guard each approach, and all through the night they took turns on guard. This tense state of affairs was kept up for two days. On their second night, a rustling noise in the nearby woods caused a general panic. Mackenzie's dog ran back and forth along the edge of the woods, growling. One of the sentries thought he saw "something like an human figure creeping along on all-fours about fifty paces from us."[42] They searched but found nothing. Mackenzie concluded that it was probably only a bear.

But when the day dawned they discovered it wasn't a bear at all—it was an old blind man who'd been left behind when the others fled. Without food for two days, he had at last crept out of his hiding place in search of something to eat. Mackenzie brought the frightened man before their fire and gave him some food. After he'd warmed himself and gained his composure, Mackenzie asked him, as best as he could through the Dene interpreters, what had caused the alarm. The old man explained that after Mackenzie's party left other natives had arrived from upriver to warn them that the strangers from over the mountains had come to kill them. This report caused a panic; the women and children fled, while the men had taken up arms. When Mackay and the Dene were spotted returning on foot, it seemed to confirm their worst fears that there was to be an attack.

Mackenzie took the old man with them on their return journey upriver so that he could explain to anyone they encountered that their intentions were peaceful. But the first native canoe they saw on the river immediately fled at their approach. A second canoe with two men in it did the same. To add to their troubles, their own canoe was again damaged, forcing them to stop for the night and search for more bark to make repairs. Indeed, it had become such an "absolute wreck" that they decided to build a new one from scratch.

It took only four days for the Canadians to fashion an entirely new canoe. With this new canoe, on July 2 the journey back upriver was resumed. It was hard, gruelling work, not helped by the bugs and shortages of food rations, as they hadn't had much chance to hunt given their uneasiness. Two days later, they at last arrived at the spot where a trail supposedly led to the ocean. Mackenzie and his men stored some of their provisions and gear to lighten their loads, then set off to follow the trail westward, leaving behind the old man who had guided them. Each of the Canadians, besides their heavy muskets, carried a ninety-pound backpack filled with pemmican and presents to ensure a friendly reception. The two Dene hunters carried lighter loads of forty-five pounds each so that they'd have the lightness of foot needed for hunting, while Mackay and Mackenzie each carried a seventy-pound pack as well as their own arms and ammunition. Mackenzie also slung his telescope over his shoulder—it proved an awkward addition, but he needed it to observe Jupiter's moons and ascertain longitude.

Over the next nine days they headed west on foot, enduring rainstorms and hail the size of "musket balls." The journey took them through thick brush sodden from the rains, over rocky terrain, up into the freezing snows of mountains whose altitudes topped two thousand metres, and then back down into swampy valleys where they sank to their knees with every step and fallen trees barred the way forward. In other places, they passed along lakeshores and across swift-flowing creeks. A few larger rivers had to be crossed in small rafts. Along the route they met with some natives, many of whom had acquired European tools from trade with the coastal tribes, who in turn received them from British and Spanish ships. But it was increasingly difficult for the Dene interpreters to understand the local dialects.

Eventually the towering Coast Mountains loomed into sight, their snowy peaks glistening in the sun. Mackenzie and his men descended from the high country into a deep, verdant valley, finding at the bottom enormous trees larger than any they'd ever seen. This dreamlike world was radically unlike any environment they'd yet encountered. It was a temperate rainforest—with moss-draped, old-growth cedar, spruce, fir, and hemlock as well as huge green ferns, colourful orchids, and other unfamiliar plants. Through this lush valley the party followed a winding river that today is known as the Bella Coola River.

Along the waterway they came across wondrously large, elaborate houses that featured ornate carvings of serpents and other artwork. These people were altogether different than the tribes east of the mountains. They were adorned with copper necklaces, arm rings, and other jewellery; their clothing was woven from cedar bark that had been turned into a hemp-like fabric in red and yellow dyes and richly embroidered with sea otter fur. Mackenzie thought their fashion sense produced "a very agreeable effect."[43] They spoke a language none could understand, and yet the party was warmly welcomed with fish, salmon roe, and fresh berries and offered finely crafted mats on which to pass the night. When they woke in the morning, Mackenzie found that the natives had already made a fire for them, and prepared a much welcomed breakfast of roasted salmon and berries.

Mackenzie admired the hospitality of these people—members of the Nuxalk tribe—and in his journal noted the "ingenuity" they showed in devising elaborate weirs with woven fish traps to catch salmon. The gooseberries and raspberries, he marvelled, "were the finest I ever saw or tasted."[44] In return, Mackenzie offered presents of iron tools and copper that he'd laboriously carried over the mountains. When, through sign language, he explained that they wanted to reach the sea, the villagers offered them one of their dugout canoes for the purpose.

Some of the villagers accompanied the party downriver in their own canoes. As they paddled along the swift-flowing river, Mackenzie observed with amazement, "I had imagined that the Canadians who accompanied me were the most expert canoe-men in the world, but they are very inferior to these people, as they themselves acknowledged, in conducting those vessels."[45] Considering that the voyageurs had canoed through hundreds of whitewater rapids, from the St. Lawrence River to the shores of the Arctic and now through the Rockies, this was high praise indeed.

When they arrived in the next village a short distance downriver, the party was mobbed by an excited crowd that hugged Mackenzie and his men and presented them with sea-otter robes. They were then ushered into a large cedar-plank house that belonged to the chief—who entertained them with a special feast consisting of salmon and a type of delicacy made from the inner bark of the hemlock. As before, all communication had to be with hand gestures, as their language was entirely different from any known to Mackenzie's party. Mackenzie admired their artwork, their wood carvings and craftsmanship, and their paintings of animals.

After spending the night in the village, the crew, along with the chief's son, embarked in a large dugout canoe. This would be the final leg of their journey to the sea. Two days later, on July 19, Mackenzie and his men at last paddled to the mouth of the river, where it emptied into the Pacific Ocean. They had crossed the continent.

They were met with a sight that exceeded their dreams. The surrounding mountains, shrouded in mist and primeval rainforest, plunged abruptly into the dark sea. The tide was out, leaving bull kelp and seaweed draping the boulders and rocky shorelines. Wildlife seemed to abound everywhere: enormous bald eagles soared overhead, hunting for salmon; porpoises and sea otters swam in the offshore waters; squawking gulls and other seabirds circled the air.

In the afternoon the winds picked up, creating large swells that forced the party to set up camp in a rocky cove beneath giant spruces and cedars. Mackenzie's hopes of taking observations with his telescope were dashed by cloudy skies. To add to his apprehensions, they were running very low on pemmican and had no nets to fish with. The chief's son killed a porcupine for food, but it wasn't enough to provide for all ten members of Mackenzie's expedition. The next morning, at low tide, Mackay gathered mussels and boiled them over a fire—although the Canadians and the Dene, unaccustomed to eating shellfish, couldn't stomach them. After breakfast the party set off in their long, leaky dugout canoe to explore more of the myriad islands and channels that make up what is now British Columbia's Pacific coastline.

As they probed these mysterious coves and inlets, three large dugout canoes, each carrying five men, suddenly appeared. These strangers were members of a coastal tribe—traditional enemies of the friendly villagers Mackenzie's party had met upriver. The coastal tribes of British

Columbia lived in villages enclosed by palisades and defended by watch-towers. Their warriors travelled in huge war canoes, each capable of transporting up to a hundred men clad in elaborate cedar-plank armour. They frequently engaged in large-scale wars with their interior rivals—whom they often abducted as slaves, much as the Vikings had.[46] And these coastal tribes had already traded not only with European ships under the command of Captain Vancouver but also with Spanish and possibly Russian ships. In contrast to those large vessels—with their dozens of cannons, crews of over a hundred sailors, and holds full of numerous precious trade items—Mackenzie's scruffy little band must have looked like paupers.

When these strangers approached, Mackenzie noted that they "examined everything we had in our canoe, with an air of indifference and disdain."[47] They did not seem very welcoming. The situation turned alarming when the strangers menacingly ordered the chief's son who was with Mackenzie and his men to leave. Evidently the young man had good reason to take the command seriously, as he departed at once. Now the strangers half-asked, half-ordered Mackenzie and his companions to come to their village. Outnumbered, the party cautiously paddled along the sea in the direction indicated, but when they neared the shore and spotted an abandoned, overgrown village, Mackenzie ordered his men to instead head for these ruins.

Soon after their own arrival there, ten canoes of the unfriendly natives beached below the deserted village and approached. Despite the language barrier, it was again clear that they wanted the party to come to their village. Mackenzie recorded: "I was very apprehensive that some hostile design was mediated against us, and for the first time I acknowledged my apprehensions to my people. I accordingly desired them to be very much upon their guard, and to be prepared if any violence was offered to defend themselves to the last."[48]

Near the seashore, Mackenzie and his men climbed atop a large rock outcrop that would allow them to defend themselves in the event of an attack. The natives appeared to be divided among themselves, with arguments going on over what they should do. It seemed that some wanted to trade with the strangers while others wanted to kill them. Apparently no consensus could be reached, and when the sun set, they simply left. The party made a fire on their rock, but had only a few depleted morsels of food left for their supper. Mackenzie wrapped himself up in his cloak and lay down, assigning his men to take turns on guard.

The next morning the chief's young son returned in a canoe with a few of his companions. He was plainly agitated. Through frantic gestures and hurried speech, he warned that they were in grave danger and had to leave immediately. He made it clear that the hostile tribe they'd met intended to return and kill them all. This news panicked Mackenzie's already highly wrought men—who had endured a sleepless night on the rock outcrop—but Mackenzie refused to budge. Inwardly he was apprehensive, but he knew that, for all their sakes, he had to retain his composure. He explained that they wouldn't move until he'd obtained his latitude and longitude readings, and for that he needed clear skies. In the meantime, he ordered his men to prime their weapons and prepare the canoe so that they'd be ready to leave quickly in the event it became necessary.

With dugout canoes soon spotted in the distance, Mackenzie completed one final task before consenting to depart: "I now mixed up some vermillion in melted grease, and inscribed, in large characters, on the South-East face of the rock on which we had slept last night, this brief memorial— 'Alexander Mackenzie, from Canada, by land, the twenty-second of July, one thousand seven hundred and ninety-three.'"[49] That simple memorial marked the end of their incredible journey to the Pacific.

For the moment, there was no time to celebrate. All about them were hostile strangers accustomed to warfare. Their immediate objective— to get back upriver—was fraught with danger; they were constantly on guard for an ambush. And given the swift current, travelling upriver was much harder than coming down had been. At one point, in the forest near the river, Mackenzie came face to face with the hostile people they'd encountered the day before—who had been tracking them. He drew his sword and a pistol as the strangers swarmed about him, prepared to fight off a dozen warriors. Fortunately, the hasty arrival of the voyageurs forced the natives to retreat. After four tense days, the party finally made it back to the friendly village, where they were out of danger—from the natives, anyway. A mother grizzly with two cubs attacked one of the voyageurs, prompting the others to shoot the bear to save their friend.

After a return journey of some thirty-two days—days that were nearly as difficult and daunting as when they'd first entered the mountains—Mackenzie, his nine men, and their trusty dog arrived safely back at their little fort. They'd been gone 107 days on a journey that had taken them off the edge of the map. They had made their way up over the Rocky Mountains and down to the Pacific Ocean, completing the first known crossing of the continent north of Mexico.

※

At age twenty-nine, Mackenzie's historical reputation was secure. Either one of his two epic journeys would have made him famous, and together they made him a legend. But for the time being, all that remained ahead. For immediate purposes, he was still just an obscure and lonely fur trader in Canada's hinterland. He spent a depressing winter after his return from the Pacific back at his isolated Fort Chipewyan. After so many adventures, the cold, dark winter proved grimmer and more monotonous than usual. Mackenzie was a man born for action; idleness was a torture to him. Shut up in his cramped quarters on the edge of the world, he fell into depression.

Like some other highly driven people, Mackenzie's supreme

self-control and confidence in action was mirrored by a correspond-ingly high-strung, short-tempered streak when not engaged in some all-consuming undertaking. He'd intended to spend the winter writing out a fair copy of his water-stained journals, since he hoped to see them one day published, but he found it impossible to concentrate. In the depths of winter, as his depression worsened, he wrote to his cousin Roderick that he intended to quit the fur trade:

> I am fully bent on going down. I am more anxious now than ever.
> For I think it unpardonable in any man to remain in this country
> who can afford to leave it. What a pretty situation I am in this winter.
> Starving and alone, without the power of doing myself or any body
> else any Service.[50]

For years Mackenzie had been consumed by his obsessive drive to chart a path to the Pacific. Now that he'd done it, he seemed rudderless, without anything to strive after.

In another letter to his cousin, Mackenzie confessed that he found it impossible to concentrate on the account of his expeditions: "Last fall I was to begin copying it, but the greatest part of my time was taken up in vain Speculations. I got into such a habit of thinking that I was often lost in thoughts nor could I ever write to the purpose."[51] What a contrast the cabin-bound, procrastinating, depressed Mackenzie made to the iron-willed, supremely efficient explorer who had conquered all obstacles.

That spring, Mackenzie's spirits partly revived with the melting of the snows. But, still only thirty, he left the Northwest for good. He had more than made his mark, and as an explorer, there seemed nothing more for him to do. Instead, he'd decided to turn his attention to greater ambitions. He now dreamed of overseeing a larger scheme: to unite the whole of northern North America into one great commercial empire. Having mapped the route to the Pacific, he now wanted to establish fur-trading posts on its shores. That way, natives and voyageurs could bring their furs to these posts rather than having to make long, arduous, expensive journeys all the way to Montreal. In order to accomplish this—and to stitch together all the posts, from Hudson Bay in the north down to the St. Lawrence and west to the Pacific—he felt strongly that all the British-controlled fur companies, including the Hudson's Bay Company, ought to merge into one giant entity. Even more crucially, Mackenzie felt that it was Canadians, not Europeans, who could make this scheme a reality. As he told Upper Canada's governor, John Simcoe, "the people of Canada being infinitely more capable of the hardships of the Indian life, & all the vicissitudes & dangers incident to the Trade, than Europeans, from thence, must draw those supplies of men without which it would not be possible to pursue the Commerce."[52]

This proposal represents, in its earliest, most embryonic stage, the idea that was to grow into the project of creating a single nation stretching across all these vast lands: Canada's Confederation. At the time, in 1794, few grasped the long-term implications of what Mackenzie had proposed—the various colonies, fur-trading companies, and competing interests remained fractious, while railroads were an undreamed-of possibility. In effect, Mackenzie was ahead of his time. It was not until after enduring the War of 1812, and realizing the dire need for better political and military coordination, that such a dream would come to fruition.

Shortly after his return from the Pacific, Mackenzie dined with Governor Simcoe and his wife in the colonial capital at Niagara. Though his table manners may have been a little rusty, he charmed Lady Simcoe with his tales of the mountains and the seacoast, of strange tribes and animals. He showed her and the governor a sea otter pelt, "proof of his having reached that coast," in Lady Simcoe's words.[53] Mackenzie submitted reports on his expeditions to both Simcoe and Lord Dorchester, governor general of all British North America.

In recognition of his accomplishments, Mackenzie was promoted within the North West Company, and tasked to act as one of its agents at the annual rendezvous of fur traders at Grand Portage on Lake Superior. Tensions had been growing between the wealthy Montreal merchants and the so-called wintering partners—those fur traders who spent the winters deep in the interior trading with the natives. Mackenzie, although now nominally based in Montreal, sympathized with the wintering partners and became a strong advocate for them. From the young traders in the interior, who of course heard all sorts of stories about his exploits, Mackenzie received something close to hero worship, a fact that made him dangerous to the wealthy businessmen in Montreal. This, and his vision of a transcontinental fur empire, brought him into rivalry with Simon McTavish, the most powerful man in the Company, who did not share Mackenzie's vision. In 1799, much to the chagrin of the young clerks and partners, Mackenzie was half-forced out and half quit the Company. It was the older McTavish who had prevailed. As one contemporary trader put it, "There could not be two Caesars in Rome."[54]

Mackenzie continued to suffer periodic bouts of depression; in the wilderness he was masterful, in complete control of himself and his men, but back in civilization he again became racked by indecision and self-doubt. There was, however, some relief—in 1801 he finally managed to publish a book about his explorations. It was an immediate success, and was soon translated into French, German, Russian, and other languages. Both Napoleon and Thomas Jefferson read it—inspiring the latter to send Lewis and Clark west to expand the American empire. And the year after his book appeared, the "Mad King," George III, knighted him Sir Alexander Mackenzie.

Sir Alexander, however, was soon back in the wilderness of Lake Superior—where he was still attempting to persuade fur traders to put aside their rivalries and unite in one great company. In this he proved only half-successful when in 1804 his old rival McTavish died and more partners joined the North West Company. Meanwhile, Mackenzie's neighbours in Lower Canada had put forward his name for election to the provincial legislative assembly. He was duly elected. After a lifetime of adventure, however, Mackenzie found colonial politics to be a bit tedious. Instead, he continued to urge the British crown to follow up on his explorations of the Pacific coastline by establishing military posts there—before the Americans, excited by Lewis and Clark's recent journey, could do so.

In 1811 Mackenzie returned to London, and there he became a founding member of the Canada Club, a group of people interested in Canada and its future. Perhaps it was a sense of sad nostalgia for his all-too-brief childhood, as well as a desire to be reunited with his long-separated sisters, that led Mackenzie in 1812 to purchase an estate in Scotland with the money he'd earned in the fur trade. That same year, at age forty-eight, he married a distant relation, Geddes Mackenzie, a teenager who was described by a contemporary as "one of the most beautiful women I ever saw."[55] Their marriage was apparently a happy one; together they had three children. But Mackenzie's health began to deteriorate, and in 1820, at the age of fifty-six, he died after a brief illness, possibly of Bright's disease.

A year after his death, the scheme Mackenzie had long promoted, a merger of the Hudson's Bay Company and the North West Company, at last came to fruition—creating an enormous fur empire stretching from the Pacific to the Atlantic, south to the Great Lakes and north to Hudson Bay. It was the far-flung fur posts, forts, and trade networks of this empire that were to provide a key foundation for Canada's Confederation. But ironically, despite the brief fame he enjoyed around the time of his knighthood, Mackenzie's name soon faded into obscurity. His two epic journeys were quickly overshadowed by the official expedition launched in 1804 by President Thomas Jefferson under the command of Lewis and Clark to explore the west, claim it for the United States, and find a route to the Pacific. When, after two years, Lewis and

Clark returned from their journey, the pair were hailed as American heroes who had conquered the west—the "first" to cross the continent. Amid all the applause, at least one shrewd observer complained in a letter to Lewis that their achievements were being exaggerated:

> Mr. M'Kenzie with a party consisting of about one fourth part the number under your command, with means which will not bear a comparison with those furnished you, and without the *authority*, the *flags*, or *medals* of his government, crossed the Rocky mountains several degrees north of your route, and for the *first time* penetrated to the Pacific Ocean. You had the advantage of the information contained in his journal, and could in some degree estimate and guard against the dangers and difficulties you were to meet.[56]

Despite the writer's protests, in the eyes of history it was Lewis and Clark who were the real trailblazers, with Mackenzie becoming a forgotten footnote. A 1965 American biography of Lewis, for example, claimed that he "stands as the greatest pathfinder" in all of North America: "He led a small band through unknown country with great tact and firmness and almost without bloodshed."[57] This claim prompted the Canadian historian W. Kaye Lamb to observe, "But surely Mackenzie did all this, with much less geographical knowledge to guide him, without the more elaborate crew and equipment available to an official party, and without any bloodshed at all."[58] Indeed, if anyone deserves the title of North America's greatest explorer, it's Alexander Mackenzie.

Merely glancing at the maps of his two epic journeys reinforces this fact. What had once been a vast blank space, entirely unknown to outsiders, is now filled with many crucial details—including the route of Canada's longest river; the outlines of one of the continent's largest lakes, Great Slave; and the location of both the Arctic and Pacific oceans.[59] In total, Mackenzie's two journeys from Fort Chipewyan spanned some ten thousand kilometres—and that doesn't even include the huge territory he had to cover to get from Montreal to his isolated fort. For the first time, the true extent of North America's landmass was revealed—and it proved larger than Pond, La Verendrye, Champlain, and others had ever dreamed. What is perhaps most remarkable of all—besides the physical hardships such journeys entailed—is that on all these immense wanderings, crossing widely different environments from the Arctic to the temperate rainforest, the Great Plains to the Rockies, the Great Lakes to the boreal forest, Mackenzie had met dozens of often very different aboriginal nations—and unlike so many previous explorers, had managed to avoid bloodshed with all of them. He strove to learn Algonquin and Athabaskan, and made as many notes as possible about the language of the friendly villagers he met near the Pacific. Moreover, in his book Mackenzie chastised those who viewed aboriginal people as any more cruel or barbaric than Europeans, and instead insisted upon their humanity and warmth. In this, as in so much else, Mackenzie was remarkable—an explorer well-fitted for his eventual recognition as among Canada's greatest.

{ 8 }

DAVID THOMPSON'S DEMONS

Here are Dragons

—TRANSLATION OF A LATIN INSCRIPTION
ON A SIXTEENTH-CENTURY GLOBE

I n the dead of winter, with bone-chilling winds sweeping down from the sombre mountains, David Thompson and his men trudged on their snowshoes deeper into the lonely, uncharted mountain pass. For days, a sense of unease had been growing in the party—the eerie silence of the mountains, the strangeness of an unfamiliar landscape, and the half-whispered legends of what might lurk in these unknown lands had frayed the nerves of the Canadians. That night, huddled on a bed of pine branches beside the flickering light of a campfire, Thompson thawed out enough ink to scribble in his journal:

> January 5 [1811]: Thermometer –26 very cold . . . We are now
> entering the defiles of the Rocky Mountains by the Athabasca
> River . . . strange to say, here is a strong belief that the haunt of
> the Mammoth is about this defile, I questioned several [Indians],
> none could positively say they had seen him, but their belief
> I found firm and not to be shaken. I remarked to them, that such
> an enormous heavy Animal must leave indelible marks of his
> feet, and his feeding . . . All I could say did not shake their belief
> in his existence.[1]

227

Two days later, having pushed deeper into the mysterious mountains, Thompson recorded finding strange tracks in the snow:

> January 7: Continuing on our journey in the afternoon we came on the track of a large animal, the snow about six inches deep on the ice; I measured it; four large toes each of four inches in length to each a short claw; the ball of the foot sunk three inches lower than the toes, the hinder part of the foot did not mark well, the length fourteen inches, by eight inches in breadth, walking from north to south, and having passed about six hours. We were in no humour to follow him; the Men and Indians would have it to be a young Mammoth and I held it to be the track of a large old grizzled Bear; yet the shortness of the nails, the ball of the foot, and its great size were not that of a Bear, otherwise that of a very large old Bear, his claws worn away; this the Indians would not allow.[2]

✳

Although David Thompson described himself as "a solitary traveller unknown to the world," the veteran surveyor J.B. Tyrell judged him "the greatest practical land geographer that the world had produced."[3] Thompson likely mapped more square miles of North American territory than any other person, and his maps were so amazingly accurate that twentieth-century surveyors retracing his routes could only marvel at his uncanny abilities. But despite his latter-day fame, Thompson died in abject poverty. His *Narrative*, an account of his journeys that spans the years 1784–1812, wasn't published until 1916, almost sixty years after his death in 1857. Contained within it are scientific and geographic musings; tales of adventure, wild animals, evil spirits, wendigo cannibals; and what may be one of the oldest "sasquatch" stories ever recorded.

Thompson was born in 1770 to poor Welsh parents who'd recently arrived in London in search of better prospects. They didn't find any.

Thompson's father died when he was two, and his mother, unable to provide for the boy, sent him at age seven to a charity boarding school. It was here that he began to learn the math fundamentals that would make him the greatest mapmaker of the era. By fourteen, Thompson's formal schooling had ended and he was shipped off to the frozen wastes of Canada's subarctic as an apprentice to the Hudson's Bay Company. Exile in a foreign wilderness must have been a horrifying prospect for a fourteen-year-old, but success in the fur trade required immersion from a young age. In Thompson's case, he had the good fortune to serve at Fort Churchill under Samuel Hearne—who assigned the newly arrived boy to copy out a legible version of his exploring notes. Thompson later recalled, "Mr Samuel Hearne was a handsome man of six feet in height, of a ruddy complexion and remarkably well made, enjoying good health."[4] Yet Thompson, who'd had religious instruction drilled into his head at boarding school, was scandalized by Hearne's free-spirited idealism, his rejection of formal religion, and his preference for Enlightenment philosophy. Later in old age it seems Thompson also became jealous of Hearne's fame, in contrast to his own obscurity.

Despite his disapproval of Hearne's philosophy, Thompson proved a quick study. He shared Hearne's facility with languages, soon mastering the Cree dialect of Algonquin, and like Hearne he took a keen interest in everything from mosquitoes to the solar system. Thompson's later "monster" stories are all the more arresting given the measured, objective tone he usually displayed in his work. A minute observer of natural phenomena, Thompson discussed mosquitoes from a scientific point of view and showed a similar interest in rocks; weather patterns; the "Esquimaux," whom he discussed in terms later anthropologists might emulate; as well as sundry other subjects. He found it worthy of mention in his *Narrative* that "It was at this Fort that Mr. Wales the Astronomer observed the Transit of Venus over the Sun in 1769."[5] He was also deeply interested in aboriginal oral history. When he was seventeen he was sent on a trading mission to the Great Plains, where he carefully recorded the history of the Peigan people, as told to him by the Peigan elder Saukamappee, with whom he lived as a guest one winter near the foothills of the Rockies. Eventually, Thompson learned to speak four different native languages and was given the name Koo-Koo-Stint by the Ktunaxa (Kootenay) people, meaning "The Stargazer."

That name, Koo-Koo-Stint, reflected Thompson's greatest passion—mapmaking. Under the Hudson's Bay Company's leading surveyor, Philip Turnor, he studied astronomy, surveying, and mathematics. It was Company policy to provide employees with a new set of clothes after they completed an apprenticeship, but on his twenty-first birthday Thompson instead requested that he be given a sextant, parallel lenses, and an astronomy book—a wish that was gratified. He spent a further six years with the Company, during which time he made numerous wilderness journeys and honed his mapmaking abilities through a growing mastery of celestial navigation.

But feeling that his talents were undervalued, in 1797 Thompson abruptly jumped ship to the rival North West Company—an act of desertion that his old employers regarded as treasonous. Thompson, however, was a headstrong, talented, ambitious young man with an unceasing itch for exploration, something that the North West Company promised to make full use of. Unlike the Hudson's Bay Company, whose forts were mostly isolated outposts in the north, the North West Company had an intricate network of inland posts stretching from the Great Lakes west to the Rockies; as such, they were alarmed by the prospect of the newly formed United States claiming possession of these territories. Thompson's new employers tasked him with surveying the proposed international border from Lake Superior westward to the Great Plains to determine which fur posts would fall on the American side. In doing so, he was engaged in an undertaking that foreshadowed the unfolding of the next century—when the tribes that had lived and fought over these lands for generations would be gradually pushed aside by two emerging powers: the United States to the south and British-controlled Canada to the north.

In 1799, in the wilderness of what is now Saskatchewan, Thompson met and married a Métis woman named Charlotte Small. Marriage between aboriginal women and fur traders had long been common—but Thompson's marriage to Charlotte proved no ordinary union. Together they had thirteen children, and by all accounts remained happily married for fifty-eight years. Charlotte, and later their children, were to become Thompson's companions on many of his surveying trips. For the next seven years he and his wife roamed across a vast area from the Great Lakes to the Rockies, exploring, mapmaking, and fur trading.

In 1806, with concern growing over the Americans' increasingly aggressive westward expansion, Thompson was dispatched by the North West Company on an expedition to reach the Pacific coast. He travelled by canoe, horse, and on foot, eventually reaching the mighty Columbia River—the largest river by volume in western North America—and then descending it to the salt water of the Pacific. To outsiders, these lands remained shrouded in myth and mystery, home to "monsters" and strange, unknown animals. Even the erudite Thomas Jefferson, president of the United States, believed that mammoths, mastodons, and giant ground sloths might still lurk in the uncharted wilderness of the West.[6] Creatures like the dreaded "grisly" bear were treated more as monsters than as real animals—and even ordinary animals that were unfamiliar to Europeans were liable to be interpreted as exotic. This included wildlife like bison, pronghorn antelope, bighorn sheep, and mountain goats, none of which were known outside the West.

It wasn't just Europeans who found the wilderness of western North America unsettling. Thompson's exploring companions were French Canadian and Iroquois explorers, both of whom regarded the west as foreign. Many of the plants, trees, birds, and other wildlife in these regions were as unknown to the Iroquois as they were to the Canadians. "Canada," after all, still referred only to the lands from Lake Huron east to the Gulf of St. Lawrence. It's easy to forget that the geography of North America is so vast and varied—the distance from the Rockies to Montreal is the same as from Germany to Iran—that our modern sense of "Canada" projects onto it an artificial sameness that it never possessed for its early inhabitants, most of whom were, by necessity, acquainted only with small parts of it.

In the late 1790s, while Thompson was busy mapping countless rivers and lakes, the western fur trade began to attract not only increasing numbers of French Canadians but also Iroquois, Algonquin, and Nipissing people from eastern Canada. These newcomers created tensions with the existing native populations of the Great Plains. In 1798, a large party of the former travelled far from their traditional homelands up the Saskatchewan and Red Deer rivers into territory that was wholly new to them. Thompson, who was based in the area at the time as a fur trader, noted, "The Algonquin and Nepissings paid every attention to the advice given to them [by the local natives], and performed the voyage without accident."[7] The Iroquois, on the other hand, as Thompson put it, "considered themselves superior to all other people," and ignored the advice of the locals, especially warnings about the dangers of pursuing bison and grizzly bears—animals not found in eastern North America.[8] The Iroquois, confident from their experiences hunting black bears and slaughtering ox on their farms back in Canada, dismissed any concerns from the natives about the local wildlife. This proved to be an error they would quickly regret.

Thompson recorded that, when attempting to hunt a large male bison, one Iroquois hunter was trampled to death and another severely wounded. A few days later, the Iroquois party encountered a grizzly bear for the first time—and discovered that they were far larger, tougher, and more aggressive than the black bears of the east. The

Iroquois shot the grizzly with their smooth-bore muskets, only to discover a grizzly could not be felled with a single shot. The enraged, wounded bear quickly turned on an unsuspecting Iroquois hunter, and then, according to Thompson,

> standing on his hind feet seized the Iroquois, hugging him with his fore legs and paws, which broke the bones of both arms above the elbow, and with it's teeth tore the skin of the head from the crown to the forehead, for the poor fellow had drawn his knife to defend himself, but could not use it; fortunately his comrade was near, and putting his gun close to the Bear shot him dead. The poor fellow was a sad figure, none of us were surgeons, but we did the best we could.[9]

Things only got worse for the Iroquois when they ignored local advice to winter in the northern forests, which held plenty of beaver and few hostile tribes. Instead, the Iroquois went south on the plains into territory controlled by powerful bison-hunting tribes like the Blackfoot, Peigan, and Blood. This incursion resulted in a quarrel that killed some twenty-five Iroquois and nearly provoked a full-scale war with the local Plains tribes. (The Nipissing and Algonquin, who were more closely related to western tribes than were the agricultural Iroquois, managed to get along without trouble.) Fortunately, though, after this rough start the Iroquois would eventually adjust to their new environment. One skilled hunter and traveller in particular among them, named Thomas, became a loyal friend of Thompson's and joined his 1811 expedition that set off for the Pacific.

There was a sense of urgency to Thompson's 1811 journey given that American ships had been sailing all the way around the tip of South America and up the North American coast to trade at the Columbia River's mouth. Thompson's orders were to continue exploring the river and to establish trading posts throughout the district before the

Americans could. But his plans to cross the Rockies through the pass he'd used before were complicated by hostile tribes in the area, who didn't want him trading with their enemies on the far side of the mountains. As a result, Thompson's party was forced to make a detour far to the north, and seek a new, previously uncharted way across the Rockies near the headwaters of the Athabasca River. It was Thomas the Iroquois who was in the lead that snowy January when the party came across the strange, unnerving tracks in the Athabasca Pass.

These supposed "mammoth" tracks left a lasting impression on Thompson. Long afterward, he continued to reflect on what he'd seen. Ever the surveyor, he'd carefully measured the tracks' dimensions:

> As the snow was about six inches in depth the track was well defined, and we could see it for a full one hundred yards from us, this animal was proceeding from north to south. We did not attempt to follow it, we had no time for it, and the Hunters, eager as they are to follow and shoot every animal made no attempt to follow this beast, *for what could the balls of our fowling guns do against such an animal*. Report from old times had made the head branches of this River, and the Mountains in the vicinity the abode of one, or more, very large animals, to which I never appeared to give credence . . . but the sight of the track of that large beast staggered me, and I often thought of it, yet never could bring myself to believe such an animal existed, but thought it might be the track of some monster Bear.[10]

Thompson clung to the belief—not without some doubt—that the creature had to have been a "monster" bear of more than ordinary size. But the question, Thompson admitted, was something that continued to weigh upon his mind. He recalled that, while camped deep in the mountain passes, his hunters had "pointed out to me a low Mountain apparently close to us, and said that on the top of that eminence, there was a Lake of several miles around which was deep moss." It was at this lake, his men believed, that the monsters fed, as they had seen a "great quantity" of moss torn up there. Despite the terror caused by the supposed creatures, the men agreed that they weren't carnivorous, but apparently lived off moss and grasses. Yet none "had ever seen the animal." Thompson noted: "I told them I thought curiosity alone ought to have prompted them to get a sight of one of them; they replied, that they were curious enough to see them, but at a distance, the search for him, might bring them so near that they could not get away."[11] Reflecting on the vastness of the unknown mountains that surrounded his small party on all sides, and the character of the Canadians, Iroquois, and Algonquin hunters who accompanied him, Thompson wrote:

> I had known these men for years, and could always depend on
> their word, they had no interest to deceive themselves, or other
> persons. The circumstantial evidence of the existence of this animal
> is sufficient, but notwithstanding the many months the Hunters have
> traversed this extent of country in all directions, and this animal
> having never been seen, there is no direct evidence of it's existence.
> Yet when I think of all I have seen and heard, if put on my oath,
> I could neither assert, nor deny, it's existence; for many hundreds
> of miles of the Rocky Mountains are yet unknown, and through the
> defiles by which we pass, distant one hundred and twenty miles from
> each other, we hasten our march as much as possible.[12]

After ample consideration, Thompson ultimately chose to hedge his bets. It was not an unreasonable stance: there were, as it turned out, large mammals still lurking in the western wilderness that were unknown to Europeans and the rest of the outside world. The kermode or spirit bear, for instance, a rare subspecies of black bear native to a small area of the Pacific Northwest, remained unknown to science until the twentieth century.[13]

As Thompson and his companions pushed on deeper into the Rockies, his men grew increasingly uneasy. In his January 8 journal entry, the day after discovering the "mammoth" tracks, Thompson wrote that one of the French Canadians, a certain Du Nord, had mercilessly beaten one of the sled dogs to death. Thompson was enraged by the man's cruelty and felt certain that he "would willingly desert if he had the courage to go alone."[14] He believed that Du Nord was no more than what the Canadians called "a 'flash' man," someone who was "a showy fellow before the women but a coward in heart."[15] That night, Thompson noted with regret that "as I am constantly ahead [I] cannot prevent his dog flogging and beating."[16] Such behaviour was likely a symptom of the psychological stress his men were under—they were dealing with incredibly adverse conditions, including not only the chilling weather and their fears of hostile natives who'd earlier pursued them on the Plains, but now rumours of a giant, dreadful creature that stalked these intimidating mountains.

Thompson, however, was at times so consumed by curiosity that he seemed almost oblivious to his companions' mounting terror. On January 10, after a hard day of marching and hauling sleds through deep snow, he scribbled in his journal:

A day of Snow and southerly Gale of wind, the afternoon fine, the view now before us was an ascent of deep snow, in all appearance to the height of land between the Atlantic and Pacific Oceans, it was to me a most exhilarating sight, but to my uneducated men a dreadful sight, they had no scientific object in view.[17]

Thompson's companions found his scientific musings and nightly star gazing rather mystifying. When he told them he did it to figure out where they were, he noted that "neither the Canadians nor the Indians believed me; for both argued that if what I said was truth, I ought to look to the ground, and over it; and not to the Stars."[18]

Despite his men's apparent lack of scientific zeal, Thompson was quick to praise their abilities. He boasted proudly, "My men were the most hardy that could be picked out of a hundred brave hardy Men."[19] Yet given the circumstances they now found themselves in, camped high above the treeline in the snowy mountains with barely wood enough for a fire, even Thompson admitted, "But the scene of desolation before us was dreadful, and I knew it, a heavy gale of wind much more a mountain storm would have buried us beneath it."[20]

Thompson found that his men, usually so active and robust, were increasingly listless, lagging behind as they cast uneasy glances over their shoulders. At night, beneath the brilliant stars, they slept with their guns close—relying upon their sled dogs to wake them if any beast should approach. The next day, pushing deeper into the uninviting mountains, the party passed by enormous glaciers, relics of the last Ice Age; one of these towered some two thousand feet and extended for miles. Elsewhere they were confronted with immense vertical rock faces, and in other places they found that the pines and spruces had been snapped off like matchsticks by deadly avalanches. In all directions lay untold mountains—uncharted and unknown.

On January 13 Thompson noted in his journal that his men were dispirited, in part because the environment was so different from what they were used to in eastern Canada. These frightening mountains, with their serrated peaks capped in eternal snows, represented to the Canadians and Iroquois a strange, terrifying new landscape that in all likelihood concealed in its caves and glaciers fearsome beasts. Thompson, in contrast, relished the chance to explore lands full of mystery: "Many reflections came on my mind; a new world was in a manner before me, and my object was to be at the Pacific

Ocean before the month of August," he wrote.[21] His head filled with thoughts of what might lie undiscovered in these wild mountains and the lands beyond, at night Thompson slept soundly on his bed of snow while his men remained on edge.

Early the next morning the party began their descent from the mountains, passing down from the barren alpine zone into a thickly forested country. In places their descent was so steep that the dogs were unable to stay ahead of the sleds, which rushed past them and slammed into trees at the bottom. Luckily none were injured, but these accidents nevertheless caused frustrating delays as the men struggled to disentangle the barking dogs and overturned sleds.

Over the next few days the party completed their descent from the mountain pass, struggling through thick, melting snow on their snowshoes and living off pemmican. Thomas brought some relief when he managed to kill two mule deer, but their sense of unease only grew when they discovered that in the night a wolverine had raided their supplies. Four of the Canadians, normally so keen for new adventures, deserted Thompson and turned back—driven away by the hardships and their fear of the "mammoth."

By January 26, after weeks of hard effort, the remaining men reached the frozen banks of the upper Columbia River. Here the party built cabins to survive the winter and a stockade around them to keep them safe. In the spring, they crafted a cedar canoe and paddled it all the way out to the Pacific Ocean in what is now Oregon. Although they'd beaten a rival American overland expedition that had also been seeking the Pacific, at the river's mouth they found that American fur trading ships had already arrived and established a fort.

The next year, 1812, Thompson returned to Montreal—after narrowly escaping capture on the Great Lakes by Americans, who had declared war that spring and invaded Canada.

In the midst of these demanding journeys Thompson found time to speculate in his journal on everything from the different shades of ice to the formation of glaciers and the effect of saltwater evaporation on mountain snows. But it's his discovery of "mammoth tracks" that is Thompson's singular contribution to one of Canada's enduring frontier legends: the sasquatch. Twentieth-century believers in "Bigfoot" cited Thompson's journal as proof of its existence, although it's not entirely clear what sort of creature the Iroquois and Canadians took the dreaded "mammoth" to be—other than that it was clearly something terrifying.

Thompson was not, it turned out, the only explorer to note the apparent dread of the Athabasca River's headwaters as home to some sort of monstrous creature. In 1831 the Irish explorer Ross Cox, while retracing Thompson's route through the Athabasca Pass, heard similar legends:

> Some of the Upper Crees, a tribe who inhabit the country in the vicinity of the Athabasca river, have a curious tradition with respect to animals which they state formerly frequented the mountains. They allege that these animals were of frightful magnitude, being from two to three hundred feet in length, and high in proportion . . . One man has asserted that his grandfather told him he saw one of those animals in a mountain pass, where he was hunting, and that on hearing its roar, which he compared to loud thunder, the sight almost left his eyes, and his heart became as small as an infant's.
>
> Whether such an animal ever existed I shall leave to the curious in natural history to determine; but if the Indian tradition have any foundation in truth, it may have been the mammoth, some of whose remains have been found at various times in the United States.[22]

Cox may well have been on to something—Alberta is a hotspot for the discovery of dinosaur bones as well the bones of other extinct creatures, so it isn't difficult to imagine that the unearthing of some of these relics could have inspired monster legends. In the 1930s, the anthropologist Diamond Jenness, who devoted his life to the study of aboriginal culture, noted the curious and apparently inexplicable fact that the area around the headwaters of the Athabasca River—the very place where Thompson and his men had found the enormous tracks—was a no man's land shunned by aboriginal people.[23]

It wasn't only strange tracks that haunted the sleep of voyageurs and explorers. In Thompson's time, when half of North America remained uncharted, the long winter nights deep in northern forests were "dark and full of terrors." Thompson's writings offer glimpses into the fascinating world of aboriginal beliefs about the supernatural, much of which he learned from his wife, whose first language was the Cree dialect of Algonquin. In his journals Thompson discussed not only legends about the mammoth, but Cree and Ojibwa stories of ghosts, good and evil spirits, and the most horrifying of all creatures in the northern forest: the dreaded wendigo. This shadowy, supernatural creature was most often represented as an evil spirit that took possession of solitary hunters, slowly driving them mad with an insatiable craving for human flesh. In Thompson's many years spent living in isolated, far-flung places across what is now western and northern Canada, he encountered several "wendigo" cases.

His first chilling encounter occurred while he was a young surveyor in 1796 in what is now northern Saskatchewan. The disturbing incident remained seared in his memory long after the event:

> Wiskahoo was naturally a cheerful, good natured, careless man,
> but hard times had changed him. He was a good Beaver worker and
> trapper, but an indifferent Moose Hunter, now and then killed one
> by chance, he had been twice so reduced by hunger, as to be twice on
> the point of eating one of his children to save the others, when he was

fortunately found and relieved by the other Natives; these sufferings had, at times, unhinged his mind, and made him dread being alone.[24]

When Wiskahoo obtained grog from the trading posts in exchange for furs (a trade practice Thompson strongly opposed), he would sit quietly alone, drinking, and "used to say in a thoughtful mood 'Nee weet to go' 'I must be a Man eater.'" Thompson understood Wiskahoo's words as meaning "I am possessed of an evil spirit to eat human flesh." Other Ojibwa trappers, upon hearing Wiskahoo's mutterings, would tie him up to prevent him from harming anyone. But Wiskahoo's demons proved too strong. Thompson reported: "Three years afterwards this sad mood came upon him so often, that the Natives got alarmed. They shot him, and burnt his body to ashes, to prevent his ghost from remaining in this world."[25]

Three years later Thompson witnessed a similar wendigo incident near Lake of the Woods. The "sad affair" involved a young man who'd confessed that he "felt a strong inclination" to eat his sister. At first, since he was a respected hunter, his comments were ignored, but his behaviour became increasingly bizarre and alarming. The man's parents, Thompson wrote, "attempted to reason him out of this horrid inclination," but it proved to no avail. The man's condition grew worse; he insisted that he "must have human flesh to eat"; and he was soon perceived as a threat to the whole camp. A council was called, and it was agreed that the young man was possessed by "an evil Spirit" that would turn him into a wendigo. The council resolved to put him to death—and that his own father should be the one to carry out the sentence. The young man accepted his fate, whereupon the "unhappy Father arose, and placing a cord about his neck strangled him." As in the earlier wendigo case, the man's body was then burned to ashes in order to prevent his "soul and the evil spirit which possessed him from returning to this world."[26]

According to Cree and Ojibwa oral histories, any individual driven to cannibalism would afterward never be satisfied with anything other than human flesh—and therefore had to be killed. The Canadian voyageurs, who had a healthy respect for aboriginal lore, believed that wendigoes were a sort of werewolf—and feared them every bit as much as their Algonquin counterparts did. Thompson was among the first outside observers to try to summarize what was known of the wendigo phenomenon. He explained that those "possessed" by the wendigo became "Man Eaters," and that such an individual "no longer keeps company with his relations and friends, but roams all alone through the Forests, a powerful wicked Man, preying upon whom he can, and as such is dreaded by the Natives." Thompson also noted that the condition appeared to afflict only people deep in the woods, as the "sad disposition to become Weetego; or Man Eaters" was wholly unknown to the people of the Great Plains or Arctic. He concluded cautiously, "There is yet a dark chapter to be written on this aberration of the human mind of this kind."[27]

Clearly, there were things to be feared in the wilderness beyond whitewater rapids, storms, and bears. Hunters and trappers who spent too much time isolated in the woods could become dangerously unhinged. Based on Thompson's observations as well as other documented cases, twentieth-century anthropologists and psychologists concluded that fur trappers and Algonquian peoples (a cultural group that includes the Cree and Ojibwa) had been occasionally afflicted by a "cultural bound" psychiatric disorder that manifested itself in a compulsion to eat human flesh. This medical condition was named "wendigo psychosis."[28]

In 1814 Thompson's wide-ranging explorations in western North America found eloquent expression in what has to be regarded as one of the greatest maps ever made. Based on his years of exploration across a vast area, the thousands of painstaking astronomical observations he'd taken under every conceivable difficulty—swarms of blackflies and mosquitoes in summer, freezing gales in winter—and reports from other explorers and aboriginal guides, Thompson created an enormous, five-by-three-metre map showing what is now western Canada. To make this huge map he glued together twenty-five separate sheets of paper, and with an ink made from growths found on apple trees, in meticulous detail he drew the principal rivers, lakes, mountain chains, and canoe routes from Lake Superior to Hudson Bay and westward to the Pacific. The finished map, a prized possession of the North West Company, was by far the most accurate ever made of western North America up to that time, and remained so for nearly fifty years. Today it sits carefully protected in a humidity- and temperature-controlled glass case in Toronto, one of the most treasured artifacts in Ontario's provincial archives. Thompson drew on it a wealth of new geographic information—including remarkably detailed outlines of Lakes Winnipeg and Superior, the course of the Saskatchewan River snaking across the Great Plains, the forbidding Athabasca Pass he'd charted through the Rockies, and a great river plunging through what is now the heart of British Columbia to the seacoast—what Thompson named the Fraser River, after his friend Simon Fraser, who had risked his life descending it in 1808. Unfortunately, time has not been kind to this more than two-hundred-year-old map; despite careful preservation, it has faded and is now difficult to reproduce. But it would be unthinkable to write about maps in Canada and not include Thompson's crowning achievement.

Examining it today, one can clearly discern the outlines of Lake Superior in the lower right corner, a lake Thompson knew well from his many canoe trips along its shores. In the top right is the southwestern shore of Hudson Bay, where he began his career, and just off the centre of the map is the vast, labyrinthine lake complex consisting of Lakes Manitoba, Winnipeg, Winnipegosis, and Cedar. Near the top of the map is Lake Athabasca—again charted in impressive detail—and on the far left appears the Fraser and Columbia rivers and the outlines of the Rockies.

Soon after completing this stupendous map, Thompson left the fur trade to pursue a career as an independent cartographer and surveyor, a line of work he would continue to excel in for decades. His talents were such that, in the aftermath of the bitter and hard-fought War of 1812, he was appointed by an international committee to authoritatively map the agreed-upon border between Canada and the United States—a task that took him through the Great Lakes, along part of the St. Lawrence, into the forests of Lower Canada, and back into his old fur-trading grounds as far west as Lake of the Woods. In completing this task with amazing precision—he used a meticulous system of triangulation to accurately plot distances across lakes, islands, and other features—Thompson had quite literally helped to make the modern map of Canada. And given that renewed war between Canada and the United States remained a distinct possibility—with violent border clashes occurring in the 1830s—he pulled it off with a high degree of professionalism under tremendous pressure.

But despite his superlative cartographic talents, Thompson's life became increasingly difficult. He was often in dire financial straits—his farming and firewood-cutting schemes in Upper Canada's Glengarry County, where he'd settled with Charlotte, proved insolvent. In 1833, now sixty-three and half-blind, he had no other option but to once more seek work as a surveyor. He still had the gift for accurate mapmaking, and with one of his sons as an assistant, he surveyed everything from rivers and lakes to proposed canal routes, farmers' lots, and even Montreal's street layout. But money was tight and the family remained in poverty, having to give up their homestead and move to rented quarters in Montreal—still little more than a town on the edge of a vast wilderness. Thompson's poverty became so galling that he had to pawn his surveying instruments, and later even his coat for food. At age seventy, he took the humiliating step of applying for a clerk position with his old employer, the Hudson's Bay Company—only to be turned down. Petitions for government support in recognition of his past services went unanswered, although payment for a copy of his magnificent map of the North West brought some temporary relief. By 1850 Thompson and his devoted wife moved in with their daughter and son-in-law in Longueil, Lower Canada. Seven years later, Thompson died. He was impoverished and forgotten, his accounts of his travels unpublished. Three months later Charlotte followed him; they were buried beside each other on Mont Royal. The family was too poor to afford headstones.

David Thompson, born a poor Welsh boy, had lived a life of undreamed-of adventures and travels across some ninety thousand kilometres of North American wilderness. And although he was forgotten in his time, long afterward he would be recognized as one of Canada's greatest explorers and a cartographer virtually without equal.

9

CANADA'S BLOODIEST BATTLEFIELD: THE SIEGE OF FORT ERIE

History is written in blood.

—UNKNOWN

Explorers might make the first maps, but the final ones are usually made by armies. On the night of July 3, 1814, under cover of darkness, a five thousand–strong American invasion force dipped their oars into the swift waters of the Niagara River opposite Buffalo, New York. They'd spent the winter and spring relentlessly drilling with a single purpose in mind: the final conquest of Canada. It was now the third year of the United States' war against Britain—a war that had been predicated on redrawing the map of the United States to include Canada—but for the Americans almost nothing had gone according to plan. In the beginning, most Americans had imagined that their war would be an easy one: after all, they outnumbered Canadians more than twenty to one—and Britain, pinned down in Europe fighting Napoleon's armies, would scarcely be able to offer any help to its distant North American colonies. Thomas Jefferson, sage of the Republic, had confidently assured his countrymen that the conquest of Canada would be "a mere matter of marching," at least as far as the fortress of Quebec, Canada's capital at the time, where even Jefferson conceded that resistance would be stiff. But as Senator Henry Clay boasted, "The conquest of Canada is in our power."[1]

It was certainly no secret that the United States, consumed with an insatiable appetite for land, had long hungered after Canada—even in the midst of the Revolutionary War, American armies had attempted to win control of the country. In the years since the Revolution, the two societies had grown further apart and looked upon each other uneasily. Now, with Britain's navy preoccupied with Napoleon, war fever gripped much of the American government; at last Canada seemed ripe for the taking. As one congressional critic lamented, "Ever since the report on foreign relations came into the house, we have heard but one word . . . Canada! Canada! Canada!"[2] Or, as Richard Johnson, a member of Congress for Kentucky and later a vice-president, put it, he'd "never die contented" until the United States had finally annexed Canada.[3]

After months of mounting tensions, on June 18, 1812, under President James Madison, the United States formally declared war on Great Britain. Madison made some brief remarks blaming his decision to launch the war on maritime shipping rights and the intolerable outrage that Canadian fur traders were friendly with "Indians" the United States wanted exterminated. But the real reasons behind the war were clear to everyone—the Americans' desire for Canadian real estate.[4]

Canada at the time consisted of two provinces, Upper Canada (what is now southern Ontario) and Lower Canada (what is now southern Quebec). The Atlantic colonies of New Brunswick, Prince Edward Island, Nova Scotia, and Newfoundland, though ruled from Quebec, were treated as distinct. The entire population of these colonies was perhaps 300,000 to 400,000—in other words, there were still more black bears than people in Canada. By far the most vulnerable to American invasion was the westernmost of the provinces, the thinly populated Upper Canada (home to some eighty thousand people). The American war leadership figured that they could seize the province without much fighting. They were wrong. It was in Upper Canada that the war's bloodiest and most protracted fighting would unfold. American invasion armies were hurled at Upper Canada's frontiers on three major fronts:

the Detroit River in the west, the St. Lawrence River in the east, and the Niagara River in the centre—all of them meeting violent resistance.

With Britain's manpower drained fighting Napoleon, few British troops were available for Upper Canada. A mere eighteen hundred British redcoats were stationed in the province—and these were thinly scattered across a vast frontier. To make up for this deficiency, the province's energetic leader, Major General Isaac Brock, had been busy transforming Canada's pioneer farmers and fur trappers into the makings of an army.

By law, all Canadian males between the ages of sixteen and sixty were required to serve as "citizen soldiers" in the militia. Most of the militia remained part-time soldiers: farmers who could be assembled to defend a village or district when the enemy appeared. But with war on the horizon, Brock had drilled some Canadian militia units to nearly professional standards, and had also made sure that the militia included specialist units devoted to artillery, horseback-mounted soldiers like the Niagara Light Dragoons, and even a Great Lakes naval force known as the Provincial Marine. These Canadians had been raised on stories of the injustices their families had suffered at the hands of cruel, intolerant Americans in the Revolution—and as such were unlikely to welcome Americans as "liberators."

Besides the militia, the British had also foreseen the need to create professional, full-time colonial regiments composed of Canadian settlers. As early as the 1790s attempts had been made to integrate French and English Canadians into a single unit, the Royal Canadian Volunteers. Known as "fencibles," these regiments differed from their British counterparts in that enlistment was restricted to Canadians, and unlike British regiments, which could be sent anywhere in the world, by law they could only be used to defend Canada. By 1812, such regiments included the Glengarry Light Infantry, the Canadian Fencibles, the French-Canadian Voltigeurs in Lower Canada, and, in the Atlantic colonies, the Royal Newfoundland Regiment, Nova Scotia Fencibles, and the 104th New Brunswick regiment—the latter of which uniquely agreed to serve anywhere in the world.

It was these troops that were called upon to defend Upper Canada when American General William Hull led his army across the Detroit River in the summer of 1812. Hull, an old veteran of the Revolution, had issued a bombastic proclamation upon his arrival on Canadian soil, declaring:

> Inhabitants of Canada! . . . The army under my command has invaded your country, and the standard of union now waves over the territory of Canada . . . In the name of my country, and by the authority of my Government I promise you protection to your persons, property, and rights . . . You will be emancipated from tyranny and oppression.[5]

Hull's words, at first conciliatory, then took on an air of menace as he promised:

> If, contrary to your own interests and the just expectation of my country, you should take part in the approaching contest, you will be considered and treated as enemies, and the horrors and calamities of war will stalk before you. If the barbarous and savage policy of Great Britain be pursued, and the savages be let loose to murder our citizens, and butcher our women and children, *this war will be a war of extermination* . . . No white man, found fighting by the side of an Indian, will be taken prisoner—instant destruction will be his lot.[6]

Since most Canadians by necessity would be fighting alongside their aboriginal allies—and many Canadians (especially French Canadians) were related through blood and marriage to aboriginal people—there was no mistaking Hull's meaning. But just to be certain, he added,

"The United States offers you peace, liberty, and security. Your choice lies between these and war, slavery and destruction. Choose, then, but choose wisely."[7] As Hull's invasion army pushed up the Thames River, his troops pillaged and burned Canadian homes and farms—dispelling any doubts about this being a "liberating" army.

Meanwhile, General Brock rallied the colony's inhabitants and acted with lightning speed to quash the invasion. Despite his troops being outnumbered, he demonstrated remarkable ingenuity, boldness, and resolve in driving Hull from the province, and then defeating him at Fort Detroit—dealing an unanticipated blow to the United States' invasion that turned Brock into the "Saviour of Upper Canada." Brock was a leader of the old school: a gallant soldier, but also a man who enjoyed classical literature. And like the ancient Greeks he admired, his principle was never to ask his troops to go where he would not lead. It was a principle he lived and would die by: in the early morning of October 13, 1812, Brock was killed in action at Queenston Heights, leading a heroic but doomed charge up a steep, wooded hill against American forces.

Brock's death was a severe loss to Upper Canada: in a pre-industrial age when populations were still small and armies numbered only a few thousand soldiers, individual leaders had an outsized influence. Brock's death did at least give the Upper Canadians a martyred hero to rally around—as the *York Gazette* put it, "Inhabitants of Canada: In the Day of Battle, Remember Brock!" But the British high command groped in the dark to find a worthy successor to the charismatic Brock—appointing a succession of generals, none of whom proved as successful on the battlefield or as popular with the people as Brock had been.

The war soon took a darker turn. Parts of Upper Canada fell under American occupation; homesteads and even whole villages were put to the torch, with much of the province transformed into a charred wasteland of burned-out farmsteads and blood-soaked fields. In the spring of 1813, the provincial capital, York, was burned by an American force, and later that year, in the midst of a December blizzard, the town of Niagara suffered the same fate. Many of these atrocities were carried out by a Canadian renegade, the traitor Joseph Willcocks, who'd been an elected member of Upper Canada's legislative assembly before throwing in his lot with the Americans. At Niagara he'd burned the homes of his own constituents—leaving them to die of hypothermia in a brutal winter. When the local Canadian troops later arrived on the scene to find their houses destroyed and their families homeless, they were, in the words of a British eyewitness, more like wild beasts than men, so great was their desire for vengeance.

The British high command, meanwhile, at last located a worthy successor to Brock—in late 1813, they named forty-one-year-old Lieutenant General Gordon Drummond as commander of the forces in Upper Canada. Drummond, by birth a Canadian from Quebec, had spent most of his life serving abroad in the British Army; he'd been posted everywhere from the deserts of Egypt to the ports of the Caribbean and the battlefields of Napoleonic Europe. As early as 1804 he'd been made a general—the first Canadian ever to obtain such a rank. Now, he was needed in his native land. In temperament, Drummond took after Brock: bold, aggressive, and eager to fight the Americans. He arrived in Niagara late in 1813 and immediately made his presence felt—striking quickly across the river on American soil and bringing victories at Fort Niagara and Buffalo.

It was General Drummond who had command of all British and Canadian troops in Upper Canada when that highly trained, new American invasion force of five thousand rowed across the waters of the Niagara River on July 3, 1814—intent on at last conquering Canada. Their first target had been Fort Erie: a small stone fort, directly opposite Buffalo, that guarded the Niagara River's head on Lake Erie. The fort's garrison, numbering only 137 troops, had quickly surrendered. From there, the Americans marched northward along the Niagara—battling British, Canadian, and First Nations warriors at the Chippawa River two days later. The Americans proved victorious, although casualties were heavy on both sides. They continued their advance north—fighting another, even bloodier battle at Lundy's Lane on July 25. Of the five generals present at Lundy's Lane, four were casualties. Drummond himself had been grazed by a bullet in the neck—a wound that almost killed him, and seems to have shaken his confidence. The bitter stalemate at Lundy's Lane resulted in the Americans retreating south to the captured Fort Erie, where they planned to dig in and await reinforcements from across the river.

The Americans quickly set about turning what had been a small, modest fort into a sprawling stronghold that one British officer aptly described as an "ugly customer."[8] Eighteen cannons now guarded the fortress, along with three American warships anchored in the waters of the Niagara River for additional firepower. This new fortified encampment could shelter over three thousand soldiers in an area stretching approximately eight hundred metres from the old British fort to a sandy knoll known as Snake Hill on Lake Erie's shoreline. Beyond the cleared "fields of fire" immediately outside the forts' walls were vast swamps and ancient forests of giant oak, maple, beech, hemlock, elm, and chestnut. It was in these woods that General Drummond camped with his own army of nearly three thousand British, Canadian, and allied First Nations warriors. John Le Couteur, a nineteen-year-old officer in the 104th New Brunswick Regiment, noted in his journal: "The woods in which we were posted were part of an endless forest marching to the North pole, for ought we knew; some of the trees of the growth of centuries, with their heads in the Clouds."[9]

Drummond's task was to contain the American army at Fort Erie—the United States' bridgehead into Upper Canada—and if possible drive them back across the river. It was not going to be easy. To attack a fortified position, a besieging army normally needed strength in numbers and enormous firepower. Drummond had neither, and was still suffering from his neck wound. Still, he took up his duty stoically; if the American army weren't contained, they would sweep through Upper Canada and spell the end of the colony.

Drummond's army was a diverse mix of British redcoats, many of them battle-hardened veterans from the Napoleonic Wars; Royal Navy sailors who'd been serving on the Great Lakes but in a pinch could double as ground soldiers; Canadian troops, including black settlers who'd fled from American slavery to freedom in Canada; and a medley of First Nations warriors, the core of which were Mohawks from the Grand River area under the command of the remarkable Major John Norton, or Teyoninhokovrawen, as he was known to the Mohawks. The colonial troops included the Glengarry Light Infantry as well as the 104th New Brunswick Regiment, which was led by the charismatic Lieutenant Colonel William Drummond, a distant relation of the General's and a man famous throughout the army for his bravery. There were also ample numbers of Canadian militia, including battle-hardened units and the Niagara Light Dragoons—cavalry formed from the local pioneer settlers.

By early August, Drummond's army began to construct fortified cannon positions in the hardwood forests a kilometre north of Fort Erie. The troops, lacking canvas tents, were forced to make their own shelters in the woods while the Americans fired cannonballs at them. One British officer noted that the Canadians, all experienced woodsmen who grew up with axes in their hands, "erected shanties, far superior, in warmth, tightness and comfort, to any canvas tent."[10] The British troops, lacking the Canadians' bushcraft skills, had to make do with primitive lean-tos that barely kept the rain out. Meanwhile, under the energetic William Drummond, raids and skirmishes in the forests around the fort became a frequent occurrence. Much of this fighting featured the dark-green-coated Canadian troops of the Glengarry Light Infantry—specialists in forest warfare and assisted by Norton's warriors—taking on elite American rifle regiments. General Drummond was impressed by his Canadian troops, writing to his superiors in Montreal of their "steadiness and gallantry" in holding off the American riflemen in the woods while the rest of the army laboured on the trench lines and defences.[11]

With the most senior American commander, General Brown, wounded, the fort was now under command of a Virginian, General Edmund Gaines, a competent soldier but one who thought the conquest of Canada would cover his army "with imperishable Glory."[12] Rounding out the American leadership was a cautious New Englander, General Eleazer Wheelock Ripley, and Brigadier General Peter B. Porter, a vain, pompous former New York congressman and a leading promoter of the war.

In the British ranks, Gordon Drummond's distant relation William Drummond warrants particular attention. Born in Scotland, this eccentric, brave, and highly charismatic warrior had served in the Caribbean and Europe before joining the 104th New Brunswick regiment. In 1813, the New Brunswickers were ordered to reinforce Upper Canada. Led by Drummond, they had arrived after marching over a thousand kilometres on snowshoes from Saint John. Drummond had a reputation for utter fearlessness; at Lundy's Lane he'd been in the thick of the action, carrying a double-barrelled shotgun and refusing to take cover when fired upon. His preferred weapon for close-quarters combat was a nine-foot-long naval pike for spearing enemies. As a mark of the awe he inspired, allied First Nations presented Drummond with sacred wampum beads, which he wore around his neck in battle—an honour that few, if any, white officers ever received. A handful of surviving letters and diaries from the time offer glimpses of this unusual officer's character. The Mohawk chief Norton referred to him as "my gallant friend" and noted his courage in battle.[13] William "Tiger" Dunlop, an army surgeon, felt that Drummond was "everything that could be required of a soldier; brave, generous, open-hearted and good-natured."[14] A French-Canadian officer, Jacques Viger, described Drummond as a "brave and excellent officer," and noted that he was "above the medium in height," with "a dignified appearance, regular and clear-cut features and a charming expression." Viger added, "So many estimable qualities, together with his reputation for courage . . . caused him to be idolized."[15] Among those who idolized Drummond was nineteen-year-old John Le Couteur, who, his head filled with the adventure stories of Sir Walter Scott, in his journal called Drummond "a splendid looking man, the personification of Rhoderic Dhu."[16] (Dhu was a hero in one of Scott's poems.)

There was certainly no shortage of heroics in the British ranks. On August 12, a Royal Navy commander, Alexander Dobbs, led a daring night raid on the American warships anchored off the fort. They managed to capture two of the three American ships in hand-to-hand combat. Dobbs, thirty years old and a veteran of naval battles across the Atlantic, had been sent to Upper Canada to put his talents to good use on the Great Lakes. There, in the port town of Kingston, he'd fallen in love with a prominent colonial politician's daughter, Mary Cartwright, and married her shortly before arriving at Fort Erie. His capture of the American warships spared the British at least some of the artillery fire that had been harassing them for weeks.

With their own cannon batteries now complete, at dawn on August 13, General Gordon Drummond ordered his artillery to open fire on Fort Erie. The Americans responded in kind, beginning a horrifying ordeal for those camped on either side, with cannonballs occasionally whistling through the air from afar and taking soldiers' heads clean off. Both sides fired a mix of solid balls, exploding mortar shells, and "hot shot," that is, cannonballs heated red hot that could ignite fires if they struck trees or buildings.

In an attempt to weaken Fort Erie and "soften" its American defenders in preparation for a ground assault, the bombardment was kept up for two straight days. Nowhere were troops entirely safe. One American soldier, while preparing dinner around a campfire, had his arm ripped off below the elbow by a flying cannonball. On a separate occasion, another American, Corporal Reed, was engaged in shaving a Sergeant Waits when a cannonball unexpectedly came whirling toward them—and in the words of an eyewitness, it "took off the Corporal's right hand, and the Sergeant's head; throwing blood, brains, hair, fragments of flesh and bones upon a tent near them, and upon the clothing of several spectators of this horrible scene."[17] Despite these grisly incidents, overall the British bombardment proved largely ineffective: their guns, placed about a kilometre north of the fort, were too far to do much damage, and General Drummond lacked the necessary cannons and artillery pieces for a proper siege. Most of their cannonballs failed to breach the fort's thick stone walls, and the ones that hit the high earthworks surrounding the buildings only "seemed to me and others to ram the earth harder," as the surprisingly poetic John Le Couteur noted in his journal.[18]

Then suddenly, on the rainy afternoon of August 14, a British cannonball sailed over the fort's walls and struck an American powder magazine, producing a tremendous explosion. The British assumed the blast must have caused many casualties. Thinking the time was now ripe for an assault, General Drummond sent word to his officers that they were to prepare for a surprise attack that night. In fact, Drummond was badly mistaken: the powder magazine had been in a relatively secluded position within the American compound, and few soldiers were harmed by its explosion. Moreover, General Gaines, having correctly anticipated Drummond's logic, had warned his men to expect a British attempt to storm the fort.

Drummond had devised an elaborate plan that entailed a three-pronged attack on the American positions, with a fourth, diversionary prong to confuse and distract the enemy soldiers during the assault. It was to be launched that night, so as to take advantage of what Drummond assumed was the American army's disarray after the powder magazine's explosion. Drummond informed his officers that inside the fortifications General Gaines couldn't have more than 1500 men—and that they were probably dispirited. In fact, Gaines had over 2800 soldiers, and they were well motivated to fight. Drummond, in contrast, had only about 3000—far fewer than what would typically be required to take a heavily fortified position like Fort Erie.

Drummond's plan was to launch his attack under cover of darkness at two a.m. The first prong, led by Colonel Victor Fischer, would strike at the southern end of the American encampment near the shores of Lake Erie. This fortified position overlooking the lake was known as Snake Hill. The Americans had enclosed it with a line of "abatis"—a tangled mass of fallen trees whose branches had been sharpened into spears protruding outward. Half a kilometre north of Snake Hill, at the opposite end of the American fortifications, two other prongs, led by Colonel Hercules Scott and Colonel William Drummond, would attack. Scott's column would advance nearest to the banks of the Niagara River, and strike at an earthen wall defended by a cannon platform that was known as Douglass's Battery after the American artillery officer who commanded it. The popular William Drummond, meanwhile, would be given the hardest and most dangerous task of all—leading the assault on the old stone fort's centre, a walled position set within a deep ditch and defended by cannons, riflemen, infantry, lines of abatis, and palisades. Finally, halfway between the north and south of the American encampment, John Norton's native warriors would undertake a diversionary movement in the woods to fool the American defenders into thinking the main attack would come from that direction.

So crucial was the element of surprise to Drummond's plan that in a letter to his three assault leaders, Fischer, Scott, and William Drummond, he urged removing the flints from the troops' muskets, permitting only the most reliable troops to keep theirs. This way, Drummond explained, the element of surprise would be preserved— there would be no premature firing by jittery troops that might alert the Americans of the attack—and moreover, without flints in their weapons, the soldiers would have no choice but to storm the fort's walls and fight hand to hand, a necessary, if horrifying, precondition of taking a fort in warfare of the era. Although this order might seem strange to modern readers, Drummond had done the same thing with success the year before during a night assault on Fort Niagara.

However, Colonels Scott and Drummond, neither of whom worried about their men's willingness to follow them into the very thick of cannon fire, ignored the recommendation. Fischer, on the other hand, less certain about his soldiers' willingness to attack, acted on it. His troops, in contrast to the others, were a motley collection of mercenaries from across Europe—a mix of Swiss, Italians, French, Poles, Hungarians, and Austrians, many of them deserters from Napoleon's armies. Fischer had reason to think that they might prove less willing to storm the fort once the fighting began—and thus he ordered their flints removed, allowing only the most experienced of the British redcoats under his command to keep theirs.

Both William Drummond—ever eager to lead from the front—and Hercules Scott, less outspoken but no less brave, had premonitions that they would not survive the attack. Certainly, the air was thick with tension that fateful, rainy evening of August 14—as those men who could write made out their wills in anticipation of what awaited them. Others cleaned their muskets, sharpened their bayonets and swords, filled their canteens, and quietly prayed.

A surgeon in one of the British regiments, William "Tiger" Dunlop, breakfasted with William Drummond the morning before the planned night attack. Dunlop noted that Drummond was evidently in "high spirits":

> We sat apparently by common consent long after breakfast was over.
> Drummond told some capital stories, which kept us in such a roar
> that we seemed more like an after dinner than an after breakfast
> party. At last the bugles sounded the turn-out, and we rose to depart
> for our stations; Drummond called us back, and his face assuming
> an unwonted solemnity, he said, "Now boys! we never will all meet
> together here again; at least I will never again meet you. I feel it and
> am certain of it; let us shake hands, and then every man to his duty,
> and I know you all too will to suppose for a moment that any of you
> will flinch it." We shook hands accordingly, all round, and with a
> feeling very different from what we had experienced for the last two
> hours, fell into our places.[19]

Young Le Couteur, who idolized Drummond, wrote in his diary on the night of August 14, "I shall never forget the solemn tone in which our good, kind and gallant Col. Drummond took leave of us. He told me that it was probable we should never meet again, something whispered this would be his last day."[20] Le Couteur, unable to believe what he was hearing, tried to cheer his commander by reminding him of his "many escapes" in the past, adding, "To look cheerfully upon this attack, we might all meet happily—under Providence!"[21] Drummond, however, merely shook Le Couteur's hand, then urged him to see that his personal effects and letters were sent to his wife. Then he "took a most affectionate farewell of us . . . which brought tears to my eyes. 'Remember the honor of the Regiment, dear boys, God Bless You!'"[22]

Elsewhere in the British camp, Colonel Hercules Scott quietly shared William Drummond's reservations about the planned attack.

Scott was less charismatic than Drummond, but no less brave—and was quietly respected by the men in his 103rd regiment. He spent the rainy day camped under a tree with one of the army surgeons, trying to encourage him by saying that they would "breakfast together in the fort in the morning." Privately, Scott was less optimistic; in a letter to his brother on the eve of the assault, he wrote, "I have little hope of success from the manoeuvre," adding that he would write more, "that is, if I get over this present business."[23]

✳

As the sun sank below the forests, cannon fire, like thunder, continued as the two sides kept exchanging shots every few minutes. The day's heavy rains had finally ceased, and in the August heat a thick mist now hung over the cleared grounds and above the rippling waters of the Niagara. Grey-coated American troops, clenching their muskets with bayonets fixed, stood guard behind their lines of felled trees, along the riverbank, or behind the parapets and stone embrasures of Fort Erie— eyes and ears alert for any hint of movement. Gaines had permitted two-thirds of the army to sleep—in their uniforms and with their weapons ready—while the other third remained on guard.

Shortly after two a.m., near the southern end of the American defences, out of the darkness emerged oncoming redcoats with bayonets at the ready. They were the advance party of Fischer's eighteen hundred–strong force, tasked with storming Snake Hill and overpowering its defenders. The American scouts, alert to the danger, could hear their steady approach through the dark and mist, and opened fire with their muskets before falling back to the main defences. Suddenly the British regiments charged out of the dark—soldiers with axes hacked away at the barricades of felled trees, clearing passages for the redcoats to swarm through. The American defenders kept up a brisk fire while scouts ran through the camp, raising the alarm with cries of "To arms! To arms!"

Half-asleep troops sprang to their feet, running out of their canvas tents to form up in order to repel the assault.

As the British struggled to fight their way through the barricade of abatis, the American artillery opened fire, mowing down redcoats as they surged toward the earthworks. The cannons perched atop Snake Hill kept firing in such rapid succession that the flashes from their muzzles illuminated the position like a lighthouse. Devastating as this cannon fire proved, it wasn't enough to keep back the charging British troops, who made it to the foot of Snake Hill and adjacent earthen embankment, where heavy musket fire greeted them. The troops, unable to return fire without flints in their muskets, threw the ladders they carried against the embankments to scale them—only to discover that the ladders were too short to reach the top. With soldiers trapped beneath Snake Hill and unable to scale it, the Americans now rained fire with impunity upon the British below—killing and wounding hundreds as they tried in vain to find a way through the American defences. Some men, in desperation, tried to circle around the American lines by plunging into the waters of the Niagara River. But in the dark many were swept away by the strong current and drowned. Those few who did make it ashore were quickly taken prisoner by American soldiers.

Still, Fischer persisted in his attack. Five times his men bravely but vainly charged the American parapets, each time being driven back with heavy losses. Finally, with the screams of the wounded around them and under relentless fire, panic seized the British corps—they turned and fled. These fleeing troops ran headlong into their oncoming reserve soldiers, the foreign mercenaries, who, in the words of an eyewitness, "became utterly terror-stricken and ran over, beat down, or swept before them" the other British redcoats still coming behind them, causing the entire attack to disintegrate.[24] The offensive had completely failed: in less than thirty minutes of intense combat, Colonel Fischer had lost 212 men and was himself severely wounded.

Meanwhile, in thick woods about four hundred metres to the north, Norton's native warriors and Canadian troops were mounting their feigned attack on the centre of the American defences. They fired with their muskets from afar and made noise, hoping to draw American forces away from the actual points of attack. The British had success- fully employed such subterfuge on the Americans earlier in the war, notably at Detroit and Beaverdams, but the American officers were now wise to the act and didn't take the bait. Although some units were kept guarding the defences opposite the warriors and Canadians, Gaines rightly concentrated his strength at the north of his stronghold—where General Drummond planned to launch his two-pronged attack.

Along the river's edge Colonel Hercules Scott advanced in the dark at the head of his 103rd regiment, leaving the relative safety of the for- ested British encampment and entering the open ground before the fort. His task was to strike at a seven-foot-high, eighteen-foot-thick embankment that the Americans had erected to connect the old stone fort to the river. At the right of this embankment, near the water, bris- tled the cannons of Douglass's Battery, an elevated and well-defended platform connected to the earth wall. Colonel William Drummond, meanwhile, had been assigned the most dangerous task—he was to lead an elite force of 104th New Brunswick regiment troops, Royal Navy sailors, and marines to storm the stone fort itself.

When the British came within a few hundred metres of the fort, although still concealed by the darkness, the Americans heard their approach, and opened fire with their cannons. These artillery pieces were loaded with "canister shot," consisting of tightly packed musket balls that when fired fanned out like a shotgun blast—capable of killing many soldiers at once. Closer to the water, the officer in command of the battery, Douglass, had ordered his troops to ram the cannons full with everything they had—solid eighteen-pound cannonballs, canis- ters, and grapeshot, creating a lethal cocktail of mixed shot flying out of each cannon. Fortunately for the attacking British and Canadians, the first American shots were aimed too high and sailed harmlessly over their heads.

But as they neared the American lines the artillery officers could now make out for the first time their foes in the dark, and adjusted their fire accordingly. It was Hercules Scott's column that caught the worst of this murderous fire—his troops made it to within fifty metres of the earth embankment when a sudden blast of cannon fire aimed straight at their ranks unleashed carnage. Lead balls smashed through bodies, splattering blood and brains as the British ranks quickly collapsed from the intensity of the fire. Scott, however, was able to rally his men from retreating, and spying a weak spot in the American defences near the river's shoreline, he led a second charge. Again, devastating fire drove them back. A third charge met with no more success. In one of these attacks, Scott was shot in the head and fell, mortally wounded. With their commander and much of their number dead, the remnants of the 103rd divided, with some retreating and others pushing forward to the stone fort, where they managed to find relative safety in the deep, dry ditch surrounding it, out of range of the roaring cannons just above them. The darkness and thick smoke from the guns helped conceal them.

Meanwhile, William Drummond led his men forward. About two hundred metres from the fort he ordered his column to halt in the shelter of a shallow ravine. Tiger Dunlop, although a surgeon and therefore not expected to fight, had felt the pull of Drummond's strange charisma, and had hurried after him when he left the camp. Drummond, however, now ordered Dunlop to remain where he was and not "expose himself" to enemy fire. He then unbuckled his sword and gave it to the surgeon, urging him to treat the wounded rather than join the fight. Dunlop, thinking Drummond perhaps "had no faith in his sword," offered the colonel his own weapon, a fine Italian blade, but Drummond declined, explaining that he preferred to carry a boarding pike.[25]

The "forlorn hope" was the name given to those soldiers in the first wave of attack on a fort—as their chances of survival were virtually nil. Drummond put himself at the head of it with the toughest Royal Navy sailors. They then ran forward through the dark, avoiding enemy fire as best they could, and slid down into the fort's ditch. With ladders they attempted to scale the fort's western wall, where a cannon was raining fire across the field and illuminating in successive flashes the oncoming attackers.

As the British reached the tops of the ladders, Americans greeted them with bayonet lunges, sword slashes, and musket fire. Le Couteur, who was in the second wave, recorded:

> We still marched at a rapid but steady pace, in a few minutes the head
> of the column, or rather the forlorn hope, got to the ditch, jumped
> in, reared the Scaling ladders and cheered us as they mounted. We
> increased our pace and cheered loudly, defying the fire of enemy.
> I jumped with our Company into the ditch. It was slow work to get
> up the ladders—of which there was not one quarter enough—there
> were palisades to be cut away, while a galling flanking fire from a
> Gun [cannon] and musquetry annoyed us sadly.[26]

The western wall, heavily defended by American infantry mounted along it, proved impossible for Drummond's men to storm—they were driven back into the dry ditch with heavy losses. Drummond, however, led his men around to a cannon bastion—a short stone tower—that was crammed with cannons pointed out through embrasures in three directions. As an artillery position, it wasn't as heavily guarded by infantry soldiers as the western wall. In the dark and smoke, the Americans were unsure where the British had gone—until suddenly Drummond and his men mounted their ladders and came rushing over the bastion's stone walls with angry shouts of "Give the damn Yankees no quarter!"[27]

The stunned artillery gunners in the bastion, their hands full loading cannons, were caught off-guard. Like a fiend, Drummond began impaling American troops on his nine-foot-long naval pike, furiously screaming "No quarter!" to encourage the others. The British swarmed over the walls, lunging at the Americans with swords, bayonets, and pikes in a bloody slaughter within the cramped confines of the bastion. One of the American officers, Lieutenant John McDonough, fell wounded and begged for mercy. But Drummond, in a rage, shouted again his command to take no prisoners, and then killed McDonough.

A narrow corridor led down from the bastion into the heart of the fort—and with Drummond in the lead, the British now attempted to fight their way along this passageway. They were greeted with musket fire, as the men in the front clashed spears and swords with their opposing number. Drummond, exposed out in front, lunged fiercely with his pike—but suddenly he was shot and staggered back. An American then stabbed him through the chest with a bayonet. He fell dead near the second door of the fort's northern barracks, a short distance from the bastion. With their commander dead, the British drew back to the bastion—where they were fired upon through the barracks' second-storey windows and loopholes.

A New Brunswick officer, Harris Hailes, led an attempt to storm the barracks by plunging back down the corridor into the fort. Hailes and his men managed to break through the door into the lower storey, where they fought hand to hand with the defenders. But, with the Americans having strength in numbers and the upper storey, they were soon driven back to the bastion. American troops in the fort's interior, meanwhile, wildly charged into the bastion in an attempt to drive off the British, only to be themselves fiercely repulsed.

The American commanders, realizing that the British were trapped in the bastion, ordered one of their cannons turned around to concentrate fire upon it. Seeing this development, in desperation the British troops managed to turn one of the American cannons inside the bastion around 180 degrees so that it now faced into the fort's interior. With this gun, they began firing upon their attackers. Unknown to them, directly beneath the bastion through a trapdoor was a powder magazine crammed full of black powder and ordnance. If so much as a spark were to hit it . . .

Meanwhile, outside the fort, the surgeon Dunlop had been waiting a few hundred metres off in the relative safety of the shallow ravine where Drummond had ordered him to remain, anxiously listening to the furious sounds of the raging battle. In the dark, he stumbled across a wounded British officer, who was bleeding from his arm and in the process of retreating. Dunlop made himself useful and fixed a tourniquet on him; then, "throwing him over my shoulder like a sack," he carried him to the British lines to receive further attention.[28] This done, Dunlop felt he could remain behind no longer. As he put it,

> A man must possess more courage than I can pretend to, who can
> stand perfectly cool, while having nothing to do, he is shot at like a tar-
> get. Accordingly, I determined to advance at all hazards, and at least
> have the pleasure of seeing what was doing for my risk of being shot.[29]

Le Couteur was still down below in the dry ditch, directing the 104th New Brunswick troops to scale the ladders into the bastion. Finally, sword in hand, he climbed up a ladder to join the others. He never made it. When he was almost at the top, a horrible quaking began to shake the entire bastion. Captain Douglass, the American officer commanding the cannon position a hundred metres away, recalled the exact moment:

> Every sound was hushed by the sound of an unnatural tremor, beneath
> our feet, like the first heave of an earthquake; and, almost at the same
> instant, the centre of the bastion burst up, with a terrific explosion;

and a jet of flame, mingled with fragments of timber, earth, stone, and bodies of men, rose, to the height of one or two hundred feet, in the air, and fell, in a shower of ruins, to a great distance, all around.[30]

Something had ignited the powder magazine directly below the British soldiers' feet in the bastion—all it would have taken was a single spark, and with all the firing to and from the bastion, such an accident was almost inevitable. The bastion's thick stone walls had concentrated the force of the explosion upward—killing men instantly and sending others hurling through the air. Some were thrown back into the dry ditch where they were impaled on the bayonets of the cramped British troops still waiting beneath the ladders. Cannons, stone masonry, and other debris were tossed through the air—one of Douglass's troops, standing some hundred metres from the blast near the water's edge, was crushed by falling debris.

Le Couteur had been thrown from his ladder just as he was about to spring into the bastion. He wrote:

I remember seeing a black volume rise from the earth and I lost my senses. After I recovered them, I was lying in a ditch fifteen or twenty feet down where I had been thrown by a tremendous explosion of gunpowder which cleared the Fort of three hundred men in an Instant. The platform had been blown over and a great beam had jammed me to the earth but it was resisting on the Scarp [edge of the ditch]. I got from under it with ease, bruised but otherwise unhurt. But what a horrid sight presented itself. Some three hundred men lay roasted, mangled, burned, wounded, black, hideous to view. On getting upon my legs, I trod on poor Lt. Horrens broke leg of the 103rd, which made me shudder to the marrow. In placing my hand on Captain Shore's back to steady myself from treading on some other poor mangled person, for the ditch was so crowded with bodies it was

almost unavoidable, I found my hands in a mass of blood and brains—
it was sickening.[31]

The explosion had wiped out most of the British attacking force,
with the dazed survivors scattered in the ditch and surrounding area.
The Americans, after recovering from the shock of the explosion,
opened fire with grapeshot on the British in the ditch. Dawn was now
breaking—revealing a horrifying scene of carnage. Le Couteur and
the others who could still stand fled back across the open plain to the
safety of the British lines, musket and cannon fire hard on their heels.
In this desperate retreat, Le Couteur stumbled upon a wounded fellow
officer, Lieutenant Fallon, and, taking his arm around his shoulders,
helped get him back to the British lines.

Dunlop, meanwhile, had been just outside the fort's dry ditch when
the explosion erupted and now:

> - found myself scouring along the road at the top of my speed, with
> a running accompaniment of grape, canister, and musketry whistling
> about my ears, and tearing the ground at my feet. When about half
> way between the ditch and the ravine, I heard a voice calling on me
> for help. I found it was a wounded officer; so, calling a drum-boy of
> the Royals, who had a stretcher, we laid him on it, and carried him . . .
> he entreated us to get into the wood, as, on the road, we were likely to
> be cut to pieces with the shot.[32]

Taking to the woods, tree branches above crashing to the ground as
cannonballs whizzed past, Dunlop and the drummer boy managed to
get the officer back to the safety of the British camp. Here, other British
survivors were slowly staggering in and being formed up to repel an
expected American counterattack.

General Gordon Drummond tried to steady his panicked troops and bring some order to the chaos caused by the failed attack. He ordered his gunners to resume firing to cover the retreat. When he spotted Le Couteur hobbling into the camp with the wounded Fallon on his arm, he asked for a report. Le Couteur, weeping uncontrollably, had to regain his composure before he could speak. Then Drummond asked the young, grieving officer whether he knew anything about what had happened to Colonel Drummond. Le Couteur recalled that he "could not articulate for grief." At last, he sobbed, "Killed, Sir." Drummond asked if he knew anything about Colonel Scott. Le Couteur responded, "Shot thro' the head, Sir," and informed him that the elite troops, the grenadiers, were bringing Scott's body in.[33] Drummond, feeling for Le Couteur's loss, tried to encourage him, then put him to work helping organize the shocked men for the anticipated counterattack.

None came—General Gaines was unsure of his own advantage, and for the moment was content just to keep up an artillery barrage on the British. In the morning light, as the smoke cleared, hundreds of charred, mangled bits of bodies, severed limbs, and burnt corpses could be seen lying scattered about the ruined bastion and dry ditch. All three prongs of the British assault had failed with heavy losses. Their combined casualties totalled nearly a thousand men—one-third of General Drummond's entire force. American casualties numbered less than a hundred.

Later that same day, the Americans dug a mass grave just outside the fort's walls and tossed the remains of British bodies into it. William Drummond's body, because he'd been in the fort's interior, was spared from the blast. The Americans treated it as a war trophy and stripped it of everything but a shirt; Drummond's fame, or notoriety, made getting any part of his uniform a valuable memento. Inside his breast pocket was found a copy of the orders issued by General Drummond. With bitter irony, immediately above the sentence "The Lieutenant General recommends a free use of the bayonet," an actual bayonet had sliced through the orders as it pierced Drummond's breast.[34] This bloodstained document now sits stashed away in an American archive. Drummond's body was left exposed to view under a cart before being added to the mass grave. But Le Couteur and Dunlop received some slight solace when, under a flag of truce, a British officer managed to recover the wampum beads he wore. These beads were divided up between Drummond's most devoted officers as a sad reminder of their fallen commander—whose premonitions had come true.

Despite the appalling losses suffered on the night of August 15, and the shortages of arms and ammunition, General Drummond refused to abandon the siege. He had little choice—his army was the only thing standing between the Americans and the rest of Upper Canada. If he couldn't retake Fort Erie by storming it, Drummond resolved to pound it into oblivion by keeping up a steady bombardment. Meanwhile, over the weeks that followed, skirmishes and raids continued almost daily in the outlying forests—with Norton's native warriors and the Canadians doing battle with American marauders. In one of these skirmishes, the hated traitor Joseph Willcocks was killed.

This war of attrition took its toll on both sides. On September 17 the Americans, desperate to break the stalemate and fearing the oncoming Canadian winter, launched a surprise attack on the British siege lines— resulting in over five hundred casualties for both sides. Before this "sortie," General Drummond had in fact already decided to withdraw his army a short distance northward to better ground. The Americans, badly weakened from the heavy fighting of the Niagara campaign, were no longer in a position to conquer anything. Worse yet, word reached the Americans that their capital, Washington, had been captured by a British force; in revenge for the torching of Canadian towns it had been burned, including the White House. Across the ocean in Europe, it turned out, the once invincible Napoleon had been defeated, meaning Britain was now free to begin sending large numbers of reinforcements to North America. With their army pinned down and demoralized at Fort Erie—a mere border fort in what was supposed to be a victorious campaign of conquest across Upper Canada—it was clear that any thought of conquering territory now had to be definitively abandoned. On November 5, 1814, the surviving remnants of the American army climbed into their boats to retreat across the river to New York state. But before the last American troops evacuated Fort Erie, they crammed it with kegs of gunpowder, set charges, and blew it up as a final act in their failed campaign.

Seven weeks later, the American government signed a peace treaty with Britain ending the war and relinquishing any claims to Canada. At the war's conclusion considerable swaths of American territory, including much of Maine and various border points, had actually been under British control. If the British had pressed their advantage in the diplomatic negotiations, the map of Canada might have been redrawn southward to include these lands—particularly the area of Maine that thrusts upward between New Brunswick and Quebec. But the British, after nearly twenty years of war with France, had considered the American conflict almost an afterthought—a purely defensive war, in which keeping Canada was victory enough. When the Treaty of Ghent restored the borders to their pre-war state, Canadians welcomed it as a hard-fought victory that kept them free of the United States.

Fort Erie was left in decaying ruins and soon forgotten. A tattered, surviving map of the siege kept in Canada's national archives reveals the geography of this bloodied corner of the country. The map was made by British Army engineers Captain Samuel Romilly and Lieutenant George Philpotts. The star-shaped old Fort Erie appears on the upper left of the map, with the American defensive lines extending southward to Snake Hill, although this portion of the map has been torn off and is now lost. Within the American encampment are a number of buildings—these housed the senior officers, including General Gaines. North is positioned on the map at the bottom of the page (the arrow beside the initials B.O. is the symbol of the British Army's Board of Ordnance, not a compass); on the left then is the Niagara River, to the south Lake Erie, and to the west, beyond the cleared plain, are the vast old-growth forests where much of the skirmishing before and after the August 15 night assault took place. The area to the west, without trees, was a morass of swamp. In the south, just beyond the fort, appears a line indicating the ravine that Dunlop had sheltered in during the initial night attack, and a short distance beyond that, screened in the woods, are the British cannon positions. These are indicated behind the bold dark lines.[35]

This map of the bitter battle waged here—the bloodiest of the War of 1812 and one of the bloodiest in Canadian history—is a solemn reminder that Canada's borders were forged at a terrible cost.

10

CANADA'S HEART OF DARKNESS: MAPPING THE ARCTIC FRONTIER

But his soul was mad. Being alone in the wilderness, it had looked within itself, and, by heavens! I tell you, it had gone mad.

—JOSEPH CONRAD, *Heart of Darkness*

D r. John Richardson was the very model of the calm, scholarly, detached gentleman. So when he cocked his flintlock pistol and blew the brains out of his exploring companion, he had his reasons. For months Richardson's party had been wandering the cruel Arctic tundra, gradually becoming reduced to mere skeletal figures— their clothing torn to rags, faces weathered and emaciated, eyes sunken in their sockets, hair long, greasy, and unwashed. These virtual walking corpses emitted a foul stench, with their gums turned black from scurvy and their yellow, crooked teeth loose in their mouths. One by one the party had dwindled as they collapsed and perished on the tundra, their corpses fed upon by wolverines and carrion birds. Of the twenty Canadian voyageurs, British sailors, and native hunters who in 1821 had set off with Richardson, only nine came back alive.

✳

In the wake of the War of 1812, most of North America's northern reaches remained on maps a vast, uncharted blank space. Across the whole northern coastline, only two spots had been explored by outsiders: the delta of the great river Alexander Mackenzie had followed to the northern sea, and, some thousand kilometres to the east, the Coppermine River's mouth, which had marked the end of Samuel Hearne's northward journey. Outside these two small points, the Arctic shores of mainland North America remained terra incognita to outsiders. Since the area was north of the treeline, and therefore beyond the range of beaver, fur traders had little incentive to risk their lives in these frozen wastes. A much earlier generation of English and Danish sea captains, in the sixteenth and seventeenth centuries, had explored by ship the easternmost Arctic, but they hadn't made it farther than Hudson Bay. Europeans at the dawn of the nineteenth century knew scarcely more about the geography of Canada's Arctic than the Vikings had nine hundred years earlier—when shaggy, bearded Northmen in their longboats had regarded these lands as the mythical home of terrifying frost giants.

With the defeat of the United States' invasion of Canada in 1814 and of Napoleon in 1815, the time had come to find out what really lurked in those mysterious regions of eternal ice. Britain now found itself as the world's undisputed leading power, with a navy that was by far the world's largest. With no enemies for the moment, the question was what to do with the idle navy. Exploration supplied the answer: the old dream of discovering a Northwest Passage—something that had haunted navigators and geographers since at least the 1500s—was revived. The Admiralty resolved to dispatch ships to search for a passage through the Arctic ice and islands—a discovery that would drastically cut the distance and time required to reach Asia and the South Seas. In addition to these maritime expeditions, in 1819 a fateful decision was made by the naval lords to dispatch a small party of sailors inland from Hudson Bay to chart the Arctic coastline on foot or by canoe.

This task was entrusted to a thirty-three-year-old naval lieutenant named John Franklin—a man who would go down in history for incompetent heroics that got himself and his entire crew killed. But in 1819, all that remained decades into the future. The youngish Franklin was a veteran of the Napoleonic Wars—he'd seen considerable action in such legendary battles as Trafalgar and Copenhagen—and whatever his shortcomings as a land explorer, he was a brilliant sea navigator. Joining Franklin was thirty-one-year-old John Richardson, a Scottish doctor, naval surgeon, and naturalist. Richardson may have been a scholar and a gentleman, but as subsequent events would show, he was also remarkably tough. Rounding out the party were two young English midshipmen and war veterans, Robert Hood and George Back, both twenty-two and both talented artists, as well as an ordinary seaman, John Hepburn. In the spring of 1819 the five of them sailed to Hudson Bay as passengers on board a Hudson's Bay Company supply ship, arriving at York Factory in late summer. They had no idea what they were getting into.

From York Factory, with the assistance of traders from the Hudson's Bay and North West companies, the sailors made their way inland. After visiting different posts and overwintering at Cumberland House, Franklin and his crew reassembled in 1820 on Lake Athabasca at what had been Alexander Mackenzie's old post, Fort Chipewyan. The route there proved arduous enough; one Canadian voyageur in a canoe carrying Richardson and Hood was swept overboard in a rapid and drowned. This, however, was an ordinary occurrence in the fur trade and thought nothing of—as grimly attested to by the graves overlooking many rivers' whitewater stretches.

Franklin had read Mackenzie's and Hearne's books about their journeys—together these amounted to his primer on wilderness survival. At Fort Chipewyan, he and Richardson arranged the logistics of their operation as best as they could, given their limited experience, eventually recruiting sixteen Canadian voyageurs to join them. Their plan was to retrace Mackenzie's route to Great Slave Lake, where a trading post now existed, and from there eventually work their way to the Coppermine River and then on to points unknown.

When on July 18, 1820, the party of three canoes pushed off from Fort Chipewyan, Franklin and his British compatriots couldn't help feeling jittery about how few provisions they had. They were plunging into what for them was an alien, sinister wilderness. In contrast, the Canadians were acting as if the whole thing was practically a summer holiday. Franklin noted: "It was gratifying, however, to perceive that this scarcity of food did not depress the spirits of our Canadian companions, who cheerfully loaded their canoes, and embarked in high glee after they received the customary dram."[1] As the party followed Mackenzie's route northward to Great Slave Lake, the Canadians did the paddling, hunting, fishing, fire-making, and guiding while Franklin took astronomical observations, Back and Hood sketched, and Richardson made notes on plants and wildlife.

A week later they arrived on Great Slave Lake at one of the world's most remote fur outposts, Fort Providence—a glorified collection of log cabins. Here they met the Canadian trader in charge, Willard Wentzel, as well as a pair of tough, experienced voyageurs, Jean-Baptiste Adam and Pierre St. Germain, who were to act as their hunters and interpreters. The following morning, Franklin and his naval companions donned their resplendent blue and gold uniforms, sword belts, and plumed hats to formally meet the leader of the local Dene tribe—a tall, imposing man in his early thirties named Akaitcho. A highly skilled hunter, Akaitcho had seven wives as well as several slaves he'd taken in battle. Fortunately for Franklin and Richardson, Akaitcho agreed to assist the party.

Franklin had intended to head down the Mackenzie River, proceed up a tributary to Great Bear Lake, and from there cross over into the watershed of the Coppermine River before descending it to the Arctic Ocean. This Akaitcho dismissed as impractical. Instead, he proposed a more direct route to the Coppermine by striking northeast from Great Slave. Franklin recorded:

They then drew a chart of the proposed route on the floor with charcoal, exhibiting a chain of twenty-five small lakes extending towards the north, about one-half of them connected by a river which flows into Slave Lake, near Fort Providence. One of the guides, named Keskarrah, drew the Copper-Mine River, running through the Upper Lake, in a westerly direction towards the Great Bear Lake, and then northerly to the sea. The other guide drew in a straight line to the sea from the above-mentioned place, but after some dispute, admitted the correctness of the first delineation.[2]

This was a remarkably accurate map—it's a shame no copy of it survives that could be reproduced here. It shows the Dene's knowledge of these lands all the way out to the seacoast, where Hearne and Matonabbee had ventured fifty years earlier. However, Akaitcho was quick to warn Franklin that he and his companions didn't know anything about the coastline much beyond the Coppermine's mouth—these were the lands of their hereditary enemies, the Inuit. Franklin, impressed by this charcoal map, deferred to the natives' expertise and accepted it as the route they would follow. He also listened to Akaitcho's advice on where they should establish their winter quarters—a lake about three days south of the Coppermine—as here there was said to be sufficient trees to allow them to build cabins.

That night, Franklin and his men pitched their tents outside the fort. But the bugs were so brutal that the British resorted to putting smouldering logs in their canvas tents to drive out the mosquitoes. This novel idea promptly resulted in a tent burning down. Fortunately, Hepburn, the sailor who was inside the flaming tent, managed to escape. For Akaitcho, however, the incident did not exactly produce a favourable impression of Franklin's intelligence.

The day after this accident, the expedition got underway. It now consisted of no fewer than twenty-eight people, including three of the

Canadians' native wives and three of their children. They travelled north in four birchbark canoes, the British riding in the middle as passengers while the voyageurs paddled. Akaitcho, meanwhile, had gone ahead of the main party with some of his wives and companions and would wait for them at the mouth of the Yellowknife River. Ascending this river, which flows into Great Slave Lake, required arduous paddling and portaging—draining their food supplies and boding ill about what awaited them north of the subarctic forests. The Canadians were already unhappy with Franklin's leadership. And now, having worked like dogs on the punishing portages that required four trips each to transport all their supplies, refused to go on unless they were given more food. In response to this insubordination, Franklin "assured them of my determination to inflict the heaviest punishment on any who should persist in their refusal to go on."[3]

This was a rude awakening to the Canadians. Earlier generations of explorers had adopted a very different style of leadership. When Alexander Mackenzie's men had become dispirited, he had inspired them with his words, his appeal to their pride, and his willingness to share every hardship. Samuel Hearne had proven himself willing to abide by the wishes of his Dene companions and follow wherever they might lead. Franklin, in contrast, was a career naval officer, accustomed to maintaining a rigid authority and issuing commands without sharing in hard labour—a style of leadership that did not sit well with the Canadians. They grudgingly carried on, but they neither respected nor trusted Franklin.

On August 19 the party reached the lake where Akaitcho had recommended they make their winter quarters. Ice was already forming at night on the small lakes, and by the end of the month snow would begin to fall. Yet, foolishly, Franklin insisted they press on. The Dene and the Canadians both rejected this mad idea. Akaitcho explained that the caribou had already begun to migrate south, and that beyond the treeline they couldn't expect to find wood for fires. Even if they did somehow manage to make it down the Coppermine River, they'd never make it back up it before the winter. In short, Akaitcho said, "the very attempt would be rash and dangerous."[4]

Franklin still wanted to press on, naively insisting that winter was not as near as Akaitcho believed. On hearing this dismissal of his advice, Akaitcho was offended and "with some warmth" told Franklin that,

> I have said everything I can urge to dissuade you from going on . . . it
> seems you wish to sacrifice your own lives, as well as the Indians who
> might attend you: however, if after all I have said you are determined
> to go on, some of my young men shall join the party, because it shall
> not be said that we permitted you to die alone.[5]

This at last brought Franklin to his senses, and he agreed not to press on until the following spring. However, in the meantime he decided to send Hood and Back, as well as nine Canadians and one Dene guide, to scout out the river. The rest of the Canadians were tasked with building log cabins before the weather turned any more severe, while Franklin, Richardson, Hepburn, and a Dene guide, Keskarrah, set off on a hiking trip to survey the surrounding area. As for Akaitcho, he and most of his companions headed south to their winter hunting grounds.

By October the parties (minus Akaitcho's band) had reunited, and the British moved into the finished dwelling—a cabin some fifteen metres long and seven and a half metres wide. This large structure was strictly for the use of the four British officers; the Canadians and Dene had to build a second, smaller structure for their own use. The big, drafty cabins proved poor shelter from the bitter Arctic cold; even with roaring fires, temperatures inside remained below freezing. Their little post Franklin rather grandly styled "Fort Enterprise." While he and the British read the books they'd brought along, the Canadians and Dene killed hundreds of caribou in order to lay up enough meat to last them through the winter when the deer would migrate south.

But dried caribou meat and what fish they could catch through the ice were insufficient to supply the whole party over the long term, and they'd also need to replenish their supplies of gunpowder, shot, and other tools. So Back, the strongest of the British officers, was sent with some Canadians on a round trip of more than sixteen hundred kilometres on snowshoes to obtain aid from the fur-trading posts on Lake Athabasca. He had little luck in finding help, and had to endure tremendous hardships and fasting during this arduous expedition. Still, it was perhaps just as well that he hadn't remained in the fort: before he left, he and his fellow midshipman, Hood, had fallen out over their rivalry for the affections of a beautiful Dene woman known as Greenstockings. Overcome by their shared infatuation, Hood and Back had done the sensible thing and prepared to fight a duel—until Hepburn intervened by removing the gunpowder from their pistols. Franklin, never one to encourage quarrels, had defused the situation by dispatching Back on the resupply mission. Hood, meanwhile, found a way to pass the winter by allegedly fathering a child with Greenstockings.

In January, the trader Willard Wentzel and the voyageur Pierre St. Germain arrived from Fort Providence with two Inuit interpreters, Tattannoeuck and Hoeootoerack, whose English names were Augustus and Junius. They were on loan from the Company forts on Hudson Bay, and given their knowledge of the tundra, both would prove an indispensable addition to the expedition.

With the spring thaw the caribou returned, relieving the party of their fasting and allowing them to depart. On June 4 Dr. Richardson, impatient to be underway, set off with an advance party travelling by dogsled and snowshoes. Back at the fort, by June 14 the birchbark canoes had been completed; they were loaded on sleds for transport to the Coppermine River. There weren't enough dogs to haul all the sleds, but, fortunately, Franklin found that, by hitching up Canadians along with the dogs, they could make decent progress. As combined teams of two dogs and four Canadians pulled the sleds, the British and their two Inuit interpreters walked alongside carrying lighter loads. Akaitcho, meanwhile, was to lead his own hunting band and supply the explorers with food caches at agreed-upon points.

The march north was extremely arduous and hazardous. When crossing some of the lakes, the men plunged through the ice and might easily have drowned. At night the temperatures plummeted, leaving them shivering in their blankets. Given the difficult conditions and heavy loads, they could manage only about ten kilometres a day. Not until June 30, after reuniting with Richardson's party, were they able to launch their canoes in the river, though there were still large chunks of ice drifting down it. The Coppermine's upper reaches were full of dangerous rapids, which in the spring melt, if not for the superb skills of the voyageurs, might have killed them.

Meanwhile, they were already running low on dried meat, which prompted Akaitcho to mount a hunting expedition for muskox. Before leaving, he warned Franklin to be "on guard against the great grizzly bears of the Barren Lands."[6] But apparently it wasn't just grizzlies that were a danger to Franklin. While the rest of the men were busy hunting, he found himself alone; suddenly a young female muskox, spooked by the hunters' gunshots, ran past him. Franklin figured he'd try his hand at hunting, and aimed a musket at the muskox, "I fired and wounded it, when the animal instantly turned and ran at me, but I avoided its fury by jumping aside and getting on an elevated piece of ground."[7] Akaitcho had rather more luck; his men sent word to Franklin that they'd killed eight muskox.

The Coppermine took the party through rugged, mountainous country, with peaks rising over three hundred metres. Most of the area was windswept tundra punctuated by a few willows and dwarf spruces. In places the narrow, snaking river plunged through steep, rapids-filled canyons whose walls were encrusted with masses of ice. The rapids weren't the only hazards. A grizzly bear attacked two Dene hunters, although Akaitcho sprang to the rescue and killed it with his musket. Franklin noted that he found the grizzly tasted "excellent."[8]

By July 12 the party had nearly reached the end of the river—and as such were alarmed by the possibility of an Inuit ambush. At night, around their camp, the Canadians and Dene took turns on guard. Franklin, meanwhile, decided to dispatch his two Inuit interpreters ahead on foot with presents to try to ensure a peaceful reception should any Inuit parties be in the area. The interpreters, Augustus and Junius, were by no means certain that they'd be well received; since they were from Hudson Bay, they weren't familiar with the people of these lands. As a precaution, they each carried a pistol. Franklin noted: "We felt great reluctance in exposing our two little interpreters, who had rendered themselves dear to the whole party . . . but this course of proceeding appeared in their opinion and our own to offer the only chance of gaining an interview."[9]

Augustus and Junius came across a small party of Inuit camped below Bloody Falls—the site where fifty years earlier Matonabbee's band had massacred the Inuit—and tried to communicate with them across the river. Their dialect differed from their own, and these Inuit were understandably wary of strangers. Later, when Franklin, Akaitcho, and the others arrived, the Inuit fled in fear—leaving behind an old man who was too infirm to escape. The elder, after his initial terror, eventually calmed down enough to speak with Franklin through the interpreters. He told them what he knew about the lands to the east, explaining that his small band, consisting of only eight hunters, spent their summers catching salmon at the river's mouth before heading a short distance west to build igloos for the winter.

Akaitcho and the Dene were uneasy about finding themselves deep in Inuit territory, as were several of the Canadians who could speak Athabaskan and understood the horror tales the Dene told of past Inuit attacks. Akaitcho now decided to quit the journey and head south to where it was safer. Franklin could do nothing to prevent him and the Dene from leaving, but he forced most of the Canadians to stay. Only Wentzel and four Canadian voyageurs, as well as the wives and children, were permitted to return to Fort Enterprise—where they were to hunt and lay up a stock of provisions to last the winter. Franklin, along with Dr. Richardson, Hood, Back, Hepburn, fifteen Canadians, and the two Inuit, Junius and Augustus, pressed on downriver.

They portaged around Bloody Falls—where the bleached bones and crushed skulls of the Inuit massacred by Matonabbee's band were still lying on the tundra—and soon reached the seacoast. Franklin noted:

> Our Canadian voyagers . . . were amused by their first view of the sea and particularly with the sight of seals . . . But these sensations gave place to despondency before the evening had elapsed. They were terrified at the idea of a voyage through an icy sea in bark canoes. They speculated on the length of the journey, the roughness of the sea, the uncertainty of provisions, the exposure to cold where we could expect no fuel, and the prospect of having to re-traverse the barren grounds to get to some establishment.[10]

If Franklin had had more sense, he might have listened to these fears rather than condemning his men to a death march. Instead he pressed blindly on—hoping to chart the seacoast as the first step in figuring out if there was a Northwest Passage.

While the frigid sea rightly terrified the Canadian woodsmen, the English sailors found it "an element more congenial with our habits," as Franklin put it.[11] Divided into two birchbark canoes outfitted with sails, they pushed off into thick fog across the water, heading eastward beneath towering rock cliffs, along desolate islands, and through drift-ing ice floes. Franklin noted with encouragement: "This part of the coast is the most sterile and inhospitable that can be imagined."[12] Fierce gales caused the ice floes to crash onto the rocky coast; if their canoes were caught between floe and shore they might have easily been crushed. At night, the merciless wind sweeping off the frigid sea was so fierce as to rip down their tents while the men huddled inside them.

Some of their bags of pemmican, having gotten wet, turned mouldy. And despite catching the occasional arctic char and shooting caribou, muskox, and even grizzly bears, their provisions quickly began to run low. Alarmed, Franklin dispatched Hepburn and the two Inuit inter-preters inland to search for any Inuit who might be willing to trade for food—but none were to be found. Given the harshness of the environ-ment, parties of Inuit were by necessity few and far between.

By August 18, the party had managed to make it over five hundred kilometres east along the indented coastline. Eventually, they came to a view of limitless ocean stretching far away to the horizon—a sight that staggered the Canadians, accustomed as they were to a life spent in forests. Exposed to the open sea, heavy squalls and violent gales pinned the party on shore, and at night repeatedly blew down their tents. "The Canadians," Franklin observed, "now had the opportunity of witness-ing the effect of a storm upon the sea, and the sight increased their desire of quitting it."[13]

For four days the fierce gales kept the party windbound on the bar-ren coast. With their food dwindling and winter coming, even Franklin realized that they had to turn back. He named the cape they'd reached Point Turnagain. It was none too soon; as they crawled out of their tents the morning of August 20, fear struck even the bravest hearts among them: ice was forming on the small tundra pools. If the weather were to trap them on the tundra, they would starve to death. It was clear to everyone that they'd never make it back to Fort Enterprise by retracing their route; a shortcut of some kind was needed. After careful consideration, they decided to try fighting their way up a river they'd come across while following the coastline. They hoped that this river (which Franklin named Hood's River after the midshipman) would take them far inland to a point where they could cut southwest back to Fort Enterprise. It wasn't going to be easy—even under the best conditions in midsummer, trying to travel *against the current* on swift-flowing, frigid Arctic rivers requires an almost Herculean effort.

The voyageurs understood what was required of them much better than Franklin and the British officers did. Franklin noted that the voyageurs, fearful of the oncoming winter, "embarked with the utmost alacrity and paddled with unusual vigour of a distance of about twenty miles before noon."[14] They were still at the mercy of the sea, however, and dangerous waves forced them to hole up on shore for the remainder of the day. At night frost covered the ground, chilling the men to the marrow inside their inadequate tents. The dawn brought no relief from the gales, but so great had their terror become at finding themselves trapped by the oncoming winter that even the voyageurs consented to risk a straight traverse across miles of open ocean to reach Hood's River. On this white-knuckle crossing the waves were so high that, although the two canoes were only a short distance apart, it was often impossible to see the masthead of the other vessel over the swells.

By August 25 they had escaped the dangers of the seacoast—having covered over a thousand kilometres of uncharted shoreline—and reached Hood's River. This unknown river proved more majestic than anything they'd ever seen—at one point it plunged through a deep gorge some sixty metres high with vertical cliffs that in some places were only a few metres apart. Along this spectacular gorge they encountered two huge waterfalls, one some twenty metres high and the other well over thirty. While the voyageurs struggled valiantly to portage their canoes and supplies around these formidable obstacles, Franklin noted that Hood and Back "took beautiful sketches of this majestic scene."[15]

Although the river's otherworldly beauty seemed like something out of a fairy tale, its fierce current and numerous rapids rendered upstream travel almost impossible. As a result, they decided to break up the two large canoes, and from their materials construct two smaller ones that could be more easily portaged. Franklin, using the one talent he did possess, astronomical navigation, had concluded that they were 149 miles in a straight line from Point Lake, a body of water they had camped on in the spring. His plan was to head overland on foot directly to this point. On September 1, with snow falling, they got underway; the canoes were now light enough that they could be carried by one voyageur each. The rest of the Canadians each shouldered a ninety-pound pack consisting of ammunition, clothing, blankets, the tents (distributed among the party), three kettles, ice chisels, hatchets, fishing nets, astronomical instruments, and dried meat. The British naval officers "carried such a portion of their own things as their strength would permit."[16]

St. Germain and Augustus, the most skilled hunters in the party, managed to track and kill a muskox, providing them with much needed food. But the weather turned bitterly cold. The winds were so strong that the voyageurs carrying the canoes were frequently knocked over—damaging one beyond repair. They made the most of this by turning the canoe into firewood—a scarce commodity on the barren tundra. But within just a few days of setting out, their situation had deteriorated. Violent gales, sleet, rain, and snow forced them to hole up in their tents all day. Snow drifts formed over a metre deep around the tents; Franklin recorded that "even inside there was a covering of several inches on the blankets." What bothered them most, though, were their empty stomachs.[17]

The party, growing weaker by the day, had less and less success hunting. In desperation they turned to subsisting on lichens, known as rock tripe, wherever any could be found. To make matters worse, on September 9 they found their progress blocked by a river about a hundred metres wide. Their sole remaining canoe could carry only four people at a time, with three paddling and a fourth riding as a passenger, but only if the passenger lay flat on the bottom, "by no means a pleasant position owing to its leakiness," as Franklin put it.[18] The three strongest voyageurs, St. Germain, Jean-Baptiste Adam, and Joseph Peltier, paddled the canoe and eventually managed to ferry everyone across in turns.

The party staggered onward across the rugged tundra in fog that made it impossible to see more than a few feet in any direction. The day after crossing the river, at noon the thick fog lifted and revealed— almost like a mirage to starving men—a herd of muskox grazing in a valley. Everyone froze at the sight of these prehistoric beasts. The best hunters were sent forward to try to bring one down, no easy task with the smooth-bore, muzzle-loading muskets of the era. It took two hours of careful, methodical stalking for the hunters to get within gunshot and kill one of the herd. From a hill, Franklin and the others had watched the hunt with "extreme anxiety."[19] With the muskox dead, Franklin noted:

> To skin and cut up the animal was the work of a few minutes. The contents of its stomach were devoured upon the spot, and the raw intestines, which were next attacked, were pronounced by the most delicate among us to be excellent . . . This was the sixth day since we had had a good meal.[20]

Within two days, even restricting themselves to one meal a day, they had devoured the entire muskox—an animal of some seven hundred pounds.

The men were now walking in knee-deep snow, the voyageurs' moccasins torn to shreds by the sharp, jagged rocks scattered across the tundra. Then, on September 13, to their "extreme mortification," they found a giant lake enclosed by high hills blocking their route.[21] They wandered along it for miles, desperately seeking somewhere to cross; finally, they reluctantly camped on its shores. As Franklin recounted, "We supped off a single partridge and some *tripe de roche*; this unpalatable weed was now quite nauseous to the whole party, and . . . produced bowel complaints. Mr. Hood was the greatest sufferer from this cause."[22] During the night one of the Canadians, Matthew Crédit, went missing. By this time the Canadian voyageurs, growing weaker by the day from their heavy packs and lack of food, insisted on lightening their loads of everything except ammunition, clothing, and the British officers' navigational instruments. Franklin, however, disagreed; he was, as he put it, "extremely distressed at discovering that our improvident companions . . . had thrown away three of the fishing-nets, and burned the floats."[23]

But even in the midst of their worsening situation there were acts of heroic selflessness. On the morning of September 14, one of the voyageurs, Ignace Perrault, approached the four British officers, who were sitting downcast around a small fire, and presented each with a small piece of meat he'd saved from his own allowance. Franklin recorded: "It was received with great thankfulness, and such an act of self-denial and kindness, being totally unexpected in a Canadian voyageur, filled our eyes with tears."[24]

There was another glimmer of hope that cold morning when Crédit, the missing voyageur, returned with news that he'd killed two caribou. They would need the strength provided by a good meal for the travails of what lay ahead—yet another perilous river crossing. They'd reached the end of the lake, but a roaring, three-hundred-metre-wide river now blocked their path. The two healthiest voyageurs, St. Germain and

Solomon Belanger, piloted the canoe while Franklin rode in the middle as a passenger and the others watched from shore.

They attempted to ferry across immediately above the rapid, but in mid-channel the wind and the current proved too strong and Belanger, trying to push them off a rock, missed his mark and upset the canoe. All three men plunged into the frigid, rushing waters, clinging to their overturned canoe until they reached a boulder, where they managed to stand up waist-deep. St. Germain and Belanger, with almost super-human effort, emptied the canoe, and while Belanger held it steady, St. Germain lifted Franklin into it. Then St. Germain, "in a very dexterous manner," also climbed in.[25] "It was impossible, however, to embark Belanger," Franklin wrote, "as the canoe would have hurried down the rapid the moment he raised his foot from the rock on which he stood. We were, therefore, compelled to leave him in this perilous situation. We had not gone twenty yards before the canoe, striking on a sunken rock, went down."[26]

The rapids were shallow enough that Franklin and St. Germain were able to stand and again empty the canoe. On their third attempt, they finally reached the opposite shore. But Belanger was still stranded in the centre of the rapid, waist-deep in the icy, rushing waters, and as Franklin noted, "suffering extremely . . . He called piteously for relief, and St. Germain on his return endeavoured to embark him, but in vain."[27] The other voyageurs on the far side bravely attempted to wade out into the swirling waters and get close enough to toss a rope to Belanger. This too failed. Finally, with Belanger's strength nearly exhausted, the rope reached him when tossed from the canoe. Franklin recorded that "he was dragged perfectly senseless through the rapid."[28] Dr. Richardson immediately ordered the men to strip Belanger's wet clothing off—then two other men undressed and were rolled up in blankets with Belanger to try to revive him with their body warmth. Gradually, the barely conscious voyageur recovered.

With the river eventually crossed at great risk, the party found themselves in increasingly hilly, rocky land. Perrault, fortunately, killed another caribou. But with the snow knee-deep, their strength was nearly depleted. The British officers were unable to keep up with the Canadians, who were more accustomed to enduring such hardships. The voyageurs, hopeful that they were nearing Point Lake, where they'd been in the spring, pushed on ahead during the day. But, as Franklin recorded, "When they failed to see the lake that night they threatened to throw away their bundles and quit us, which rash act they would probably have done had they known what track to pursue."[29] With the Canadians carrying the heavy loads and doing all the hunting, it's no wonder that they felt like abandoning the British. However, the fact that only the naval officers could work out their positions and navigate ruled this out. With things getting increasingly desperate, Dr. Richardson, ever the dedicated naturalist, at last abandoned the plant and mineral specimens he'd collected along the seacoast.

On September 22, ragged and starving, they came to a large lake that they assumed was a branch of Point Lake. During the day's hard marching, half-delirious from famine, the party increasingly became separated from each other as stragglers fell behind and the strongest hunters pushed on ahead. Their last canoe, meanwhile, was abandoned after it was broken beyond repair by the wind repeatedly knocking over the voyageur carrying it. This alarmed Franklin—he knew that they might encounter yet more rivers blocking their path. Tensions began to mount; the voyageurs threatened again to abandon the officers, who likewise threatened violence to any man who should desert them. That evening, around a sputtering fire of dwarf willows, the men desperately gnawed on their old leather shoes.

The morning after this dreadful night, the hunters managed to kill five small caribou—restoring their hopes and giving them strength to push on. On September 26 they at last reached the Coppermine River. But crossing its swift rapids without a canoe would be another matter entirely. As they scoured the area for any stunted spruces that could be used to build a raft, Franklin sent Back, Pierre St. Germain, and Beauparlant to look for a place to cross. Franklin noted the mounting desperation: "Our people, through despondency, had become careless and disobedient and had ceased to dread punishment or hope of reward."[30] During their search along a lake, the party came across the rotten remains of a caribou carcass in the cleft of a rock, into which it had evidently fallen months earlier. "We supped on the remains of the putrid deer," Franklin wrote, "and the men . . . scraped together the contents of its intestines which were scattered on the rock and added them to their meal."[31]

By September 29, with any hope of finding stunted spruces abandoned, the desperate decision was made to attempt crossing on a raft. The voyageurs cut huge numbers of willows and bound them together, eventually completing a small raft that was barely able to support the weight of a single man. Two voyageurs, Benoit and Belanger, nonetheless tried valiantly and repeatedly to traverse the frigid waters of the Coppermine—but it proved impossible to make any headway in the swift current, especially without paddles, which they'd burned earlier when in dire need of firewood. With hope fading, Dr. Richardson volunteered to risk his life to save them. Franklin recorded:

> Dr. Richardson . . . proposed to swim across the stream with a line and haul the raft over. He launched into the stream with the line round his middle, but when he got a short distance from the bank, his arms became benumbed with cold, and he lost the power of moving them; still, he persevered, and turning on his back, had nearly gained the opposite bank, when his legs also became powerless, and to our infinite alarm, we beheld him sink. We instantly hauled upon the line and he came again to the surface and was gradually drawn ashore in an almost lifeless state. Being rolled up in blankets, he was placed

before a good fire of willows . . . He recovered strength gradually . . .
I cannot describe what everyone felt at beholding the skeleton which
the Doctor's debilitated frame exhibited.[32]

Meanwhile, one of their Inuit interpreters, Junius, had gone missing;
Augustus's attempt to track him proved to no avail. On October 1,
Back, St. Germain, and Beauparlant, having failed to find any way to
cross the river, rejoined the main group. But then St. Germain, the
most experienced of the voyageurs, came up with a new plan to cross
the river. He thought it might just be possible to fashion a canoe by
sewing together the waterproof canvas the men used as backpacks and
then stretching it over a frame of willows.

There was no time to lose—a fierce snowstorm had struck and the
men were reduced to eating rock tripe and old caribou bones they'd dug
up on the tundra. The four British officers had become so weak from
starvation that they were almost unable to walk—of the British, only
Hepburn, the common sailor, was left standing. St. Germain and Adam
worked frantically on the canvas canoe, and by October 4 had it ready.
In this frail little vessel, St. Germain, with exceptional courage, managed to cross the river. It was then drawn back across the water with a
rope, and in this manner, one by one, the party was conveyed over.
Junius, the still missing Inuit interpreter, was sadly given up for lost.

They were still a long way from Fort Enterprise—and, with the
snow deepening, their trek became a death march. Stragglers could no
longer keep up; two of the voyageurs, Registe Vaillant and Crédit, collapsed and fell behind. Some of the other voyageurs urged permission
to abandon their loads and push on with all speed to Fort Enterprise,
where they would seek help. At first, Franklin refused. He pointed out
that none of them knew the course to pursue, and that none of the officers who could navigate were capable of maintaining the Canadians'
pace. But after much discussion and bickering, it was clear that something

had to be done. Dr. Richardson and Hood were so weakened that they volunteered to remain behind with a single attendant, the still relatively strong Hepburn, rather than slow the party down and condemn them all to death. St. Germain, Belanger, and Beauparlant, the strongest voyageurs left, along with Back, were sent ahead. Franklin and the other voyageurs would follow as best as they could.

But soon after leaving Richardson, Hood, and Hepburn at the tent, several of Franklin's party became too weak to continue. Perrault felt dizzy and kept collapsing after only a few steps. All they could offer him for relief was some Labrador tea and scraps of burnt leather. Two other voyageurs, Michel Teroahaute and Jean-Baptiste Belanger, were in an equally bad state; all three gave up and tried to stagger back to the tent. A short time afterward, a fourth voyageur, Antonio Fontano, also collapsed in exhaustion and had to turn back. Meanwhile, the sole remaining Inuk, Augustus, impatient with these delays, pressed on by himself and caught up with Back's advance party.

Franklin's party was reduced to just himself and four voyageurs. For days they staggered through the deep snow, living off only a few morsels of rock tripe and leather clothing. The cold had by now frozen the rivers solid, so at least they no longer had difficulty crossing them. On the morning of October 12 the starving men at last reached Fort Enterprise. But, to their horror, they found no one there and the cabins destitute of all provisions. A letter left by Back—who'd reached the post with St. Germain and Solomon Belanger a few days before—explained that, having found the cabins deserted, they'd pressed on in search of Akaitcho and the Dene, who were now their only hope of survival.

Back's party, in reality led by the voyageur St. Germain, had risked crossing half-frozen rivers in their speed to reach Fort Enterprise. Twice Belanger had fallen through the ice and was nearly killed; the other men had desperately fastened their belts together to haul him out. They'd managed to reach the fort five days after leaving Franklin and the others—only to find it abandoned. With no other choice, St. Germain had led them onward to where they hoped to catch fish or find the Dene. On this grim march, Beauparlant, almost paralyzed with hunger, fell behind. He froze to death overnight.

After reading Back's note, Franklin and the exhausted voyageurs desperately searched around the fort for anything to eat. They found a few old hides and some discarded bones buried in the ashes of the fire-places; for firewood, they tore up the floorboards. Meanwhile, Augustus emerged, himself weakened by hunger. A few days later, Solomon Belanger, who'd gone ahead with Back, staggered into the cabin half-frozen to death; he'd fallen into a rapid and nearly died of hypothermia. When he recovered enough to speak, he explained that Back had been unable to find Akaitcho or the Dene and was camped some distance away awaiting instructions. Franklin decided that he, along with Augustus and the voyageur Joseph Benoit, would set out to find Back. With him they would march all the way to Fort Providence on Great Slave Lake for aid—a horrifying prospect given the distance involved. The other weakened Canadians would be left at Fort Enterprise.

But Franklin was unable to keep up with his two companions, and after a day he gave up and staggered back to the fort, leaving Augustus and Benoit to push on alone. Throughout October the men at Fort Enterprise slowly starved—only one of them, Peltier, had strength enough to chop wood to keep them from freezing. Rock tripe, old hides, and bones were their only sustenance.

Meanwhile, back at the lonely campsite on the snowy barrens where Dr. Richardson, Hood, and Hepburn had been abandoned, things were even more appalling. Of the four voyageurs who'd been unable to keep up with Franklin's party, only one, Michel, had found his way back to the tent. The other three, Jean-Baptiste Belanger, Perrault, and Fontano, had disappeared. During a snowstorm they'd become separated from each other. Michel had spent the night somewhere to the north of the tent, and only managed to find it in the morning. The others were presumably lost somewhere on the barrens. Fortunately, Michel, a skilled hunter, had managed to kill a partridge and a hare, which he shared with Richardson, Hood, and Hepburn. He'd also spotted a clump of stunted spruces about a kilometre and a half from their camp, and asked for a hatchet to go back and gather wood; he preferred, he said, to stay there by a fire rather than shiver inside the tent.

After a few days, with Hood's vision fading from the effects of starvation, Dr. Richardson resolved that they ought to use what strength they still had to drag the tent and themselves to Michel's clump of spruces—where at least there'd be wood for a fire. But when they arrived Michel was nowhere to be found; they feared he'd become disoriented and lost like the others somewhere on the tundra. It was a surprise, then, when a short time later he emerged out of the snow carrying some fresh meat. Michel had found, he explained, the remains of a dead wolf that had been gouged by a caribou's antler; he'd been busy cutting it up. The starving men eagerly devoured the wolf meat he gave them.

But Michel's behaviour over the following days became increasingly suspicious. He'd leave the camp each morning in search of food, rebuffing Richardson's offer to accompany him, and at night he refused to sleep in the tent with the others, saying that he preferred to remain by the fire. On October 13 a snowstorm kept him in camp, but, as Richardson noted, the next day, "the gale abating, Michel set out as he said to hunt, but returned unexpectedly in a very short time. This conduct surprised us, and his contradictory and evasory answers to our questions excited some suspicions."[33] Dr. Richardson and Hepburn assumed that he'd hidden a stash of caribou meat and was keeping it for himself.

The men became increasingly suspicious of each other. Michel would disappear for days—his evident strength suggesting that he'd been eating something more nourishing than lichens or old caribou bones. On the morning of October 20, Michel and the ailing Hood were arguing around their campfire when Richardson wandered off to gather rock tripe and Hepburn struggled to chop down a nearby tree. Richardson had been gone only a short time when he heard a gunshot. When the doctor staggered back into the camp, he saw Hood lying dead—a gunshot wound in his forehead. His first thought was that Hood, yielding to despair, had put an end to his own life. But he soon realized that the bullet had passed through the back of Hood's head; moreover, his hair was singed, indicating that the shot had been fired at point-blank range. Michel offered only vague explanations, insisting that he'd been alone inside the tent when the gun went off. Richardson and Hepburn were too weak to argue, and unable to bury Hood's body, they feebly dragged it into a nearby clump of willows. Returning to their fire, Richardson gave a brief eulogy in addition to their evening prayers.

The next afternoon Michel managed to kill several ptarmigans, which he shared with the starving Hepburn and Richardson. But the men remained wary of each other and kept their pistols at their sides at all times. On October 23, they felt strong enough to continue hiking in the direction of Fort Enterprise. As they wandered, a horrible realization began to eat away at Dr. Richardson. Turning the matter over in his troubled mind, he found it increasingly difficult to avoid the conclusion that the "meat" Michel had been bringing to camp for the past week was from the corpses of the dead voyageurs who'd gone missing. With horror, he recalled Michel's having asked for the hatchet the night he'd gone off; in retrospect, it seemed clear that it was for chopping up the frozen bodies of Belanger and Perrault. The supposed meat from a wolf gouged by a caribou that they'd all so eagerly devoured had more than likely been the remains of one of the dead voyageurs. Whether the three missing men, after falling behind from Franklin's group, had been murdered by Michel or had died of starvation and Michel only ate their bodies afterward was uncertain. At minimum, it was plain that Michel had murdered Hood, presumably after the food supply offered by the other corpses had run out.

When Michel was out of earshot, Richardson confided in Hepburn, who concurred with his suspicions. Both felt that Michel's plan was to cannibalize them in order to survive the march back to Fort Enterprise. Since they were weaker than Michel—who had strength from the corpses he'd been feeding upon—they would have to plan their attack with stealth. Moreover, Michel, besides his musket, was armed with two flintlock pistols, a bayonet, and a large knife. When Michel halted briefly to gather some rock tripe from an exposed boulder, Hepburn and Richardson were afforded their chance. Richardson cocked his pistol, and in his own words, "Immediately upon Michel's coming up to us I put an end to his life by shooting him through the head."[34]

Thus ended Michel Teroahaute. Richardson and Hepburn now staggered on alone for another six days in an almost delirious state from hunger. At one point they came upon the track of a wolverine, which had evidently been dragging something—they followed it and found the clean-picked carcass of a caribou. They eagerly crushed the spinal cord to get at the marrow inside, devouring it raw. Finally, on October 29, they reached a rocky ridge overlooking Fort Enterprise. Smoke was rising from one of the chimneys. Richardson recorded:

> Upon entering the now desolate building, we had the satisfaction of embracing Captain Franklin, but no words can convey an idea of the filth and wretchedness that met our eyes on looking around. Our own misery had stolen upon us by degrees, and we were accustomed to the contemplation of each other's emaciated figures, but the ghastly countenances, dilated eye-balls and sepulchral voices of Captain Franklin and those with him were more than we could at first bear.[35]

Although they were reunited, without immediate assistance the log walls of the cabin would become their tomb. The remaining Canadian voyageurs, Peltier, Adam, and François Samandre, were incapable of rising from their beds. Franklin was only slightly better, with barely the strength to crawl on his hands and knees in the snow outside the cabin searching for old bones to eat. Dr. Richardson and Hepburn were strong enough to go on short walks in search of rock tripe and ptarmigan. But both grew weaker by the day. By November 1 Peltier's condition had worsened still further; he slipped in and out of consciousness. As Franklin reported, "We were alarmed by hearing a rattling in his throat and, on the doctor examining him, he was found to be speechless. He died in the course of the night."[36] That same night, Samandre also died. Franklin and the others were too weak to remove the bodies, let alone bury them. All they could do was drag the corpses to the far side of the cabin.

For another week the four remaining survivors subsisted on crushed bone that they turned into a thin soup. Then, suddenly, came the sound of musket fire. They could scarcely believe their eyes: out of the woods emerged three Dene natives whom they recognized as belonging to Akaitcho's band. St. Germain, Back, and Augustus, it turned out, had reached Akaitcho's camp two days earlier and informed them of the expedition's distress. Akaitcho had at once dispatched his three fastest companions to aid Franklin and his men.

One can only imagine the Dene's horror when they entered the cabin and beheld the two corpses and the four skeletal figures of the survivors. The trio, only one of whom, Crooked Foot, is known by name, set about to save Franklin and the others. They fed them dried caribou meat, fat, and caribou tongues, which, although saving their lives, proved more than their shrunken stomachs could handle and caused them all to become violently ill. But gradually they recovered. The Dene cleaned up the cabin; hauled in firewood and kept a blazing fire going to warm the half-frozen men; and fished and hunted to keep them fed. Then, after nursing them back from the brink of death, the Dene, in Franklin's words, "next turned their attention to our personal appearances and prevailed upon us to shave and wash ourselves."[37]

By November 16, nine days after they'd been rescued, the four survivors had recovered sufficiently to leave Fort Enterprise and begin the
trek to Akaitcho's camp. Franklin, amazed at the kindness shown to
him by Crooked Foot and his two companions, noted of their trek:

> The Indians treated us with the utmost tenderness, gave us their snow
> shoes, and walked without, themselves, keeping by our sides so that
> they might lift us when we fell. The Indians prepared our encamp
> ment, cooked for us and fed us as if we had been children; evincing
> humanity that would have done honour to the most civilized people.[38]

After a ten-day journey under the care of their Dene saviours,
Franklin and the others reached Akaitcho's winter camp. Here they
found their Inuit interpreter, Augustus, in good health, and learned that
Back, St. Germain, and Belanger had recovered enough strength to push
on to Fort Providence on Great Slave Lake, where there were sufficient
provisions to survive the winter. Fifteen days later, Franklin, Richardson,
Hepburn, and Adam—the sole surviving Canadian in Franklin's
group—made it to Fort Providence, where they were reunited with the
other survivors of their disastrous ordeal.

At Fort Providence Franklin had intended to repay Akaitcho and his
band's kindness as richly as he could with gifts of iron tools, kettles, muskets, ammunition, tobacco, and other trade goods, only to discover that
there were none to distribute. Akaitcho, however, took this disappointment in stride, explaining rather philosophically,

> The world goes badly. All are poor. You are poor, the traders appear
> to be poor, I and my party are poor likewise. Since the goods have not
> come, we cannot have them. I do not regret having supplied you with
> provisions, for a Copper Indian cannot permit white men to suffer
> from want of food on his lands.[39]

Of the twenty men who'd set off under Franklin's command to chart the Arctic shoreline, eleven never returned. Nine Canadian voyageurs had died—Joseph Peltier, Ignace Perrault, Jean-Baptiste Belanger, François Samandre, Antonio Fontano, Michel Teroahaute, Matthew Crédit, Gabriel Beauparlant, and Registe Vaillant—as had the Inuit interpreter Junius and the English midshipman Robert Hood. Whatever their failings, they had shown tremendous fortitude and courage as they endured extreme deprivations and suffering in what to them was an alien environment. But their heroics had been made necessary only by Franklin's ignorance, which put all their lives in jeopardy.

Incredibly, after this disastrous ordeal, the British Admiralty decided that Franklin was just the man to lead another overland Arctic expedition. Four years later, in 1825, Richardson, Back, and Hepburn willingly joined him on a second journey that, compared with their first nightmarish undertaking, went smoothly. Together they added a thousand kilometres of previously uncharted Arctic coastline to the map. But Franklin was still no wiser than he'd been on his first journey. Twenty years after that, in 1845, he led a final, doomed quest to discover the Northwest Passage. This time he had two ships and 132 men under his command—none of whom ever saw England again. They perished from starvation, hypothermia, scurvy, and possibly lead poisoning.

Ironically, it was Franklin's incompetence that ultimately led to the successful charting of the Northwest Passage and the rest of North America's mainland Arctic coastline. Numerous expeditions were dispatched to find Franklin and his lost ships—the British navy and others launched them by sea, and the Hudson's Bay Company mounted them overland. And although none of them could quite find Franklin, in the process of searching for him they filled in much of the remaining blank spots on the Arctic map.

The most successful of the overland quests were led by Franklin's old companion Dr. Richardson and the formidable Dr. John Rae, a self-sufficient explorer who excelled in snowshoeing, hunting, igloo building, and navigation. It was Rae who, through conversations with Inuit hunters, eventually ascertained the fate of Franklin's ill-fated crews. Meanwhile, the fur trade explorers Peter Warren Dease and Thomas Simpson together charted much of the northwest Arctic by canoe from 1836 to 1839. Dease and Simpson proved a remarkably effective exploring duo (until Simpson went insane, murdered two companions, and then shot himself).

✳

The adventures, follies, tragedies, and heroic accomplishments of the first phase of this "golden age" of Arctic exploration are told in a splendid 1828 map that accompanied the publication of Franklin's account of his explorations. The map, "Shewing the discoveries made by the British Officers in the Arctic Regions from the year 1818 to 1826," combines the discoveries of Franklin's expeditions with those of the British Royal Navy captains Sir James Ross and Sir William Edward Parry, both much more competent explorers than Franklin and yet much less famous. The map reveals the complete outline of Hudson Bay, including the westward indent of Chesterfield Inlet, which geographers had earlier hoped might prove to be a passage straight across the continent to the Pacific. As the map makes clear, that was wishful thinking. To the west, across the barren interior, lie the vast inland waters of Great Slave and Great Bear Lake; traced on the map through these lakes are Franklin's exploration routes down the Coppermine to the Arctic Ocean, his overland traverse from the Hood River back to Fort Enterprise, and his later 1825 expedition down the Mackenzie River, along the Arctic coastline, and through Great Bear. The map's details, given improvements in the measuring of latitude and longitude—again, one skill Franklin did possess—are thoroughly impressive. But enormous blank spaces remain uncharted, in particular a large gap on the northern Alaskan coastline and along the coast east of Point Turnagain, the farthest point Franklin reached. Most strikingly, the Northwest Passage itself remains uncharted, impenetrable ice having so far defeated all attempts to find a way through the Arctic maze. Not until the early twentieth century would a ship, under the command of the explorer Roald Amundsen, manage to make it all the way through the ice from the Atlantic to the Pacific. And well into the twentieth century there were still unmapped portions of Canada's High Arctic—the final frontier, as it were, of North American exploration.

Franklin and his fellow naval officers had believed that, in charting these frozen lands, they were claiming them henceforth for the British Empire—lest the Americans, Danes, or Russians seek an Arctic domain of their own. As for the Canadians who had accompanied Franklin— and in fact performed most of the hard work of exploration—they never thought of these icy lands as part of Canada. To them, "Canada" was a land far away in the southeast: the forests and farms of the Great Lakes– St. Lawrence River corridor. And although by the time of Franklin's journeys the Canadians had formed a strong sense of their own identity, with their own set of folk heroes, songs, customs, and even national symbols, they hadn't dreamed of Canada one day claiming an empire of its own. However, in their journeys far beyond the country's existing limits, these voyageurs and explorers were inadvertently planting the seeds of a new and greatly enlarged Canada—an idea that, in just a few generations, would germinate into Canadian Confederation. Alexander Mackenzie had earlier envisioned something like it, and by the 1860s his colonial successors spoke openly of building a transcontinental nation: an expanded Canada that would claim as its own the lands explored by generations of its explorers, voyageurs, and fur traders—including, ultimately, the farthest reaches of the Arctic. It's a legacy that, for better or worse, created the modern Canada we know today.

AFTERWORD

He said he should prefer not to know the sources of the Nile, and that
there should be some unknown regions preserved as hunting-grounds for
the poetic imagination.

—GEORGE ELIOT, *Middlemarch*, 1874

If there's been one constant throughout Canada's history, it's been our wilderness. Vast, forbidding, mysterious, at times both grim and enticing—Canada's wilderness is many things. For centuries it nurtured and sustained First Nations. European explorers were challenged and awed by its immensity, its strangeness, and it lured and enchanted generations of voyageurs, coureurs de bois, and other pathfinders. For French and English settlers it loomed large, surrounded as they were in their fledgling farms and tiny frontier outposts by its ancient, unbroken forests. It was the stage for the great dramas of Canada's past—its struggles, wars, tragedies, crimes, follies, and odd acts of heroism. The wilderness, much more than hockey or the canoe or some bland modern platitude, is the real soul of Canada.

But as more and more of Canada has become mapped—and mapped in ever greater detail—we've gradually lost a sense of mystery about what might lie beyond the seas, over the mountains, around the next river bend. Our modern Google Maps doesn't generally include lands of frost giants, sasquatch, or wendigoes. Nor do we often find blank spaces labelled "these parts entirely unknown." As the scope of our maps has expanded, it seems the scope for our imaginations has shrunk. Exploration and mapmaking made possible the spread of knowledge and the intermingling of cultures and people worldwide, in the process bringing about the concept of a place called "Canada." But they also spelled the end of ancient ways of doing things and the destruction of much of the natural world. It's not just fantastic beasts that have vanished from our maps; there's less mystery in the woods in part because there are *less woods*—and fewer plants and animals—than there once were.

Many species once known intimately to Canada's First Nations are now either severely diminished or gone forever. The great auks, Labrador ducks, and sea minks that greeted Jacques Cartier are extinct; blue whales, humpbacks, and other sea creatures that adorned early maps are much reduced. The giant sturgeons and alligator gars found in Champlain's journals have become rare; other freshwater fish like the blue walleye have vanished. So has the eastern elk, and to that we can add the near extinction of the Plains bison and the eastern cougar, among others. The Carolina parakeet that bewitched Champlain into losing his way will never be seen again; the huge flocks of passenger pigeons that could blot out the skies are gone. Immense old-growth forests that once cloaked much of southern Canada—and that awed the young officer John Le Couteur at Fort Erie—have nearly all been cleared to make way for farms, cities, highways, and shopping malls. Trees like the American chestnut—its nuts an essential food source for Eastern Woodland peoples, and something that Champlain munched on as he marched with the Wendat—have been destroyed by invasive blight. A similar fate has befallen the ash (dying rapidly from emerald ash borer), the elm (devastated by the invasive Dutch elm disease), and the butternut (killed by an invasive fungus). The latter's delicious nuts had been a welcome discovery for the Vikings, but it's now scarcely found anywhere in Canada.

A few years ago I went back to my family home to revisit my old haunts in the woods—the place where I first learned about maps and dreamed, as did earlier generations of Canadians, of what might lie hidden beyond the horizons. But it felt surreal, like a nightmare: the numerous ash trees, once the most common in the forest, had been stripped, seemingly overnight, of their bark. All around me, every last one of them was dead or dying from the invasive emerald ash borer. These were the trees I'd known since childhood—the trees I'd climbed up or scampered over when they blew down across swamps, and from whose wood I'd fashioned arrows for my bow and carved the walking stick I still carry. Not one had been spared—even the largest ash in the heart of the forest, beneath whose ancient branches I'd so often camped with my brother and cousins, was dying. Seeing it now, I could barely keep myself from weeping. If we lose our forests, our *wilderness*, we lose a huge part of what makes "Canada" Canada.

Soon after writing this book—having spent more time staring at maps than is probably healthy—I set off on a journey alone across Canada's North. In doing so I was following in the footsteps of Hearne and Matonabbee and all those others who'd felt the pull of unknown places beyond the edge of the map. Nominally, I was crossing the Arctic to celebrate "Canada's 150th Birthday." But from a historical point of view, "Canada" is a changing thing, something that exists in our imaginations. It could be home to frost giants or sasquatches, to unicorns or ostriches. To some, it's a nation, to others, an empire—and an unwelcome one. Yet the truth is, I undertook my journey not so much to celebrate the past as to mourn the future—the Canada we're losing. We may not have many blanks on our maps anymore, but we still have unspoiled wilderness, and I wanted to experience as much of it as I could while it still exists. It's the bedrock of our country—the harsh but beautiful reality that gives meaning to our national identity.

Where we go from here is an open question. What would a Canada without true wilderness be like? Maybe we should stop looking at our wild places as "needing" to be developed, exploited, paved over, turned into parks, or otherwise parcelled up. There are other ways of looking at the world—of visualizing it, of putting it on the map. The Haudenosaunee concept of "Turtle Island"—the idea that all North America is a fragile, interconnected ecosystem that humans share equally with plants and animals—offers one such possibility. Perhaps the revival of indigenous cultures provides a vision for a society that gets us past seeing the natural world in terms of dollars and cents, gross domestic product, a means to an end. Indigenous knowledge holds out the hope that we'll recognize Canada's remaining wild lands and wildlife for the irreplaceable gifts that they are.

In 1867, there were still scarcely more people than bears in Canada. Any home, anywhere in the country, was a short hike or horse ride away from wilderness. It was simply the character of the country— and the omnipresent reality for those who lived in it and shaped it. When American armies had invaded Canada in 1775 and 1812, it was the wilderness as much as anything that defeated them. Ill-equipped and poorly clothed, exposed to brutal winters and vast, unnerving forests, many were rendered ragged and starving. "Canada" soon seemed a country not worth having. The French crown in 1763 had felt the same—better to get rid of the land Voltaire had summed up as "covered with snows and ice eight months of the year, inhabited by barbarians, bears and beavers" than try to carve something out of it.[1] For most of the past thousand years, few people ever found Canada a place worth settling. The Vikings abandoned their settlements; Cabot and Cartier wanted only a route to Asia. Over more than a century and a half, New France was chronically unable to attract more than small numbers of colonists. Right up until the twentieth century, prospective settlers preferred, by huge margins, the milder climes of the United States. Those who did come—and choose to stay—were the exceptions. They, uniquely, had to make their peace with northern wilderness.

Canada's 150th has come and gone. Whether in another 150 years it'll still be possible to experience the magic of unspoiled wilderness and ancient old-growth forests is uncertain. But I hope we can find the courage to chart a new path that will leave room on our maps for true wilderness—metaphorical "blank spaces" where the imagination still roams free.

ACKNOWLEDGMENTS

This book wouldn't have been possible without the help, expertise, and encouragement of a number of people. First and foremost, I'm indebted to Nick Garrison, my editor. Nick's keen insight on matters big and small helped sharpen the book's focus and make it a much more compelling story than it otherwise would've been. Without his vision, this book wouldn't have happened.

I've also been fortunate to benefit from the expertise and professionalism of a great team at Penguin Random House. David Ross, the managing editor, kept everything on schedule and running smoothly, despite the complications introduced by my expedition across Canada's North. Leah Springate designed the book layout, and Jessica Cooney handled the book's publicity (again no easy task with an author who disappears off the grid). I'm thankful for all their hard work on this project.

The copyeditor, Karen Alliston, carefully scrutinized the manuscript and helped correct errors. I'm much in her debt for her attention to detail. Any errors that remain are my own.

My literary agent, Rick Broadhead, steered me through the publishing world as expertly as any guide could. I've benefited much from his encouragement and expertise.

I must also thank family and friends who were kind enough to read early stages of this book and offer their thoughts. In particular, I want to thank Ben Shoalts, Mark Shoalts, Catherine Shoalts, Aleksia Wiatr, and Katelyn Chung. Finally, I wish to thank those people who over many years have encouraged, nurtured, and shared my passion for history and geography. This includes my old school teachers, university professors, archaeological dig companions, work colleagues, wilderness canoe partners, and many others too numerous to list. Though they may not have known it at the time, by enriching my understanding of the past, they helped make this book come to fruition.

NOTES

INTRODUCTION

1   See Michael A. Rappenglück, "Palaeolithic Timekeepers Looking At The Golden Gate Of The Ecliptic; The Lunar Cycle And The Pleiades In The Cave Of La-TETe-Du-Lion (Ardéche, France) – 21,000 BP," *Earth, Moon, and Planets*, Vol. 85, Issue 0, January 1991: 391–404; and Rappenglück, "Ice Age people find their ways by the stars: A rock picture in the Cueva de El Castillo (Spain) may represent the circumpolar constellation of the Northern Crown (CrB)," *Migration Diffusion International Journal* 1 (2), 2000: 15–28.

2   Alexander Wolodtschenko and Thomas Forner, "Prehistoric and Early Historic Maps in Europe: Conception of Cd-Atlas," *e-Perimetron*, Vol. 2, No. 2, Spring 2007: 115.

3   Jeremy Harwood and A. Sarah Bendall, *To The Ends of the Earth: 100 Maps That Changed the World* (David & Charles, 2006), 15.

4   James A. Harrell, "Turin Papyrus Map from Ancient Egypt," University of Toledo, http://www.eeescience.utoledo.edu/Faculty/Harrell/Egypt/Turin%20Papyrus/Harrell_Papyrus_Map_text.htm.

5   Eratosthenes estimated the earth's circumference was 250,000 stades, an Ancient Greek unit of measurement. There is much debate among scholars over what a stade represented, as it seems to have varied from place to place. The traditional assumption is that one stade equals 176.4 metres, which would result in an estimate of the earth's circumference of 44,100 kilometres, an error of only 10 percent larger than the earth's true circumference. However, other scholars have argued that the stade Eratosthenes used was of greater length, which would make Eratosthenes's estimate less accurate. See Newlyn Walkup, "Eratosthenes and the Mystery of the Stades - How Long Is a Stade?," *Convergence* (August 2010).

6   See Katherine L. Brown and Robin J.H. Clark, "Analysis of Pigmentary
     Materials on the Vinland Map and Tartar Relation by Raman
     Microprobe Spectroscopy," *Analytical Chemistry* 74 (15), 2002:
     3658–3661; and K.M. Towe, R.J.H. Clark, and K.A. Seaver, "Analysing
     the Vinland Map: A Critical Review of a Critical Review," *Archaeometry*
     50 (5), 2008: 887–893.

7   Daniel Harmon, *A Journal of Voyages and Travels in the Interiour of
     North America* (Andover: Flagg and Gould, 1820), 371-372.

8   Charles Francis Hall, *Life with the Esquimaux*, Volume I, (London:
     Sampson Low, Son, and Marston, 1864), 128.

9   Derek Hayes, *Historical Atlas of Canada: Canada's History Illustrated
     with Original Maps* (Vancouver: Douglas & McIntyre, 2002), 152.

10   Judith Hudson Beattie, "Indian Maps in the Hudson's Bay Company
     Archives: A Comparison of Five Area Maps Recorded by Peter Fidler,
     1801-1802," *Archivaria* 21 (Winter 1985-86): 166.

11   Malcom Lewis, "Frontier Encounters in the Field: 1511-1925," in
     *Cartographic Encounters: Pespectives on Native American Mapmaking and
     Map Use*, edited by Malcom Lewis (Chicago: University of Chicago
     Press, 1998), 24.

12   See, Katherine Woollett and Eleanor A. Maguire, "Acquiring 'the
     Knowledge' of London's Layout Drives Structural Brain Changes,"
     Current Biology, Vol. 21 (December 2011): 2109–2114.

13   Bradford Angier, *Field Guide to Edible Wild Plants* (Mechanicsburg,
     Penn: Stackpole Books, 1974).

14   As a constitutional state, or nation-state (*as opposed to a nation*), Canada
     predates almost every polity in Africa, the Middle East, Eastern Europe,
     and much of Asia, as well as Australia, New Zealand, and even many
     western European states, notably Germany (1871), Norway (1905), and
     Ireland (1921). While many Latin American states were formed earlier,
     none have constitutional settlements that have lasted as long as
     Canada's. The same is true of many of the western European states
     that although formed before 1867, do not have as old a constitution
     (i.e., France, Spain, Portugal).

15   Pierre Trudeau, "Exhaustion and Fulfillment: The Ascetic in a Canoe,"
     in *Wilderness Canada*, edited by Borden Spears, 1970.

1 THE VIKINGS: THE SKÁLHOLT MAP

1   The date of the Skálholt Map is often given as 1570. This, however,
    is an error. The more likely correct date is 1590, as Stefánsson was too
    young to have created it in 1570.

2   As quoted in Else Roesdahl, *The Vikings*, revised edition, translated
    by Susan M. Margeson and Kristen Williams (London: Penguin, 1987,
    1998), 190.

3   "The King's Mirror," in *The Viking Age: A Reader*, second edition,
    edited and translated by Angus A. Somerville and R. Andrew
    McDonald (Toronto: University of Toronto Press, 2014), 310.

4   In fact, the Vikings had likely visited Iceland as early as 860, but 870 is
    when the first permanent settlers arrived.

5   There are some who believe that the Norse never made maps, since
    none survive. This logic, however, does not seem very compelling.

6   *The Vinland Sagas: The Norse Discovery of America*, translated with
    an introduction by Magnus Magnusson and Hermann Palsson,
    (London: Penguin, 1965). *Vinland Sagas*, 49.

7   *Vinland Sagas*, 53.

8   *Vinland Sagas*, 54.

9   *Vinland Sagas*, 55.

10 From *The Saga of the Greenlanders*, as quoted in, Birgitta Linderoth
    Wallace, *Westward Vikings: The Saga of L'Anse aux Meadows*
    (St. John's: Historic Sites Association of Newfoundland and Labrador,
    2006, revised edition 2012), 17.

11 *Vinland Sagas*, 55.

12 *Vinland Sagas*, 55-56.

13 *Vinland Sagas*, 7.

14 Ibid.

15 Ibid.

16 Ibid.

17 Ibid.

18 Ibid.

19 *Eirik the Red's Saga* states that Thorvald, a pagan, led a party of ten,
    including himself, in a separate ship after the first winter while the rest
    stayed with Karlsefni. *Vinland Sagas*, 97.

20   This is based on the archaeological excavations carried out in Greenland at the Norse settlements. Based on the 144 skeletons excavated at Thjodhild's church, the average height for adult women was 156 cm, and 171 cm for adult men, but some men measured 184-185 cm tall. See Helge Ingstad, *The Viking Discovery of America: The Excavation of a Norse Settlement in L'Anse aux Meadows, Newfoundland* (St. John's, NL: Breakwater Books, 2000), 22. In contrast, adult male Inuit in the eastern Arctic averaged around 158 cm.

21   The two sagas do not agree on what the Norse traded in exchange for skins; the *Saga of the Greenlanders* says it was milk, but *Eirik the Red's Saga* says it was red cloth. Presumably, they may have traded both.

22   *Vinland Sagas.*

23   *The Vinland Sagas: The Icelandic Sagas about the First Documented Voyages Across the North Atlantic: The Saga of the Greenlanders and Eirik the Red's Saga* translated by Keneva Kunz, edited by Gisli Sigurosson (London: Penguin, 2008), 44.

24   Kirsten A. Seaver, *The Frozen Echo: Greenland and the Exploration of North America, Ca. A.D, 1000-1500* (Stanford: Stanford University Press, 1996), 28.

2   THE BIRTH OF "CANADA"

1   Older estimates placed the death toll at around ⅓ to ½ Europe's population; but more recent estimates have tended toward the higher estimate, with some arguing for a figure of 60 percent. See, Ole J. Benedictow, *The Black Death: The Greatest Catastrophe Ever*, Vol. 55, Issue 3, March 2005.

2   See Jack L. Schwartzwal, *The Collapse and Recovery of Europe, AD 476-1648* (McFarland, 2015), 121-122; and Ole Jørgen Benedictow, *The Black Death, 1346-1353: The Complete History* (Boydell, 2004), 212.

3   Giovanni Boccaccio, *The Decameron of Giovanni Boccaccio*, translated by Richard Aldington (New York: Dell 1930), 30-36.

4   Philip Daileader, "The Late Middle Ages," audio/video course produced by *The Teaching Company* (2007).

5   Ole J. Benedictow has estimated that the Black Death killed 60 percent

of Europe's population. He also argues, in contrast to other scholars, that death rates were as high in northern Europe as in southern Europe. See, Ole J. Benedictow, *The Black Death: The Greatest Catastrophe Ever*, Vol. 55, Issue 3, March 2005.

6   See Maanasa Raghavan et al., "The Genetic Prehistory of the New World Arctic," *Science*, Vol. 345, 2014: http://science.sciencemag.org/content/345/6200/1255832.

7   W.J. Eccles, *The Canadian Frontier* (Albuquerque: University of New Mexico Press, 1983), 2.

8   As quoted in R. A. Skelton, "John Cabot" in *Dictionary of Canadian Biography*, Vol. 1 (University of Toronto/Université Laval, 1966–).

9   Ibid.

10   Ibid.

11   See E.T. Jones, "Alwyn Ruddock: 'John Cabot and the Discovery of America,'" *Hist. Research* (Oxford, Eng.) *81* (2008): 224–54; and E.T. Jones, "Henry VII and the Bristol expeditions to North America: the Condon documents," *Hist. Research* 83 (2010): 444–54.

12   English, Basque, and Portuguese fishermen were likely crossing the Atlantic in these early days; certainly by the early 1500s the Basque had established a fishery, including whaling, along Labrador's southern coast.

13   Jacques Cartier, *The Voyages of Jacques Cartier*, edited and translated by Henry Percival Biggar and Ramsay Cook (Toronto: University of Toronto Press, 1993), 117.

14   As quoted in *The Tragic History of the Sea*, edited by C.R. Boxer, (St. Paul: University of Minnesota Press, 2001), 8.

15   Cartier, *Voyages*, 10.

16   Cartier, *Voyages*, 16.

17   Cartier, *Voyages*, 22.

18   Cartier, *Voyages*, 24.

19   Cartier, *Voyages*, 26.

20   As quoted in "The Explorers: Jacques Cartier, 1534-1542," *Virtual Museum of New France, Canadian Museum of History*, http://www.historymuseum.ca/virtual-museum-of-new-france/the-explorers/jacques-cartier-1534-1542/.

21   Ibid.

22   Gustave Lanctot, "Troilus de, Marquis de La Roche de Mesgouez," in
      Dictionary of Canadian Biography, Vol. 1 (University of Toronto/
      Université Laval, 1966–).

23   Ibid.

3   CHAMPLAIN'S MAP OF NEW FRANCE

1   Samuel de Champlain, *The Voyages of the Sieur de Champlain of
      Saintonge* . . . (Paris: 1613), CWB 1: 209–210.

2   Samuel de Champlain, *The Works of Samuel de Champlain*, Vol. I, edited
      by Henry Biggar, translated by John Squair (Toronto: Champlain
      Society, 1922–1936), 54.

3   This view of Champlain owes much to the historian David Hackett
      Fischer. Fischer has argued that Champlain was a "humanist" who was
      very tolerant in his views toward other cultures. See David Hackett
      Fischer, *Champlain's Dream* (Toronto: Random House, 2008).

4   Champlain, *The Works of Samuel de Champlain*, Vol. II (Toronto:
      Champlain Society, 1922–1936), 12.

5   Champlain, Vol. II, 54.

6   Archaeology, particularly forensic anthropology or bioarchaeology, has
      revealed that Canada's pre-contact past was far from peaceful. See Patricia
      M. Lambert, "The Archaeology of War: A North American Perspective,"
      Journal of Archaeological Research, Vol. 10, No. 3, 2002: 207–241.

7   Champlain, Vol. II, 67.

8   Champlain, Vol. II, 91.

9   Champlain, Vol. II, 101–102.

10   For a discussion of torture and trophy taking, see *The Taking and
      Displaying of Human Body Parts as Trophies by Amerindians*, edited by
      Richard J. Chacon and David H. Dye, *Interdisciplinary Contributions to
      Archaeology* (Berlin: Springer Science and Business Media, 2007).

11   Champlain, Vol. II, 129.

12   As quoted in Fischer, 295.

13   Champlain, Vol. II, 185.

14   Champlain, Vol. II, 184.

15   Champlain, Vol. II, 275.

16   Champlain, Vol. II, 276.

17   Champlain, Vol. II, 307.

18   Champlain, Vol. III, 38.

19   Champlain, Vol. III, 45.

20   Champlain, Vol. III, 45–46.

21   Champlain, Vol. III, 86.

4   THE RISE AND FALL OF THE FRENCH EMPIRE: JACQUES-NICOLAS BELLIN'S MAP OF NORTH AMERICA

1   Pierre Esprit Radisson, *Voyages of Peter Esprit Radisson . . . Transcribed from the Original Manuscripts in the Bodleian Library of the British Museum*, edited by Gideon Scull (Boston: Prince Society, 1885), 198.

2   See Derek Hayes, *Historical Atlas of Canada: Canada's History Illustrated with Original Maps* (Vancouver: Douglas & McIntyre, 2006).

3   As quoted in Don Gilmour and Pierre Turgeon, *Canada: A People's History*, Vol. I (Toronto: McClelland & Stewart, 2001), 92.

4   See Céline Dupré, "Cavelier de La Salle, René-Robert," in *Dictionary of Canadian Biography*, Vol. 1 (University of Toronto/Université Laval, 1966–).

5   Louis Hennepin, *A New Discovery of a Vast Country in America . . .* (London: 1698), 29.

6   As quoted in Gilmour and Turgeon, Vol. I, 89.

7   See José António Brandão, *Your Fyre Shall Burn No More: Iroquois Policy Toward New France and Its Native Allies to 1701* (Lincoln: University of Nebraska Press, 2000).

8   For a study of Iroquois military tactics, see Craig S Keener, "An Ethnohistorical Analysis of Iroquois Assault Tactics Used Against Fortified Settlements of the Northeast in the Seventeenth Century," *Ethnohistory*, Vol. 46, No. 4, 1999: 778.

9   See Brendan D. O'Fallon and Lars Fehren-Schmitz, "Native Americans Experienced a Strong Population Bottleneck Coincident with European Contact," *Proceedings of the National Academy of Sciences of the United States of America*, Vol. 108, No. 51, 2011: 20444–20448.

10   *Jesuit Relations and Allied Documents*, Vol. 51, edited by Reuben Gold Thwaites (Cleveland, OH: Burrows Brothers, 1901), 117. Allouez's reference to the "Assinipoulac" is presumably the Assiniboine.

11   Henry Kelsey, *The Kelsey Papers*, with an introduction by John Warkentin, Arthur G. Doughty, and Chester Martin (Regina: Canadian Plains Research Center, 1994), xxiv.

12   Kelsey, *The Kelsey Papers*, 8.

13   Kelsey, *The Kelsey Papers*, 2.

14   Pierre Gaultier de Varennes, sieur de La Vérendrye, *Journals and Letters of La Vérendrye and His Sons*, edited by Lawrence J. Burpee (Toronto: Champlain Society, 1927), 247–248 and 51.

15   La Vérendrye, *Journals*, 46.

16   La Vérendrye, *Journals*, 51.

17   La Vérendrye, *Journals*, 58.

18   La Vérendrye, *Journals*, 58–59.

19   La Vérendrye, *Journals*, 51.

20   Ibid.

21   La Vérendrye, *Journals*, 56.

22   La Vérendrye, *Journals*, 169.

5   PETER POND'S MAP OF THE NORTHWEST

1   Thomas Jefferson, "Letter to James Monroe," November 24, 1801, *Thomas Jefferson Foundation*, http://tjrs.monticello.org/letter/1743.

2   As quoted in Harold Innis, *Peter Pond: Fur Trader and Adventurer* (Toronto: Irwin & Gordon, 1930), 1.

3   Innis, *Pond*, 11.

4   Innis, *Pond*, 14.

5   Voltaire, *Candide* (Paris: 1758).

6   As quoted in Barry M. Gough, "Peter Pond," in *Dictionary of Canadian Biography*, Vol. V (University of Toronto/Université Laval, 1983–).

7   Ibid.

8   Gough has speculated that Pond learned surveying in the army (see the entry listed above). This is highly unlikely; only Royal Engineers were trained in surveying, and Pond was never in the Engineers. He may conceivably have learned some rudimentary cartography from other fur traders or during his brief career as a merchant sailor. But more likely, he was limited to educated guesswork.

9   The total number of Loyalists who would eventually arrive in Canada

may have been as many as fifty thousand. However, many of the "late" Loyalists weren't directly fleeing persecution in the aftermath of the American Revolution; they were more attracted by other consider- ations, such as cheap land.

10 Gough, "Peter Pond," *DCB*.

6 SAMUEL HEARNE'S MAP OF THE COPPERMINE RIVER

1 Samuel Hearne, *A Journey from Prince of Wales's Fort in Hudson's Bay, to the Northern Ocean* . . . (London: A. Strahan and T. Cadell, 1795), xxix.

2 As for the copper, the Hudson's Bay Company saw a chance to reap an easy windfall by using it, instead of ordinary gravel, as ballast in Company ships sailing back to England. It could then be sold, thus maximizing the amount of valuable cargo a ship could transport.

3 Hearne, *Journey*, xxxxviii.

4 Hearne, *Journey*, 53.

5 Hearne, *Journey*, 351.

6 Hearne, *Journey*, 350.

7 Some modern readers find Hearne's account of Matonabbee's views on women off-putting and degrading, and for those reasons, prefer to believe it must not be true. This is understandable, but on the other hand, if we try to set aside twenty-first-century perspectives and examine things from the context of the 1770s, Matonabbee's views can be seen in another light. Matonabbee was in essence saying to Hearne, "Women are important in our society; they're essential to our success; they're not like your delicate English women, our women are strong and healthy, and the reason you failed before is that your exploring parties didn't have them." Hearne himself upholds this view later on when he talks about how astonished and impressed he is that, after giving birth, Dene women are still able to keep up with the others. For Hearne's discussion of Matonabbee's views on women, see Hearne, *Journey*, 55. For a discussion of aboriginal women's role in the fur trade, see Sylvia Van Kirk, *Many Tender Ties: Women in Fur-Trade Society, 1670–1870* (Norman: University of Oklahoma Press, 1983).

8 Hearne, *Journey*, 66–67.

9 Hearne, *Journey*, 83.

10   Hearne, *Journey*, 97.

11   Hearne, *Journey*, 103–104.

12   Hearne, *Journey*, 349–352.

13   Hearne, *Journey*, 106–107.

14   Hearne, *Journey*, 116.

15   Hearne, *Journey*, 121–122.

16   Hearne, *Journey*, 134.

17   Hearne, *Journey*, 146.

18   Hearne, *Journey*, 152.

19   Hearne, *Journey*, 153–154.

20   Hearne, *Journey*, 154–155.

21   Hearne, *Journey*, 155–156.

22   Hearne, *Journey*, 158–159.

23   Hearne, *Journey*, 161–162.

24   Because it's so shocking to modern sensibilities, there may be an understandable temptation to dismiss Hearne's account of the massacre as an exaggeration. However, aboriginal oral history, other historic accounts from the time, archaeological excavations in Canada's Arctic, and more recently, genetic studies of ancient DNA all suggest that such violence was part of life in Canada's North. For an ethnographic study of Dene–Inuit relations, see Strother E. Roberts, "Trans-Indian Identity and the Inuit 'Other': Relations Between the Chipewyan and Neighboring Aboriginal Communities in the Eighteenth Century," *Ethnohistory*, Vol. 57, No. 4, 2010: 597–624. For the archaeology, see J. Melbye and S.I. Fairgrieve, "A Massacre and Possible Cannibalism in the Canadian Arctic: New Evidence from the Saunaktuk Site (NgTn-1)," *Arctic Anthropology*, Vol. 31, 1994: 57–77, and Patricia M. Lambert, "The Archaeology of War: A North American Perspective," *Journal of Archaeological Research*, Vol. 10, No. 3, 2002: 207–241. For a study of ancient DNA in Canada's Arctic, see Maanasa Raghavan et al., "The Genetic Prehistory of the New World Arctic," *Science*, Vol. 345, 2014: http://science.sciencemag.org/content/345/6200/1255832.

25   Hearne, *Journey*, 173.

26   Hearne, *Journey*, 359.

27   See Thomas Pennant, *Arctic Zoology*, Vol. I (London: Henry Hughs,

1784), 62–64; and Charles Darwin, *The Origin of Species* (Edison, NJ: Castle Books, 2004), 220.

7   FIRST ACROSS NORTH AMERICA: ALEXANDER MACKENZIE'S QUEST

1   These contemporary descriptions of Mackenzie can be found in W. Kaye Lamb's Introduction to *The Journals and Letters of Sir Alexander Mackenzie* (Toronto: MacMillan, 1970). For Mackenzie's description of himself, see Lamb's edition of Alexander Mackenzie, *Voyages from Montreal, on the River St. Laurence, Through the Continent of North America to the Frozen and Pacific Oceans* . . . (first edition, London: T. Cadell, Jun. and W. Davies, Strand, 1801, edition cited here, Toronto: MacMillan, 1970), 57.

2   Lamb, "Introduction," *Journals and Letters*, 2.

3   Mackenzie, *Voyages*, 57.

4   Mackenzie, *Voyages*, 85.

5   Mackenzie, *Voyages*, 176.

6   Mackenzie, *Voyages*, 180.

7   Mackenzie, *Voyages*, 182–183.

8   Mackenzie, *Voyages*, 196.

9   Ibid.

10   Mackenzie, *Voyages*, 197.

11   Ibid.

12   Mackenzie, *Voyages*, 200.

13   Mackenzie, *Voyages*, 200–201.

14   Mackenzie, *Voyages*, 201.

15   Mackenzie, *Voyages*, 212.

16   Mackenzie, *Voyages*, 213.

17   Ibid.

18   Mackenzie to Lord Dorchester, Governor-General of North America, November 17, 1794, reprinted in *Journals and Letters of Sir Alexander Mackenzie*, 457.

19   This observations was made by the experienced land surveyor Franck C. Swannell, who retraced portions of Mackenzie's route through British Columbia. See Lamb, "Introduction," *Journals and Letters*, 20–21.

20   Mackenzie, *Voyages*, 237.

21   Mackenzie to Roderick, January 10, 1791, *Journals and Letters*, 450.

22   Mackenzie, *Voyages*, 252.

23   Mackenzie, *Voyages*, 256.

24   Mackenzie, *Voyages*, 257.

25   Mackenzie, *Voyages*, 262.

26   Mackenzie, *Voyages*, 264.

27   Mackenzie, *Voyages*, 264–265.

28   Mackenzie, *Voyages*, 265.

29   Mackenzie, *Voyages*, 266.

30   Mackenzie, *Voyages*, 267.

31   Ibid.

32   Mackenzie, *Voyages*, 271.

33   Mackenzie, *Voyages*, 272.

34   Mackenzie, *Voyages*, 278.

35   Mackenzie, *Voyages*, 280.

36   Mackenzie, *Voyages*, 287.

37   Mackenzie, *Voyages*, 295.

38   Both quotes in the paragraph are from Mackenzie, *Voyages*, 299.

39   Mackenzie, *Voyages*, 321.

40   Mackenzie, *Voyages*, 324.

41   Ibid.

42   Mackenzie, *Voyages*, 329.

43   Mackenzie, *Voyages*, 363.

44   Mackenzie, *Voyages*, 361.

45   Mackenzie, *Voyages*, 364.

46   For an archaeological study of West Coast aboriginal warfare, see
      Herbert D.G. Maschner and Katherine L. Reedy-Maschner, "Raid,
      Retreat, Defend (Repeat): The Archaeology and Ethnohistory of
      Warfare on the North Pacific Rim," *Journal of Anthropological
      Archaeology* 17 (1998): 19–51. See also Donald Leland, *Aboriginal
      Slavery on the Northwest Coast of North America* (Berkeley: University of
      California Press, 1997); and for West Coast aboriginal armour, see also
      the Museum of Canadian History's collections, www.historymuseum.
      ca/cmc/exhibitions/aborig/haida/havwao1e.shtml.

47 Mackenzie, *Voyages*, 375.

48 Mackenzie, *Voyages*, 376.

49 Mackenzie, *Voyages*, 378.

50 Mackenzie to Roderick, January 13, 1794, *Journals and Letters*, 453.

51 Mackenzie to Roderick, March 5, 1794, *Journals and Letters*, 454.

52 John Graves Simcoe's letter appears in *Journals and Letters*, 24.

53 Elizabeth Simcoe, *The Diary of Mrs. John Graves Simcoe*, with notes and a biography by J. Ross Robertson (Toronto: Prospero, 2001), 243.

54 This was Alexander Henry; see *Journals and Letters*, 30.

55 *Journals and Letters*, 45.

56 David McKeeham to Lewis, *Journals and Letters*, 52.

57 Richard Dillon, *Meriwether Lewis: A Biography* (New York: Coward-McCann, 1965), xvi.

58 Lamb, "Introduction," *Journals and Letters*, 52.

59 The map accompanied the publication of Mackenzie's account of his "voyages" in 1801 and was made by the English cartographer Aaron Arrowsmith in collaboration with Mackenzie. Arrowsmith produced many such maps based on the sketch maps of explorers.

8 DAVID THOMPSON'S DEMONS

1   David Thompson, *David Thompson's Narrative of His Explorations in Western America, 1784–1812*, edited by Joseph Burr Tyrell (Toronto: Champlain Society, 1916), 444–445.

2   Thompson, 445.

3   Tyrell, *Thompson's Narrative*, xxxii.

4   Thompson, 10.

5   Thompson, 9.

6   See Stephen Ambrose, *Undaunted Courage: Meriwether Lewis, Thomas Jefferson, and the Opening of the American West* (New York: Simon and Schuster, 1996), 55 and 91. Lewis and Clark found mammoth bones on their travels.

7   Thompson, 312.

8   Thompson, 311.

9   Thompson, 313.

10 Thompson, 537.

11　All quotes in the paragraph are from Thompson, 538.

12　Ibid.

13　*Ursus americanus kermodei*, commonly called the kermode or spirit bear, was first identified by the zoologist William Hornaday in 1905 from the skins and skulls of specimens he obtained from aboriginal hunters.

14　Thompson, 446.

15　Ibid.

16　Ibid.

17　Ibid.

18　Thompson, 105.

19　Thompson, 446.

20　Thompson, 446–447.

21　Thompson, 448.

22　Ross Cox, *The Columbia River; Or Scenes and Adventures During a Residence of Six Years on the Western Side of the Rocky Mountains, Among Various Tribes of Indians Hitherto Unknown: Together with a Journey Across the American Continent.* Vol. II (London: Henry Colburn and Richard Bentley, 1831), 207–208.

23　Diamond Jenness, *The Indians of Canada* (Toronto: University of Toronto Press, Seventh Edition, 1977, first edition: 1932).

24　Thompson, 125.

25　All quotes in this paragraph are from Thompson, 125.

26　All quotes in this paragraph are from Thompson, 259–260.

27　All quotes in this paragraph are from Thompson, 260–261.

28　See, for example, Morton I. Teicher, *Windigo Psychosis: A Study of the Relationship Between Belief and Behaviour Among the Indians of Northeastern Canada* (Seattle: American Ethnological Society, 1960).

9　CANADA'S BLOODIEST BATTLEFIELD: THE SIEGE OF FORT ERIE

1　Henry Clay's speeches are reprinted in Julius W. Pratt, *Expansionists of 1812* (Gloucester, Mass: P. Smith, 1957), 40–42.

2　As quoted in Louis Hacker, "The Desire for Canadian Land," in *The Causes of the War of 1812: National Honor or National Interest?* edited by Bradford Perkins (New York: Holt, Rinehart and Winston, 1962), 49–50.

3   Ibid.

4   Although in American popular history the cause of the war is sometimes
     represented as arising from maritime shipping rights or even "national
     honour," these arguments are not taken seriously by most historians, nor
     were they by the actual proponents of the war in 1812. For example, see
     the above-cited Louis Hacker, "The Desire for Canadian Land," and
     Julius W. Pratt, *Expansionists of 1812* (Gloucester, Mass: P. Smith, 1957).
     For President Madison's "War Address," see James Madison, "Madison's
     War Message," in *Basic Documents in American History*, edited by Richard
     Brandon Morris (Princeton: Princeton University Press, 1956), 89–92.

5   William Hull, *Memoirs of the Campaign of the North Western Army of the
     United States* (Boston: True & Greene, 1824), 45–46.

6   Ibid.

7   Ibid.

8   John Le Couteur, *Merry Hearts Make Light Days: The War of 1812
     Journal of Lieutenant John Le Couteur, 104th Foot*, edited by Donald E.
     Graves (Ottawa: Carleton University Press, 1993), 189.

9   Le Couteur, *Journal*, 186.

10   William "Tiger" Dunlop, "Recollections of the American War," in
     The Literary Garland and British North American Magazine, New Series,
     Vol. V (Montreal: Lovell & Gibson, 1847), 355.

11   As quoted in Donald E. Graves, *And All Their Glory Past: Fort Erie,
     Plattsburgh, and the Final Battles in the North, 1814* (Montreal: Robin
     Brass Studio, 2013), 47.

12   "Attack on Fort Erie," *Naval and Military Chronicle of the United States*
     (Philadelphia: Vol. 1, No. II, February 1816).

13   John Norton, *The Journal of John Norton*, edited by Carl F. Klinck
     (Toronto: Champlain Society, 1970), 356.

14   Dunlop, "Recollections," 355.

15   Jacques Viger, *Reminiscences of the War of 1812–14: Being Portions of
     the Diary of a Captain of the "Voltigeurs Canadiens"* . . . translated by
     J.L. Hubert Neilson (Kingston, 1895), 10–11.

16   Le Couteur, *Journal*, 73.

17   Jarvis Hanks, "The Siege of Fort Erie, August to September 1814,"
     in *Soldiers of 1814: American Enlisted Men's Memoirs of the Niagara*

Campaign, Jarvis Hanks, Amasiah Ford, and Alexander McMullen; edited, with an introduction and notes, by Donald E. Graves (Youngstown, NY: Old Fort Niagara Association, Inc., 1995), 42.

18 Le Couteur, *Journal*, 189.

19 Dunlop, "Recollections," 361.

20 Le Couteur, *Journal*, 189.

21 Ibid.

22 Ibid.

23 Both Scott quotes are from Graves, *And All Their Glory Past*, 68 and 70.

24 General Gordon Drummond to General Provost, as quoted in Graves, *And All Their Glory Past*, 81.

25 Dunlop, "Recollections," 361.

26 Le Couteur, *Journal*, 189–190.

27 William Drummond's command was reported afterward by various Americans; see, for example, "Attack on Fort Erie," *Naval and Military Chronicle of the United States* (Philadelphia: Vol. 1, No. 2, February 1816); and *Soldiers of 1814: American Enlisted Men's Memoirs of the Niagara Campaign*.

28 Dunlop, "Recollections," 361.

29 Ibid.

30 David B. Douglass, "Reminiscences of the Campaign of 1814, on the Niagara Frontier," *The Historical Magazine*, Vol. II, No. 1, July 1873.

31 Le Couteur, *Journal*, 190.

32 Dunlop, "Recollections," 361–362.

33 All quotes in the paragraph are from Le Couteur, *Journal*, 191.

34 See Benson Lossing, *The Pictorial Field-Book of the War of 1812* (Harpers & Brothers, 1869), 832.

35 I spent three seasons working at Old Fort Erie National Historic Site for the Niagara Parks Commission, and an additional three seasons participating in archaeological excavations of the site under Dr. John Triggs of Wilfrid Laurier University. Those experiences—shifting through the traces of the siege on archaeological digs; working with muskets, cannons, and other weapons and tools of the era; and treading the grounds and becoming intimately acquainted with the layout of the site—did much to assist me in reconstructing the history recounted in this chapter.

10 CANADA'S HEART OF DARKNESS: MAPPING THE ARCTIC FRONTIER

1   John Franklin, *Narrative of a Journey to the Shores of the Polar Sea: In the Years 1819-20-21-22* (London: John Murray, 1824), 193.

2   Franklin, 204.

3   Franklin, 217.

4   Franklin, 224.

5   Franklin, 224–225.

6   Franklin, 220.

7   Franklin, 331.

8   Franklin, 373.

9   Franklin, 343–344.

10 Franklin, 358.

11 Franklin, 362.

12 Franklin, 365.

13 Franklin, 386.

14 Franklin, 393.

15 Franklin, 398.

16 Franklin, 398.

17 Franklin, 401.

18 Franklin, 405.

19 Franklin, 406.

20 Franklin, 406–407.

21 Franklin, 407.

22 Franklin, 408.

23 Ibid.

24 Franklin, 409.

25 Ibid.

26 Ibid.

27 Franklin, 410.

28 Ibid.

29 Franklin, 415.

30 Franklin, 421.

31 Franklin, 422.

32 Franklin, 423–424.

33   John Richardson, in John Franklin, *Narrative Journey to the Shores of the Polar Sea: In the Years 1819-20-21-22* (London: John Murray, 1824), 452.

34   Richardson, 458. Ironically, Franklin's final, doomed Arctic expedition in 1845 ended with cannibalism among his starving Royal Navy crews.

35   Richardson, 461.

36   Franklin, 463.

37   Franklin, 468.

38   Franklin, 470.

39   Franklin, 474.

AFTERWORD

1   Voltaire, *Essai sur les moeurs et l'esprit des nations, et sur les principaux faits de l'histoire, depuis Charlemagne jusqu'a Louis XIII* (Geneva: 1771, first printed 1756), 42.

INDEX

Note: HBC = Hudson's Bay Company; NWC = North West Company